S

15.

A fi
aft
ite
be
Rep
da
w

B100088   201400057

The Economics of Wellbeing

Wellbeing: A Complete Reference Guide, Volume V

Wellbeing: A Complete Reference Guide

Volume I: Wellbeing in Children and Families
Edited by Susan H. Landry and Cary L. Cooper

Volume II: Wellbeing and the Environment
Edited by Rachel Cooper, Elizabeth Burton, and Cary L. Cooper

Volume III: Work and Wellbeing
Edited by Peter Y. Chen and Cary L. Cooper

Volume IV: Wellbeing in Later Life
Edited by Thomas B. L. Kirkwood and Cary L. Cooper

Volume V: The Economics of Wellbeing
Edited by David McDaid and Cary L. Cooper

Volume VI: Interventions and Policies to Enhance Wellbeing
Edited by Felicia A. Huppert and Cary L. Cooper

The Economics of Wellbeing

Wellbeing: A Complete Reference
Guide, Volume V

Edited by David McDaid
and Cary L. Cooper

WILEY Blackwell

Library of Congress Cataloging-in-Publication Data

The economics of wellbeing / volume editor, David McDaid; editor-in-chief, Cary L. Cooper.
        pages cm. – (Wellbeing : a complete reference guide; volume V)
    Includes bibliographical references and index.
    ISBN 978-1-118-60838-8 (cloth : alk. paper)
1. Health behavior–Economic aspects.   2. Economics–Sociological aspects.   3. Well-being
I. McDaid, David.
    RA776.9.E3266 2014
    362.1–dc23   2013030509

A catalogue record for this book is available from the British Library.

Cover image: © Ekely / Getty
Cover design by cyandesign.co.uk

Set in 10.5/14pt Galliard by Laserwords Private Limited, Chennai, India
Printed and bound in Singapore by Markono Print Media Pte Ltd

1   2014

Contents of this Volume

Contents of this Volume

Richard Layard

About the Editors

David McDaid is Senior Research Fellow in Health Policy and Health Economics at LSE Health and Social Care and the European Observatory on Health Systems and Policies at the London School of Economics and Political Science, U.K. He is involved in a wide range of work on the economics of mental and physical health and wellbeing in the United Kingdom, Europe, and beyond. He has served as an advisor to organizations including the European Commission, World Health Organization, and national governments. He has published over 200 peer-reviewed papers and reports, including studies looking at the case for investing in measures to promote and protect health and wellbeing. He is coeditor of *Mental health policy and practice across Europe* (2007) and coauthor of *Because it's worth it: A practical guide to conducting economic evaluations in the social welfare field* (2003).

Cary L. Cooper, CBE, is Distinguished Professor of Organizational Psychology and Health at Lancaster University Management School, U.K. He is the author/editor of over 150 books, has written over 400 scholarly articles for academic journals, and is a frequent contributor to national newspapers, TV, and radio. He is the Chair of the Academy of Social Sciences (comprised of 46 learned societies in the social sciences, with nearly 90,000 social scientists), President of RELATE, President of the Institute of Welfare, and immediate past President of the British Association of Counselling and Psychotherapy. He was the Founding President of the British Academy of Management, Founding Editor of the *Journal of Organizational Behavior*, and is currently Editor-in-Chief of the international scholarly journal *Stress & Health*. He has received honorary doctorates from a number of universities (e.g., University of Sheffield, Aston University, and Heriot-Watt University). He has been awarded honorary fellowships by the Royal College of Physicians, Royal College of Physicians of Ireland, British Psychological Society, European Academy of Occupational Health Psychology, and Institute of Occupational Safety and

Health. In 2010 Professor Cooper was awarded the Lord Dearing Lifetime Achievement Award at the *The Times Higher Education* Awards for his distinguished contribution to higher education. He was lead scientist on the U.K. Government's Foresight program on Mental Capital and Wellbeing, which had a major impact in the United Kingdom and Europe. Professor Cooper was Chair of the Global Agenda Council on Chronic Diseases in the World Economic Forum in 2009–2010. In 2012, *HR* magazine voted him the Fourth Most Influential HR Thinker. In 2001, he was awarded a CBE by the Queen for his contribution to occupational health.

Contributors

Tinna Laufey Ásgeirsdóttir, University of Iceland, Iceland

Cary L. Cooper, Lancaster University, U.K.

Hope Corman, Rider University, U.S.A.

Candice Currie, University of St Andrews, U.K.

Anna K. Forsman, National Institute for Health and Welfare (THL), Finland and Nordic School of Public Health NHV, Sweden

Arthur Grimes, Motu and Economic Public Policy Research, New Zealand

Brendan Kennelly, NUI Galway, Ireland

Richard Layard, London School of Economics and Political Science, U.K.

David McDaid, London School of Economics and Political Science, U.K.

Kelly Noonan, Rider University, USA

Þórhildur Ólafsdóttir, University of Iceland, Iceland

Lars Osberg, Dalhousie University, Canada

Les Oxley, University of Waikato, New Zealand

A-La Park, London School of Economics and Political Science, U.K.

Nancy E. Reichman, Robert Wood Johnson Medical School, U.S.A.

Andrew Sharpe, Centre for the Study of Living Standards, Canada

Laura Stoll, New Economics Foundation, U.K.

Nicholas Tarrant, GT Research and Consulting, New Zealand

Kristian Wahlbeck, Finnish Association for Mental Health, Finland

Cara Zanotti, University of South Australia, Australia

Full Contents of *Wellbeing: A Complete Reference Guide*

Volume I   Wellbeing in Children and Families
Edited by Susan H. Landry and Cary L. Cooper

Volume II   Wellbeing and the Environment
*Edited by Rachel Cooper, Elizabeth Burton, and
Cary L. Cooper*

Volume III Work and Wellbeing
Edited by Peter Y. Chen and Cary L. Cooper

Volume IV   Wellbeing in Later Life
Edited by Thomas B. L. Kirkwood and
Cary L. Cooper

Volume V   The Economics of Wellbeing

Edited by David McDaid and Cary L. Cooper

Volume VI   Interventions and Policies to Enhance Wellbeing

Edited by Felicia A. Huppert and Cary L. Cooper

Introduction to *Wellbeing: A Complete Reference Guide*

Cary L. Cooper
Lancaster University, U.K.

This series of six volumes explores one of the most important social issues of our times, that of how to enhance the mental wellbeing of people, whether in the developed, developing, or underdeveloped world, and across the life course from birth to old age. We know that 1 in 4–6 people in most countries in the world suffer from a common mental disorder of anxiety, depression, or stress. We also know that mental ill health costs countries billions of dollars per annum. In the United Kingdom, for example, mental health-care costs have amounted to over £77 billion per annum, the bill for sickness absence and presenteeism (people turning up to work ill or not delivering due to job stress) in the workplace is another £26 billion, and the costs of dementia will rise from £20 billion to an estimated £50 billion in 25 years' time (Cooper, Field, Goswami, Jenkins, & Sahakian, 2009). In Germany, the leading cause of early retirement from work in 1989 was musculoskeletal disease but by 2004 it was stress and mental ill health, now representing 40% of all early retirements (German Federal Health Monitoring, 2007). In many European countries (e.g., Finland, Holland, Norway, and Switzerland) the cost of lost productive value due to lack of mental wellbeing is a significant proportion of gross domestic product (McDaid, Knapp, Medeiros, & MHEEN Group, 2008). Indeed, the costs of depression alone in the European Union were shown to be €41 billion, with €77 billion in terms of lost productivity to all the economies (Sobocki, Jonsson, Angst, & Rehnberg, 2006).

The issue of wellbeing has been around for sometime but has been brought to the fore more recently because of the global recession and economic downturn, which have made the situation worse (Antoniou & Cooper, 2013). But it was as early as 1968 that politicians began to talk about the inadequacy of gross national product as a measure of a society's success. In a powerful speech by Bobby Kennedy at the University of Kansas, when he was on the campaign trail for the Democratic Party nomination for U.S. President, he reflected:

> But even if we act to erase material poverty, there is another greater task, it is to confront the poverty of satisfaction—purpose and dignity—that afflicts us all. Too much and for too long, we seemed to have surrendered personal excellence and community values in the mere accumulation of material things. Our gross national product, now, is over $800 billion a year, but that gross national product—if we judge the United States of America by that—that gross national product counts air pollution and cigarette advertising, and ambulances to clear our highways of carnage. It counts special locks for our doors and the jails for the people who break them. It counts the destruction of the redwood and the loss of our natural wonder in the chaotic sprawl. It counts napalm and counts nuclear warheads and armoured cars for the police to fight the riots in our cities. . . . Yet the GNP does not allow for the health of our children, the quality of their education or the joy of their play. It does not include the beauty of our poetry or the strength of our marriages, the intelligence of our public debate or the integrity of our public officials. It measures neither our wit nor our courage, neither our wisdom nor our learning, neither our compassion nor our devotion to our country, it measures everything in short, except that which makes life worthwhile.
>
> University of Kansas, March 18, 1968,
> http://www.americanswhotellthetruth.org/portraits/robert-f-kennedy

Since that time there have been numerous studies to show that the wealth of a country is not related to its happiness (Cooper & Robertson, 2013); indeed, as you earn far beyond your means you may become less happy or content. More recently, we have had politicians like former President Sarkozy of France, Prime Minister Cameron of the United Kingdom, and the King of Bhutan extol the virtue of gross national wellbeing; that is, that the goal of a nation's politicians should be to enhance wellbeing among its citizens, with gross national product being only one indicator of a country's success. Indeed, Prime Minister Cameron has instituted an annual assessment of this through the U.K. Office of National Statistics which measures wellbeing among a large sample of the U.K. population, publishing the results, highlighting concerns, and ultimately considering policies to deal with them. The World Economic Forum of leading global companies, nongovernmental organizations, international bodies, and global charities now has one of its Global Agenda Councils on "mental health and wellbeing." Happiness and wellbeing indices abound (e.g., The Happy Planet), and many countries are being compared and assessed on a range of quality-of-life metrics. Indeed, in April 2012, 79 countries in the General Assembly of the United Nations signed the Bhutan Agreement, supporting the view that an overarching goal of a country should be to enhance the wellbeing and happiness of its people.

The biggest study of its kind undertaken by any government was the 2 year U.K. Government's Foresight project on mental capital and wellbeing, the aim of which was "to produce a challenging and long-term vision for optimising mental capital and wellbeing in the United Kingdom in the 21st century—both for the benefit of society and for the individual" (Cooper et al., 2009). Mental capital was defined as the metaphorical "bank account of the mind," which gets enhanced or depleted throughout the life course (see figure). Mental wellbeing was defined as "a dynamic state that refers to individuals' ability to develop their potential, work productively and creatively, build strong and positive relationships with others and contribute to their community" (Beddington et al., 2008).

Over 85 international science reviews were commissioned to assess the factors that influence an individual's mental capital and wellbeing throughout life, from early childhood to school years to working life to old age. There were numerous findings in this report, which were costed and developed as potential government policy and/or interventions. An example of some of the findings were: (a) if society does not catch learning difficulties in children early enough, there will be increased personal and economic costs downstream, leading to depleted mental wellbeing in terms of increased antisocial behavior as well as significant health costs; (b) if society does not identify the common mental disorders (CMDs) of anxiety, depression, and stress early enough, and provide appropriate treatment and support, society won't be able to tackle the 1 in 4–6 people suffering from depression and other CMDs; (c) with the workplace being more insecure, people working longer hours, and being more overloaded, occupational stress in many countries is now the leading cause of sickness absence and presenteeism, which has implications for the viability of businesses and their productivity; and, finally, (d) with the doubling of over-65-year-olds and the tripling of over-80-year-olds over the next 30 years, society needs to deal with the consequences of dementia now with preventative strategies, better early diagnosis, and more successful and evidence-based treatment regimes. The Foresight project developed many recommendations to enhance mental capital and wellbeing not only in the United Kingdom but also for other countries (Cooper et al., 2009), and its legacy has provided a roadmap for how other countries should think about this in the future, in terms of both policies and interventions for wellbeing.

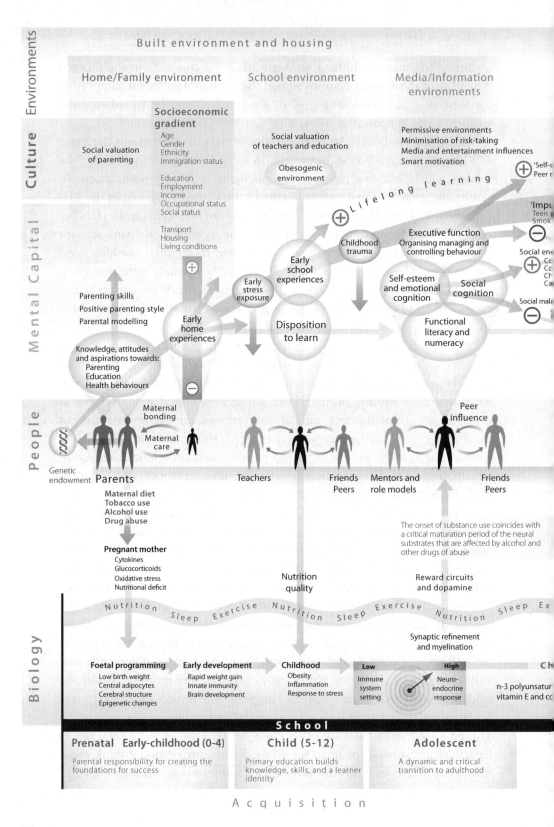

Figure. Synthetic View of the Mental Capital Trajectory.

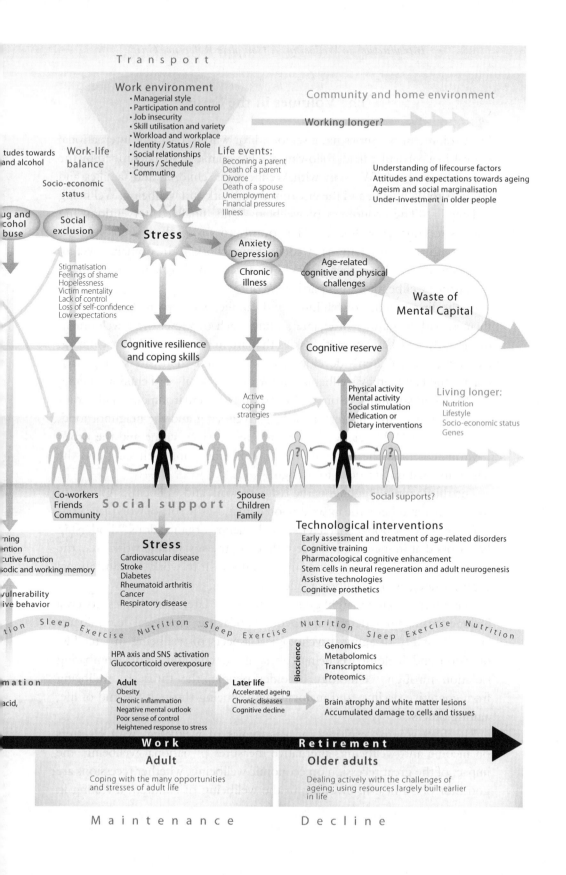

The Volumes in the Series

Each volume in the series has a senior editor who is a leading international scholar in a particular field, following the life-course model described by the Foresight program. We start with Wellbeing in children and families and progress to Wellbeing and the environment, Work and wellbeing, Wellbeing in later life, The economics of wellbeing, and, finally, Interventions and policies to enhance wellbeing. The contributors to each of these volumes are distinguished international academics who work in the domain covered, reviewing the evidence that can help to develop policies and interventions to enhance wellbeing in that particular context.

In the first volume on children and families we explore four different themes, with a number of chapters under each of these: the development of the early social and cognitive skills that are important in child wellbeing, parenting and children's development, school and child care-settings that impact child and family wellbeing, and stress and family and child wellbeing.

The second volume is on wellbeing and the environment. This comprises sections, with chapters in each, on wellbeing and the neighborhood, wellbeing and buildings, wellbeing and green spaces, crime and the urban environment (and the implications for wellbeing), and wellbeing and the environmental implications for design.

The third volume highlights the issues of work and wellbeing. A range of topics is covered here: the impact of job demands, the role of workplace control, the organizational characteristics of "happy organizations," leadership behaviors that influence employee wellbeing, the sustainable workforce, the "working wounded" (including stigma and return to work), organizational coping strategies and wellbeing, and many more.

The fourth volume highlights wellbeing in later life. Topics covered include the changing demographic context of aging, biological determinants and malleability of aging, psychological aspects of wellbeing in later life, nutrition and lifelong wellbeing, physical exercise and aging, combating isolation through technology in older people, the threat to wellbeing from cognitive decline, and maintaining wellbeing through the end of life, among others.

The fifth volume explores the economics of wellbeing, with chapters on income and wellbeing, alternative measures of national wellbeing, the impact of the great recession on economic wellbeing, whether recessions are good for one's health, investing in the wellbeing of children, investing in wellbeing in the workplace, promoting health and wellbeing of older people and protecting population mental health, wellbeing during an economic crisis, and many others.

Finally, the sixth volume highlights interventions and policies that can enhance wellbeing throughout the life course. There are three sections, with chapters on the state of wellbeing science, individual/group interventions on childhood and adolescence, promoting mental health and wellbeing in schools, mindfulness training for children and adolescents, interventions in working years and post retirement, mental health promotion in the workplace, intergenerational interventions to enhance wellbeing among retired people, interventions to create positive organizations and communities with wellbeing as a business priority, the power of philanthropy and volunteering, and creating community connections. Finally, policies are discussed, such as mental health and wellbeing at the top of the global agenda, how subjective wellbeing can influence policy, media and the public's mental health, and promoting wellbeing through new technology.

These volumes contain the leading-edge research, practice, and policies to help government, businesses, local authorities, and global institutions consider how we can action some of what Bobby Kennedy suggested were an important set of outcomes for a successful society. Our institutions need to change, and we as individuals need to do so as well, if we are to achieve personal wellbeing, or as Abraham Lincoln wrote during the American Civil War, "it is not the years in your life which are important, but the life in your years." Winston Churchill reflected on this as well, when he wrote in an essay on how he dealt with the excessive pressures of life and found solace: "many remedies are suggested for the avoidance of worry and mental overstrain by persons who, over prolonged periods, have to bear exceptional responsibilities and discharge duties upon a very large scale. Some advise exercise, and others, repose. Some counsel travel, and others, retreat. . . no doubt all of these may play their part according to individual temperament. But the element which is constant and common in all of them is Change. . . a man can wear out a particular part of his mind by continually using it and tiring it, just in the same way as he can wear out the elbows of his coats. . . but the tired parts of the mind can be rested and strengthened, not merely by rest, but by using other parts. . . it is only when new cells are called into activity, when new stars become the lords of the ascendant, that relief, repose, refreshment are afforded."

I hope that these volumes will provide you with the science, practice, and tools to enhance the mental wellbeing of people in your own work.

References

Antoniou, A., & Cooper, C. L. (Eds.) (2013). *The psychology of the recession on the workplace*. Cheltenham: Edward Elgar Publishing.

Beddington, J., Cooper, C. L., Field, J., Goswami, U., Huppert, F., Jenkins, R., . . . Thomas, S. (2008). The mental wealth of nations. *Nature*, *455*(23), 1057–1060.

Cooper, C. L., Field, J., Goswami, U., Jenkins, R., & Sahakian, B. (Eds.) (2009). *Mental capital and wellbeing*. Oxford: Wiley Blackwell.

Cooper, C. L., & Robertson, I. (Eds.) (2013). *Management and happiness*. Cheltenham: Edward Elgar Publishing.

German Federal Health Monitoring (2007). *Trends in causes of early retirement*. http://www.gber.bund.de.

McDaid, D., Knapp, M., Medeiros, H., & MHEEN Group (2008). *Employment and mental health*. Brussels: European Commission.

Sobocki, P., Jonsson, B., Angst, J., & Rehnberg, C. (2006). Cost of depression in Europe. *Journal of Mental Health Policy and Economics*, *9*(2), 87–98.

1

Introduction

David McDaid
London School of Economics and Political Science, U.K.

Cary L. Cooper
Lancaster University, U.K.

This volume reflects on different perspectives on the economic aspects of wellbeing. Debates and discussions on how we both measure the progress of society and understand what we as human beings value the most in our lives are nothing new. We have pondered these questions since the very dawn of time, but with comparatively little discussion of the interaction between economics and wellbeing until the latter half of the twentieth century.

The approach to economics set out by the Scottish philosopher and economist Adam Smith in *The wealth of nations* set the tone for much of the discourse on economics over the next two centuries (Smith, 1776/1977). Progress in society would be best achieved through economic growth brought about by ever more efficient production processes, with free and open markets governing the supply and demand for goods and services. The population would maximize their satisfaction and enjoyment of life in such a society. Dissenting views using alternative ways of organizing the means of production and distributing resources, most notably those based on of some of the ideas first set out in *Das Kapital* (Marx, 1867), were often seen to be failed experiments that caused stagnant levels of economic growth and were mainly used by authoritarian regimes, which entailed the restriction of many individual freedoms.

As Laura Stoll illustrates in her chapter looking at the history of wellbeing research from the time of Socrates, Plato, and Aristotle to the present day,

The Economics of Wellbeing: Wellbeing: A Complete Reference Guide, Volume V.
Edited by David McDaid and Cary L. Cooper.
© 2014 John Wiley & Sons, Ltd. Published 2014 by John Wiley & Sons, Inc.
DOI: 10.1002/9781118539415.wbwell01

although economists such as Francis Edgeworth expressed an interest in trying to develop machines to measure levels of happiness or other forms of subjective wellbeing (Edgeworth, 1881), this line of inquiry was condemned by neoclassical economists and not pursued in mainstream economics for many years. Doubting that income and happiness were close correlates was deemed to constitute an important challenge to traditional economics (Stutzer & Frey, 2012).

The interest of economists in wellbeing research only really reemerged in the 1970s; Stoll highlights comments made by then U.S. presidential candidate Robert Kennedy in 1968 as a catalyst, questioning the value of conventional measurement of economic output through gross national product or gross domestic product (GDP) as satisfactory measures of "everything that makes life worthwhile." Kennedy questioned the merits of all economic growth, recognizing that growth could be achieved through negative actions such as pollution and other destruction of the natural environment or engagement in unhealthy behaviors such as smoking.

Kennedy himself was probably influenced by the economist J. K. Galbraith, who had acted as an advisor to his brother President John F. Kennedy. Galbraith was well known for his book *The affluent society*, which a decade earlier had also questioned the value of GDP because of its failure to look at other aspects of personal and societal wellbeing (Galbraith, 1958). Another economist to question the status quo in the early 1970s, Ernst F. Schumacher, developed a set of principles that he termed "Buddhist Economics," in which he challenged the conventional wisdom of the pursuit of economic growth, again questioning the impact of growth and its importance to our wellbeing in his seminal work *Small is beautiful: A study of economics as if people mattered* (Schumacher, 1973).

Most famously, Richard Easterlin was able to make use of social indicator research data in the United States to observe that, despite rising GDP per capita, average happiness in the United States rose through the late 1950s and then fell for the following 20 years, returning to near its 1946 level by 1970 (Easterlin, 1974). This so-called 'Easterlin Paradox' has been at the root of much subsequent work in the economic literature on what is as often referred to as the economics of happiness or the economics of wellbeing (Layard, 2005).

Today, the focus in economics is still very much on measurement issues: just what exactly constitutes wellbeing and do we need to go beyond conventional economic measures that use GDP as a primary indicator of social progress as well as economic performance? In 2008 the French government under President Sarkozy asked Joseph Stiglitz (President of the Commission), Amartya Sen (Advisor) and Jean Paul Fitoussi (Coordinator) to establish an international Commission on the Measurement of Economic Performance and Social Progress (Stiglitz, Sen, & Fitoussi, 2010). It recognized wellbeing to be multidimensional, including issues of income and wealth, the level of insecurity in our lives, including in our economic and health status, the strength of social networks, political accountability and democracy, quality of education, employment status and the environment in which we all live.

In the United Kingdom, following a request from Prime Minister David Cameron (Cameron, 2010), the Office of National Statistics embarked on a program to "develop and publish an accepted and trusted set of national statistics that helps people to understand and monitor national wellbeing" (Beaumont, 2012). The first set of data looking at aspects of wellbeing in the UK was published in 2012, with work continuing to further develop indicators (Self, Thomas, & Randall, 2012). This includes traditional economic indicators, supplemented by many of the same broad indicators of wellbeing suggested in the Stiglitz Commission's report.

Much of this volume is thus concerned with the issue of the measurement of wellbeing. Brendan Kennelly in his chapter reviews the fundamental relationship between income and subjective wellbeing, looking at some of the more serious methodological issues in the latter's measurement. He suggests that there have been some significant flaws in the measurement of subjective wellbeing over time that challenge the validity of responses to population surveys. As he notes, 43% of people in a poll in the United States in 1970 described themselves as very happy, the highest possible response available on the survey. But what could they then say the following year, or 5 years later, if they were asked again about their happiness and regarded themselves as even happier?

He also notes that people in higher income countries generally evaluate their lives in a more positive way than people in poorer countries, yet that relationship does not hold for measures of experienced wellbeing. He is in agreement with American economists Deaton and Stone who argue that a measure of hedonic wellbeing that shows that the average European is worse off than the average person from Mozambique, Sudan, or Rwanda is basically meaningless (Deaton & Stone, 2013). He concludes that the balance of recent evidence suggests that, on average, more income is better for individuals and that great caution should be exercised before income measures are replaced or even complemented by measures of subjective wellbeing for policy purposes.

Lars Osberg and Andrew Sharpe describe their Index of Economic Wellbeing and how it can be used to look at cross-country changes in wellbeing following the onset of the global economic crisis in 2008. Their measure of wellbeing focuses on economic dimensions of wellbeing and does not look at more subjective issues, or what they call quality of life issues. They make the point that "there is more to economic wellbeing than GDP per capita, and it is useful to have better measures of the economic wellbeing of society because better measurement may help guide better decisions" (Osberg & Sharpe, 2005).

Their measure considers issues of income, but also issues to do with the distribution of income in society, accumulated stocks of wealth after taking account of the negative impacts of wealth generation to the environment, and economic security, including financial risk due to poor health. They find that the global recession of 2008 had very different impacts in different countries and that economic security for populations plays a key role in protecting them from the greatest negative impacts on their wellbeing. This, potentially, has important policy implications. They identify Finland and Norway as two nations that do well in insulating their citizens against the hazards of the business cycle, for any given size of business cycle shock.

Arthur Grimes and colleagues compile and compare a range of alternative measures of wellbeing including: material measures (e.g., GDP per capita), surveyed measures (e.g., life satisfaction) and composite measures (e.g., on ecological sustainability and development) covering a range of countries. They argue that revealed preference indicators such as migration choices—where the choices are made so as to improve life outcomes now and into the future—are also objective indicators of wellbeing. They then test the predictive power of wellbeing measures against net migration patterns over a 50-year timespan. They conclude that material wellbeing such as GDP, while being an important predictor of migration, is an insufficient index for measuring aggregate wellbeing for potential migrants. A broader measure of life satisfaction must also be included in the definition of aggregate wellbeing for these individuals.

An important policy implication of their empirical analysis is that increases in income may sometimes come at the cost of decreases in other aspects of life satisfaction. This means that economic studies that look at the case for different policy actions need to include a monetary valuation of life satisfaction in their calculations for cost–benefit analyses and not focus solely on material issues. While income does improve wellbeing, their analysis indicates that it should not be the sole basis for assessing the merits of alternative public policies.

Making the Economic Case for Investing in Wellbeing

Thinking further about policy implications, much of the current research on economics and wellbeing has focused on its measurement rather than on how we can use this information to change and improve society. It is not enough to know what factors contribute to wellbeing, we then need to carefully evaluate the cost-effectiveness of actions to promote better wellbeing in society. This economic case for investing in measures to improve wellbeing forms a major component of the volume. Different actions across the life course are considered.

Much of this case for action looks at issues affecting mental wellbeing, which Richard Layard in his chapter contends is the biggest single influence on life satisfaction, with mental health status 8 years earlier a more powerful explanatory factor than current income. Layard demonstrates that our state of mental health also affects earnings and educational success, but, most strikingly, affects employment and physical health. He notes that in high-income countries mental health problems are the main illness of working age—amounting to 40% of all illness under 65.

Cost-effective interventions to treat mental health problems do exist, but it remains the case, even in high-income countries, that only between a quarter and a third of all people who could benefit from mental health services actually receive treatments (Demyttenaere et al., 2004). Layard argues that psychological therapies such as cognitive behavioral therapy would, if more widely available, pay for themselves in savings on benefits and lost taxes.

It has been argued that actions to promote wellbeing in the early years of life will generate the greatest economic returns on investment (Heckman, 2006). In Chapter 8, McDaid and colleagues look in detail at the economic arguments for investing in measures to promote and protect the wellbeing of young people. The strength of the economic case in this area has benefited greatly from the availability of cohort studies that have followed groups of children over many decades. These studies consistently indicate that there can be many adverse health, social, and economic consequences in adulthood of poor wellbeing in childhood. Highly cost-effective actions not only to protect psychological wellbeing, but also to address overweight and obesity and reduce risks from alcohol, smoking, and sexual behavior, were highlighted. In addition, there is compelling evidence, largely from a U.S. context, suggesting that investing in preschool educational interventions can generate positive returns on investment by the time that children reach adulthood (Nores & Barnett, 2010).

Another key area where there is a good economic case for promoting wellbeing is in the workplace. Effective prevention of excess psychosocial stress, as well as promotion of mental wellbeing and investment in return to work activities can all contribute to better outcomes for business. Not only can rates of poor functioning at work, as well as absenteeism and withdrawal from work, be reduced, but a healthy workplace environment can foster creativity and innovation (Robertson & Cooper, 2011; Wang & Samson, 2009). McDaid and Park indicate in Chapter 9 of this volume that not only is there a business case for workplace health promotion, but that there are other additional benefits including reduced use of health-care services and less need to claim long-term disability benefits as a result of work-related mental health problems. Healthy workplaces should not be the preserve of large companies and major public sector organizations; but financial and regulatory incentives may be needed to stimulate investment in workplace health promotion in small enterprises, particularly in contexts where health-care costs are not paid for by employers.

Turning to the wellbeing of older people, many societies do not put enough value on the wisdom and benefits of age, instead having very negative conceptions of aging. A not often reported statistic is that, even beyond official retirement age (in countries where this concept still exists), older people make a positive net economic contribution to the economy, even when their higher rates of disability and health problems are taken into account.

Promoting wellbeing is integral to a healthy aging process and cost-effective measures to tackle risk factors to wellbeing such as social and geographical isolation, bereavement, poor lifestyle behaviors and loss of role are identified in the chapter by Park and colleagues. The importance of prioritizing actions to promote the health of older people will become ever more acute given changing population demographics in many high-income countries and a growing recognition of the importance of protecting the health of older workers, as well as the countless millions of older people who are providing care and support not only for spouses but also for other groups such as their grandchildren. The cost to any policy maker of having to substitute professional carers for informal family carers should also be a powerful incentive for investing in measures to protect wellbeing at older ages.

We have already highlighted how Osberg and Sharpe in this volume have looked at impacts of the current economic downturn on wellbeing in many nations. We can also learn much at individual country level about the impacts on health and wellbeing behaviors in times of austerity and uncertainty. Perhaps no other country was as affected by the 2008 economic crisis as Iceland. Tinna Laufey Ásgeirsdóttir and colleagues were able to use longitudinal survey data that include pre- and post-reports from the same individuals on a range of health-compromising and health-promoting behaviors. They found that the crisis led to significant reductions in some poor behaviors, including smoking and drinking alcohol and sugary drinks, but also a decrease in the consumption of fruit and vegetables. Because of the small size of the population, as well as its concentration around the capital city Reykjavik, it was possible to control for many confounding factors in this analysis, helping to better identify factors that contributed to health behavior change. Reduction in disposable income and dramatic increases in the price of some goods were found to be key variables.

Having a better understanding of how economic shocks, whether boom or bust, impact on health and wellbeing is important to making contingency plans for any future adverse events. McDaid and Wahlbeck explore some of the potential economic consequences of these economic shocks and look at what is known about the effectiveness and cost of actions to alleviate some of the potential risk factors to mental health and wellbeing. A better understanding of local context, as in the Icelandic case, is critical. The magnitude of adverse events and the populations most affected can vary considerably. The chapter stresses that the promotion and protection of mental wellbeing cannot be achieved by the health sector alone. The determinants of mental wellbeing often lie outside of the remits of the health system and all sectors of society have to be involved in its promotion and protection.

We can see from contributions here that research on economics and wellbeing has moved on considerably in the last quarter millennium and there is nothing to suggest that interest is going to wane any time in the near future. Traditional economic measures of growth, while far from being defunct, need to be supplemented with other ways of measuring and putting an economic value on the different dimensions of wellbeing. Care must however be taken in the development of these measures. Policy makers also need to carefully consider how they will best make use of new approaches to wellbeing measurement so as to better evaluate what works best to promote wellbeing, at what cost, and in what context.

References

Beaumont, J. (2012). *Measuring national wellbeing: A discussion paper on domains and measures*. London: Office for National Statistics.

Cameron, D. (2010). *Speech on wellbeing*. London: Cabinet Office. https://www. gov.uk/government/speeches/pm-speech-on-wellbeing.

Deaton, A., & Stone, A. A. (2013). Two happiness puzzles. *American Economic Review, 103*(3), 591–597.

Demyttenaere, K., Bruffaerts, R., Posada-Villa, J., Gasquet, I., Kovess, V., Lepine, J. C.,. . . Chatterji, S. (2004). Prevalence, severity, and unmet need for treatment of mental disorders in the World Health Organization World Mental Health Surveys. *Journal of the American Medical Association, 291*(21), 2581–2590.

Easterlin, R. (1974). Does economic growth improve the human lot? Some empirical evidence. In P A. David & M. W. Reder (Eds.), *Nations and households in economic growth: Essays in honor of Moses Abramovitz* (pp. 89–125). New York: Academic Press.

Edgeworth, F. (1881). *Mathematical psychics: An essay on the application of mathematics to the moral sciences*. New York: Augustus M. Kelly.

Galbraith, J. K. (1958). *The affluent society*. New York: New American Library.

Heckman, J. (2006). *The economics of investing in children. Policy Briefing No 1*. Dublin: UCD Geary Institute.

Layard, R. (2005). *Happiness: Lessons from a new science*. London: Penguin Books.

Marx, K. (1867). *Das Kapital. Kritik der politischen Ökonomie*. Hamburg: Verlag von Otto Meissner.

Nores, M., & Barnett, W. S. (2010). Benefits of early childhood interventions across the world: (Under)Investing in the very young. *Economics of Education Review, 29*(2), 271–282.

Osberg, L., & Sharpe, A. (2005). How should we measure the "economic" aspects of well-being. *Review of Income and Wealth, 51*(2), 311–336.

Robertson, I., & Cooper, C. (2011). *Wellbeing: Productivity and happiness at work*. Basingstoke: Palgrave Macmillan.

Schumacher, E. F. (1973). *Small is beautiful: A study of economics as if people mattered*. London: Blond & Briggs.

Self, A., Thomas, J. & Randall, C. (2012). *Measuring national well-being: Life in the UK, 2012*. London: Office for National Statistics.

Smith, A. (1776/1977). *An inquiry into the nature and causes of the wealth of nations*. Chicago: University of Chicago Press.

Stiglitz, J., Sen, A., & Fitoussi, D.-P. (2010). *Mismeasuring our lives: Why GDP doesn't add up. The report by the Commission on the Measurement of Economic Performance and Social Progress*. New York: The New Press.

Stutzer, A., & Frey. B. (2012). *Recent developments in the economics of happiness: A selective overview* (IZA Discussion Paper no. 7078). Bonn: IZA.

Wang, H., & Samson, K. (2009). *Wellness and productivity management: A new approach to increasing performance*. Philadelphia: Right Management.

Part 1

Perspectives on the Economics of Wellbeing

2

A Short History of Wellbeing Research

Laura Stoll

New Economics Foundation, U.K.

Introduction

"Research" into what constitutes "the good life" began with the origins of philosophy itself. Its foundations lie in Ancient Greece: ideas that began there have shaped the way in which scientists and policy makers still think about wellbeing. After a period characterized by the rise of religious thinking about wellbeing, the Enlightenment signaled a change in the way that wellbeing was conceptualized: it was no longer based in faith and tradition, and could be treated as a science, much like physics or chemistry. This was followed by a growth of interest in wellbeing from sociologists, political philosophers, and psychologists. More recently, over the past 40 years or so and alongside the maturation of wellbeing psychology, there has been a rise in wellbeing as a field of study within economics, tightly linked to the development of its measurement in the second half of the twentieth century.

Ancient Greece

Any introduction to the history of wellbeing research must begin in Ancient Greece, where philosophers documented their theories on what constituted "wellbeing" or "the good life" and how it was to be obtained. These philosophies still form the basis of much of the subjective wellbeing research

The Economics of Wellbeing: Wellbeing: A Complete Reference Guide, Volume V.
Edited by David McDaid and Cary L. Cooper.
© 2014 John Wiley & Sons, Ltd. Published 2014 by John Wiley & Sons, Inc.
DOI: 10.1002/9781118539415.wbwell02

today (Haybron, 2008), and their different conceptualizations of wellbeing as hedonism, *eudaimonia,* and stoicism still guide much of the thinking about the different kinds of subjective wellbeing measures that scientists and policy makers are currently using.

Greece was rich, with an extensive trade network that had expanded across the Mediterranean and several colonies. The first monetary trading system was in existence and in Athens, a burgeoning metropolis, democracy had arrived. Self-government was an incredibly important and very radical departure from the way societies had been ruled up to this point (and also for quite a lot of them after) (Raaflaub, Ober, & Wallace, 2008). Suddenly, the men of Greece had moderate democratic control over important aspects of their lives. This opened up the debate about how one could control one's life to live well and flourish (McMahon, 2006).[1]

Socrates (470–399 B.C.E.)[2] was the first philosopher to consider in detail the necessary conditions for happiness. Although there are no extant texts written by Socrates himself, his thoughts about wellbeing are captured in the writings of Plato, his most famous student and one of his most loyal proponents. In Plato's *Symposium,* Socrates describes happiness as what the gods possess (Griffith, 1989). He says that happiness is not found through hedonism—the pursuit of pleasure—it is not found in good fortune, power, riches, fame, or even health or familial love. In place of these things, Socrates preaches philosophy. His recipe for living well is through lifelong learning: beginning in youth, men learn not to desire physical beauty but to put a higher value on beauty of the mind. Through this process they learn gradually to desire wisdom and to become philosophers. Plato believed that through this process of learning self-control, humans could acquire wellbeing (Griffith, 1989).

Plato's most famous student, Aristotle, is also a key figure in the history of wellbeing. Aristotle's complex moral philosophy cannot be summarized easily, but one of the concepts central to the current conceptualization of wellbeing is that of *eudaimonia.* Aristotle proposed that the aim of life is *eudaimonia*—sometimes translated as happiness—but, in Aristotle's words, is "pretty well defined as a sort of well-living and well-acting." Well-living and well-acting involve satisfactory performance of those things that are particularly characteristic of us as human beings. Happiness is therefore excellent performance of the tasks that are typical of a man:

> Just as a good lyre-player is someone who performs well at the tasks which lyre-players perform professionally or qua [the characteristics of] lyre-players,

so a good man is someone who performs well at the tasks which men perform typically or qua men.

Barnes (2004), p. xxvi

The question thus becomes what are these things that are particularly characteristic or *qua* of us as humans? Aristotle's answer is that man is a rational animal and, accordingly, the most characteristic human activity is contemplation, by which Aristotle means a quasi-aesthetic appreciation of knowledge and truth. However, only a god-like few can achieve this for much of their life, and therefore the exercise of practical rationality, following reason in day-to-day life, should be the aim of most people. This requires us to foster and exercise *areté*, normally translated as virtue but perhaps more accurately as good character or excellence, and including such characteristics as justice, courage, temperance, and wittiness (Barnes, 2004). This often involves ensuring that extreme forms of behavior are avoided and being careful to judge the right way of behaving. It is the excellent performance itself that counts for those who cannot achieve a life of contemplation.

This performance lasts a lifetime and the resulting *eudaimonia* is not a momentary state but something that characterizes an entire life. Indeed, one can only determine whether people are happy after their lives are over. Accordingly, Aristotle prescribes a lifelong training for acquiring virtue.

Aristotle systematized this thought by proposing three sorts of goods contributing to happiness: goods of the soul, including the moral and intellectual virtues; goods of the body, such as strength, good health, beauty, and sound senses; and external goods, such as wealth, friends, good birth, good children, good heredity, good reputation, and others. External and bodily goods might be necessary, or at least make it easier, to perform virtuous actions, although on their own they are insufficient for achieving *eudaimonia*. In other words, Aristotle drew a clear distinction between wellbeing and the necessary conditions for wellbeing, a distinction very much recognized by the current treatment of subjective wellbeing measures as *outcomes* of several other conditions of people's lives, from employment to health and marriage.

By the end of the fourth century B.C.E., happiness variously defined was the ultimate goal of all the Greek philosophical schools, including Stoicism and Epicureanism. Both Zeno (born c. 335 B.C.E.), founder of the Stoics, and Epicurus (born c. 341 B.C.E.), founder of the Epicureans, believed that wellbeing was a private state and therefore was ours to control. This message resonated in a time of social and political change in Greece: Athenian democracy had collapsed and its independence was destroyed following Alexander's death in 323 B.C.E. and the incorporation of its dominions into the Macedonian empire (McMahon, 2006). It has been posited that this period of disruption and dislocation led to the citizens of Greece experiencing a sense of powerlessness and perhaps a loss of cultural identity, making them particularly welcoming of the kinds of messages that were being proposed by the Stoics and Epicureans: that wellbeing was independent of those external conditions that lay outside an individual's control, and instead was within the realms of private agency (Bok, 2010). Unlike Plato and Aristotle, Zeno and Epicurus also offered a much more inclusive vision of wellbeing: Epicurus theorized that women and slaves could aim for happiness, whilst Zeno preached the natural kinship of all humankind.

Epicurus famously argued that "pleasure is the beginning and the goal of a happy life" (McMahon, 2006), but his main concern was not positive pleasure but the absence of pain and mental illness. He thought that the examination of our personal motives and the development of self-knowledge would enable us to free ourselves from these sources of pain. By pursuing happiness in this way virtue would be the result—but it did not need to be consciously cultivated. Zeno and the Stoics, by contrast, argued that people must bring their individual natures into harmony with nature as a whole using virtue and wisdom. This process required attention and cultivation; striving to be virtuous was the only way of attaining a flourishing life.

There was, of course, a continuing evolution of thinking and writing about wellbeing over the next two millennia. The development of the Abrahamic religions, the Renaissance, and the Reformation all brought about changes in the ways that philosophers, political leaders, and the public viewed the attainment of wellbeing, although there was an enduring focus on tradition and faith. For reasons of brevity, this chapter will not attempt to detail this extended period, but instead will begin again in the second half of the seventeenth century, with the rise of reason and science.

The Enlightenment: Seventeenth- and Eighteenth-Century Europe

Increasingly, in the late seventeenth century, writers agreed that it was possible to construct a science of wellbeing—just as Isaac Newton and others had shown that it was possible to construct a science of physics. Wellbeing might have to be pursued individually, but it was possible to work out what that required. Enlightenment thinkers preached social progress through knowledge, putting forth a picture of a world that could be understood and governed by discernible laws (Reill, 2003). What is more, just as physics had its basic substance—atoms—so any science of wellbeing would have its basic substance, namely pleasure. Like atoms, this could be analyzed, quantified, and measured. The result was a much greater emphasis on wellbeing as a series of good experiences rather than as arising from the entire narrative of one's life or a series of good relationships—ideas that had played a more prominent role in the past.

This new view of wellbeing as a topic of scientific research was reflected in a sudden increase of works on happiness in the last two decades of the seventeenth century (McMahon, 2006). By the middle of the eighteenth century there was a huge explosion in studies, reflections, treatises, discourses, sketches, and essays on happiness from France, Britain, the Low Countries, Germany, Italy, and America. Amongst them, Voltaire in 1734, and Diderot in 1749 both wrote about happiness and religion, criticizing the Christian argument that earthly life was wretched and true happiness was only achievable, if at all, in the afterlife.

In 1772, Francois-Jean de Chastellux attempted to write the world's first history of happiness—a piece of comparative sociology to find out the levels of happiness in different populations at different times (McMahon, 2006). Chastellux argued that this, in theory, required knowledge of complex variables such as levels of taxation, daily and yearly totals of the working hours expended to secure basic necessities and ease, estimates of the leisure time available to workers, and calculations of the hours individuals could labor "without succumbing to despair." However, in practice he used an easier approach, which used measures of slavery and war as the greatest impediments to public happiness, followed by religious superstition (which he thought led to ascetic self-denial, unnecessary fear, and the misappropriation of resources). Chastellux also contended that levels of population and the productivity of agriculture correlated directly with *félicité publique* (McMahon, 2006).

Chastellux epitomizes the desire of Enlightenment thinkers to use science and measurement in the quest for wellbeing and their extension of the responsibility for creating the conditions for flourishing lives to society itself. This desire to explain human behavior according to natural laws is a legacy of the Enlightenment that continues to have a powerful grip on modern society, as is the idea of the rational pleasure-maximizing individual, the *Homo economicus* of orthodox economics.

This emphasis on wellbeing as pleasure also led to widespread conviction in the principle of utility: "the greatest happiness of the greatest number." This principle, of maximizing pleasure and minimizing pain, could now be used to judge the usefulness of all actions and objects. However, this relied on pleasure and pain being measurable. Jeremy Bentham, an author and proponent of utilitarianism had the notion of constructing a "felicific calculus" that would allow decision makers to calculate the net pleasure or pain connected to every action and for everyone affected by that action, with public policy choices made to get the greatest net pleasure or least net pain for the greatest number of people (Sirgy et al., 2006). He assigned values to the "intensity, duration, certainty or uncertainty, propinquity [physical or psychological proximity between people] or remoteness, fecundity, and purity" of pleasure and pain which could be used to follow his principle (Bentham, 1789/2007). This attempt to sum pleasure and pain is seen by some as the forefather of subjective wellbeing research (Bok, 2010; Powdthavee, 2010). Julian Offray de La Mettrie took the principle to its logical extreme, rejecting all hope of immortality and arguing that sensation was all that counted (Bok, 2010).

Not that pleasure trumped religion and virtue during this period. The link between virtue and happiness was also being preached across the Christian world: over the course of the eighteenth century there were hundreds of sermons that linked social welfare and the pursuit of happiness to the pursuit of Christian ethics. There was also a popular belief that desire without limits was dangerous, as was desire focused only on the self. Men and women continued to look to God for guidance in how to live, and Christian doctrines were regarded by many as an authoritative guide to the pursuit of happiness.

Even economists emphasized virtue. Adam Smith (1723–1790) thought that true happiness lay in "tranquillity and enjoyment," which he thought had less to do with economic conditions than with virtue. He recognized that most men pursued happiness through wealth but argued that this was a devious path. Smith also believed that the division of labor, and the subsequent lack of control and connection that workers felt over the goods they produced, would lead men to become alienated from each other and to become more ignorant; he believed that the solution to this lay in public schooling and civic education (Smith, 1776/1977).

Another prominent figure in the Scottish Enlightenment, Francis Hutcheson (1694–1746), maintained that the most effective way to promote private pleasure was to do publicly useful things—in other words, happiness is pursued by being good (McMahon, 2008). So the link between virtue and happiness discussed by Aristotle, Plato, Epicurus, and others, was emphasized once more, this time in the period of development of modern governments. The theory and numerous variations on it were very popular in Britain, Europe and America.

Looking to Other Societies: The Nineteenth Century

When Alexis de Tocqueville was sent by the French government to America in 1831 to research the criminal justice system, he wrote about the evolution he saw towards freedom and democracy in this relatively new nation. He noted that a great many Americans believed that the pursuit of happiness and the pursuit of wealth were one and the same. They therefore often sought nothing more than the freedom to pursue their happiness according to this idea, attempting to create a better life for themselves and their families, and enjoying the fruits of their labor in the process. But de Tocqueville felt that there were two countervailing factors that prevented America from becoming a purely hedonistic society: first, there was a strong norm encouraging people to find those places where their own individual interests and those of the whole society coincided—a belief that at least sometimes by serving others they could serve themselves; and second, religion played an important social role, acting as a necessary check on the desire for physical pleasure (De Tocqueville, 1838).

At a similar time, a similar observation was being made by John Stuart Mill. Mill, who had been educated by his father and his father's friend Jeremy Bentham, had followed Bentham's principles of utilitarianism until 1826, when he began to disagree with several of the premises. He started to think of human progress not just in terms of maximizing the number of outward sources of pleasure and minimizing those of pain, but also as a nurturing of long-stifled emotions. He proposed that happiness could only be attained if it was not made the direct end but gained through the pursuit of other ends. Throughout the body of his philosophical work, Mill considers candidates for the "end," including justice, self-sacrifice, beauty, dignity, love, independence, diversity, and liberty. He also disagreed with Bentham that all kinds of pleasures were of the same quality. Mill argued that there were better and worse types of happiness: happiness was not the same as contentment; it involved the pursuit of "nobler feelings," "higher pleasures," and higher things. He thought that residual Christian moralism, as exemplified by Calvinism from the sixteenth and seventeenth centuries, had made it more difficult for people to experience self-realization and self-actualization (Mill, 1863/2001). In order to overcome this Christian culture of conformity and to have a true definition of self required for happiness, people needed to be more self-assertive.

In 1904, a visit to the United States by another European sociologist, Max Weber, prompted a theory on the source of the "spirit of capitalism" that de Tocqueville had witnessed so strongly (Weber, 1930). Weber proposed that Protestant anxiety over the fate of individual salvation had motivated people to accumulate capital, which was regarded as a sign (and a partial assurance) of God's blessing. More specifically, the ascetic renunciation and the notion of work as a divine calling associated with the Protestant faith, combined with a critically rational disposition, had brought together capitalism's essential qualities: the restriction of consumption in favor of the accrual of capital, and a religious ethic of discipline, industry, thrift, and delayed gratification.

Writing in the 1840s in England, the philosopher, writer, and historian Thomas Carlyle provided a quite different response to the individualist development of capitalism and the pleasure principle. Describing economics as "the dismal science," he wrote of the false promises of happiness: falling wages, abominable working conditions, political disenfranchisement, and the rising cost of bread had sparked protests across England (McMahon, 2006). Carlyle argued that if you looked at history, it was clear what people needed: a close-knit community, purposeful labor, and a sense of God.

Friedrich Engels, a contemporary of Carlyle's, agreed with much of his analysis. He thought that there was a route to happiness that was common to all men. This route was to be found through communism, which, he and Karl Marx argued, would deliver community and purposeful labor as well as a more equitable distribution of the fruits of that labor. The result would be a more meaningful life and profound, indeed spiritual, satisfaction. Marx discounted the current ideals of domestic happiness and depicted the nuclear family and marriage as a bourgeois institution. Above all, work was to be an important source of satisfaction in the future. Marx, like Adam Smith before him, argued that the division of labor had led to alienation of man from his product and society. His solution, though, was different: in order to address this, private property must be completely abolished (Engels, 1884/1983; Marx & Engels, 1888/2009).

The nineteenth century was also a prolific period for utopian experiments as people reacted to industrialization, with a particular concentration in the United States (Pitzer, 1997). A typical example is the several hundred New Icarian socialists who arrived in Nauvoo, Illinois, in 1849 to found their ideal city, New Icaria, where they would put an end to social strife and put into practice true Christianity, a kind of egalitarian communism. Private property was to be abolished and everyone would work in harmony towards the common good.[3]

There were many different ideas as to how to create utopia (Pitzer, 1997). Étienne Cabet (of New Icaria) and Robert Owen, a Welsh social reformer, envisioned the common ownership of goods, equality, and grassroots autonomy as the conditions of a prosperous society; Henri de Saint-Simon imagined a technocratic hierarchy in which science and industry would be managed by highly skilled elites in order to serve the masses; and Charles Fourier thought that since individuals' needs and abilities varied widely, total equality would be unsuitable, instead proposing to match personality types (of which, in his slightly idiosyncratic psychology, there were 810) to complement one another (Christensen & Levinson, 2003). All these men inspired, or attempted to create themselves, utopian societies in Europe and America. But although these early socialists often disagreed about what was needed to live a good life, they generally agreed about the causes of unhappiness in the present world: the swings of the business cycle that left entire sectors of the workforce in poverty on a periodic basis; the terrible conditions of workplaces, especially factories and mines; the terrible living conditions and overcrowding of slums, which caused sickness and disease to spread. And they all argued that wellbeing must be extended to all—unless all were happy, none could be happy.

Psychology and Wellbeing

At the end of the nineteenth century the new-found field of psychology began to develop its own theories—and empirical research—on wellbeing. This arose out of much earlier works such as that of John Locke (1632–1704), who proposed that wellbeing involved satisfying an uneasiness that is natural to men and women; and that there was no single version of how humans could flourish, a template forged in heaven for us to follow: different things made different people happy, and to try to satisfy them using the same means was not possible. Psychologists began to think about the internal, rather than external, drivers of wellbeing.

In *Principles of psychology*, the philosopher and psychologist William James theorized that humans rely on introspective observation for insight into understanding the nature of their experiences (James, 1890/1950). In his work on the study of wellbeing, he used observation and experimental findings on introspection, as well as works of art and autobiographical writings, including the self-narratives of Rousseau, Teresa of Avila, Thoreau, Tolstoy, and others. In *The varieties of religious experience* he illustrates the many ways that people used meditation, prayer, and soul-searching to focus on happiness (or unhappiness) in different spiritual traditions (James, 1902/1985).

Friedrich Nietzsche also recognized that religion, specifically Christianity, was a source of wellbeing, albeit, in his eyes, an impoverished one (McMahon, 2006). For the people who led difficult or oppressed lives it offered the opportunity of being "God's elect," transforming present suffering into preparation for the wellbeing that would be experienced at some future point. Nietzsche argued that the Christian and Socratic faiths undermined the possibility of developing "faith in oneself." The legacies of these philosophical traditions were a human denial of our own nature—our most basic instincts, dispositions, and driving motivations. It also lead to the guilt and "shame at being man" that humans felt. In order to develop faith in ourselves, we would have to unlearn this loathing, and only then could self-realization replace self-denial.

Sigmund Freud, whose work formed the beginning of psychoanalysis, maintained that the pursuit of the good life had two sides to it: a positive and a negative. The negative was the absence of pain and suffering and the positive was the experience of strong feelings of pleasure (Freud, 1930/2002). Freud thought that the best path to wellbeing, rather than drugs, hedonism, withdrawal from society, or the practice of asceticism, was that of "becoming a member of the human community and working for the good of all" (McMahon, 2006). He dismissed religion and the aesthetic approach—where happiness is found in art and beauty—as illusory, arguing that the pleasures to be had through creative and productive work were far more promising. Freud particularly commended "professional activity" and especially "physical and intellectual work," and also argued that erotic love was perhaps closer to the goal of wellbeing than any other method. He was a proponent of the long tradition according to which a life well lived involved effective action; also observing that humans should not seek out complete satisfaction from any single source.

Wellbeing in the Twentieth Century

From William James' work on wellbeing at the turn of the century, it was not long before more empirical studies of subjective wellbeing in psychology followed. In 1925 Flügel studied moods by asking people to record their emotional experience of events and then summing their emotional reactions across these moments (Flügel, 1925). Subsequently a number of scholars investigated the effects of positive mood (Diener, Oishi, & Lucas, 2009; Hersey, 1932; Johnson, 1937).

But while psychological research on wellbeing was becoming a burgeoning field, economists' interest in subjective wellbeing did not experience the same level of growth. The origins of economic interest in wellbeing can be traced back to welfare economists such as A. C. Pigou, Francis Edgeworth, Henry Sidgwick, and Alfred Marshall. A. C. Pigou, for example, thought that "there is a clear presumption that changes in economic welfare indicate changes in social welfare in the same direction, if not the same degree" (Pigou, 1929). Edgeworth, following in the footsteps of his Utilitarian forefathers, went so far as to envisage the "hedonimeter," a machine that continually registers the "height of pleasure experienced by an individual . . . the delicate index now flickering with the flutter of the passions, now steadied by intellectual activity, low sunk whole hours in the neighbourhood of zero, or momentarily springing up towards infinity" (Edgeworth, 1881, p. 101).

But with the dominance of the "preference satisfaction" account of wellbeing in neoclassical economics, and subjective wellbeing measures condemned by economists such as Jevons, Pareto, and Robbins, wellbeing fell out of favor in mainstream economics for much of the twentieth century (MacKerron, 2011).

Despite, or perhaps because of, the lack of interest in wellbeing within mainstream economics, the 1930s saw the rise of the social indicators movement, signaled by a couple of key publications—*Recent social trends in the United States* (Ogburn, 1933) and *Southern regions of the United States* (Odum, 1936). This "movement" reflected a desire not only that research using social indicators should exert an influence on the field of social sciences, but also that these indicators should be used to measure and monitor levels of quality of life and social progress across time and geographical areas (Noll, 2002).

After the Second World War questions on happiness and life satisfaction began to be included on global polls. George Gallup and Hadley Cantril pioneered the use of large-scale surveys as an assessment technique (Diener et al., 2009). These questions tended to be fairly simple, with simple response options, but were still valuable in the study of subjective wellbeing. As the subjective wellbeing research field has matured, more multi-item scales have appeared, with greater reliability and validity than single-item instruments (See further discussion on this issue in the Chapter 3 in this volume).

Then, in the 1960s, the U.S. National Aeronautics and Space Administration (NASA) supported the development of the National Commission on Technology, Automation, and Economic Progress and *Social indicators* (Bauer, 1966), which explored the potential of social indicator developments (Sirgy et al., 2006). After further encouragement from sociologists (Moore & Sheldon, 1965), the Federal Government set up a Panel on Social Indicators and, following this, launched a program to produce chart books of indicators in time series (U.S. Bureau of the Census, 1981; U.S. Office of Management and Budget, 1974, 1976).

The rise of the use of social indicators by statisticians was accompanied by recognition amongst certain politicians that welfare needed to be measured in a more comprehensive way than purely by economic growth. In a now oft-quoted speech from 1968, Robert Kennedy criticized the use of gross national product (GNP) as a measure of welfare:

> Gross National Product counts air pollution, and cigarette advertising and . . . the destruction of the redwood and the loss of our natural wonder in chaotic sprawl. It does not allow for the health of our children, the quality of their education or the joy of their play . . . the beauty of our poetry or the strength of our marriages. It measures everything, in short, except that which makes life worthwhile.
>
> Kennedy (1968)

It was also in the 1960s that a few psychology researchers began to focus on happiness as a central topic. Warner Wilson published a review paper in 1967 focused on "correlates of avowed happiness" in which he described the characteristics of a happy person (Wilson, 1967). This provided a starting point for the empirical study of subjective wellbeing in psychology (Wilson, 1967). In 1969 Bradburn introduced the "Affect Balance Scale" which was intended to assess negative and positive affect.[4] Findings demonstrated the relative independence of positive affect and negative affect and supported the idea (discussed by Freud) that they represented separate factors within the encompassing construct of subjective wellbeing (Sirgy et al., 2006).

Although government support dwindled, the 1970s saw a flourishing in social indicators research and publications (Sirgy et al., 2006). This included a large growth in studies using subjective wellbeing data and theories in psychology, economics, and public policy; "happiness" was first listed by *Psychological Abstracts International* as an index term in 1973 (Sirgy et al., 2006). Large-scale national quality of life surveys, which included assessments of subjective wellbeing, such as the Eurobarometer, were also conducted in the 1970s (Andrews & Withey, 1976; Campbell, Converse, & Rodgers, 1976).

In 1974 a new journal, *Social Indicators Research*, was published. This focused on quality of life (QoL) research and represented an important publication outlet for subjective wellbeing researchers (Sirgy et al., 2006). Also in 1974, Robert Nozick, the political philosopher, proposed a now famous thought experiment: the experience machine. Nozick asked: would we choose to be connected to a machine that simulated a life of continuously experienced pleasure, and contentment more generally, or would we choose reality? (Nozick, 1974). The rise of wellbeing as a topic in political philosophy (public policy) mirrored the rising interest from psychologists.

The first attempt within economics to assess the trend of wellbeing in terms of personal reports of happiness or life satisfaction was that of Easterlin in 1974, an article which was famously rejected by the *American Economic Review* before eventually being published as a chapter in a book on economic growth (Powdthavee, 2010). The research found that, despite rising GDP per capita, average happiness in the United States rose through the late 1950s and then fell for the following 20 years, returning to near its 1946 level by 1970 (Easterlin, 1974). After this now infamous study, the results eventually dubbed the 'Easterlin Paradox', economic research on subjective reports of wellbeing—wellbeing economics—languished over the next two decades with only a few exceptions (Frank, 1985; Scitovsky, 1976), such as Bernard M. S. Praag who made notable advances in the analysis of subjective data on the adequacy of income (Sirgy et al., 2006).

In about 1990 there began to be a small upsurge in economic research on subjective wellbeing. Considerable credit for this has been given to the work of British economist Andrew Oswald and colleagues, as well as to Bruno Frey, a Swiss academic in economic psychology (Frey & Stutzer, 2002; Oswald, 1997). By contrast, the 1990s witnessed an explosion in *psychological* research

Barnes, J. (2004). Introduction. In Aristotle, *The Nicomachean ethics*. London: Penguin Books.

Bauer, R. A. (1966). *Social indicators*. Cambridge, MA: The MIT Press.

Bentham, J. (1789/2007). *An introduction to principles of morals and legislation*. New York: Dover Publications.

Bok, S. (2010). *Exploring happiness: From Aristotle to brain science*. New Haven: Yale University Press.

Campbell, A. C., Converse, P. E., & Rodgers, W. L. (1976). *The quality of American life*. New York: The Russell Sage Foundation.

Christensen, K., & Levinson, D. (2003). *Encyclopaedia of community: From the village to the virtual world*. Great Barrington, MA: Berkshire Publishing Group.

De Tocqueville, A. (1838). *De la démocratie en Amérique* [Democracy in America]. New York: George Dearborn & Co. and Adlard & Saunders.

Diener, E., Oishi, S., & Lucas, R. (2009). Subjective well-being: The science of happiness and life satisfaction. In C. R. Snyder & S. J. Lopez (Eds.), *Oxford handbook of positive psychology* (pp. 63–73). Oxford: Oxford University Press.

Easterlin, R. (1974). Does economic growth improve the human lot? Some empirical evidence. In P. A. David & M. W. Reder (Eds.), *Nations and households in economic growth: Essays in honor of Moses Abramovitz* (pp. 89–125). New York: Academic Press.

Eckman, P., Davidson, R. J., & Friesen, W. V. (1990). The Duchenne smile: Emotional expression and brain psychology II. *Journal of Personality and Social Psychology, 58*(2), 342–353.

Edgeworth, F. (1881). *Mathematical psychics: An essay on the application of mathematics to the moral sciences*. New York: Augustus M. Kelly.

Engels, F. (1884/1983). *The origin of the family, private property and the state*. New York: Pathfinder Press.

Flügel, J. C. (1925). A quantitative study of feeling emotion in everyday life. *British Journal of Psychology, 15*, 318–355.

Foresight Mental Capital and Wellbeing Project (2008). *Final project report—Executive summary*. London: Government Office for Science.

Frank, R. H. (1985). The demand for unobservable and other nonpositional goods. *American Economic Review, 75*(1), 101–116.

Freud, S. (1930/2002). *Civilization and its discontents*. London: Penguin.

Frey, B. S., & Stutzer, A. (2002). What can economists learn from happiness research? *Journal of Economic Literature, 40*(2), 402–435.

Griffith, T. (Trans.). (1989). *Plato: The symposium*. Berkeley: University of California Press.

Haybron, D. (2008). Philosophy and the science of subjective well-being. In M. Eid & R. Larsen (Eds.), *The science of subjective well-being* (pp. 17–43). New York: The Guildford Press.

Hersey, R. B. (1932). *Workers' emotions in shop and home—A study of individual workers from the psychological and physiological standpoint*. Philadelphia: University of Pennsylvania Press.

James, W. (1890/1950). *The principles of psychology*. New York: Dover Publications.

James, W. (1902/1985). *The varieties of religious experience*. London: Penguin Classics.

Johnson, W. B. (1937). Euphoric and depressed moods in normal subjects I & II. *Journal of Character and Personality*, 6, 79–98.

Kahneman, D., & Krueger, A. (2006). Developments in the measurement of subjective well-being. *Journal of Economic Perspectives*, 20(1), 3–24.

Kennedy, R. F. (1968). *Robert F. Kennedy on what GNP means*. Retrieved from http://www2.mccombs.utexas.edu/faculty/michael.brandl/main%20page%20items/Kennedy%20on%20GNP.htm

MacKerron, G. (2011). Happiness economics from 35,000 feet. *Journal of Economic Surveys*, 26, 705–735.

Marx, K., & Engels, F. (1888/2009). *The communist manifesto*. Middlesex: The Echo Library.

McMahon, D. M. (2006). *The pursuit of happiness: A history from the Greeks to the present*. London: Penguin Books.

McMahon, D. M. (2008). The market and the pursuit of happiness. In J. M. Imber (Ed.), *Markets, morals and religions* (pp. 99–114). New Brunswick, NJ: Transaction Publishers.

Mill, J. S. (1863/2001). *Utilitarianism*. Indianapolis: Hackett Publishing Company.

Moore, W. E, & Sheldon, E. B. (1965). *Monitoring social change: A conceptual and programmatic statement*. Washington, DC: Social Statistics, Proceedings of the American Statistical Association.

Myers, D. G., & Diener, E. (1995). Who is happy? *Psychological Science*, 6, 10–19.

Noll, H.-H. (2002). Social indicators and quality of life research: Background, achievements and current trends. In N. Genov (Ed.), *Advances in sociological knowledge over half a century*. Paris: International Social Science Council.

Nozick, R. (1974). *Anarchy, state and utopia*. New York: Basic Books.

Odum, H. W. (1936). *Southern regions of the United States*. Chapel Hill, NC: The University of North Carolina Press.

Ogburn, W. (1933). *Recent social trends in the United States: Report of the President's Commission on social trends*. New York: McGraw-Hill.

Oswald, A. J. (1997). Happiness and economic performance. *Economic Journal*, 107, 1815–1831.

Pigou, A. C. (1929). *The economics of welfare* (3rd ed.). London: Macmillan.

Pitzer, D. E. (1997). *America's communal utopias*. Chapel Hill: University of North Carolina Press.

Powdthavee, N. (2010). *The happiness equation: The surprising economics of our most valuable asset*. London: Icon Books Limited.

Raaflaub, K. A., Ober, J., & Wallace, R. W. (2008). *Origins of democracy in ancient Greece*. Berkely, CA: University of California Press.

Reill, P. H. (2003). The legacy of the scientific revolution: Science and the Enlightenment. In R. Porter (Ed.), *The Cambridge history of science, volume 4:*

Eighteenth-century science, (pp. 23–43). Cambridge: Cambridge University Press.

Sandvik, E., Diener, E., & Seidlitz, L. (1993). Subjective well-being: The convergence and stability of self and non self report measures. *Journal of Personality and Social Psychology*, *61*(3), 317–342.

Scitovsky, T. (1976). *The joyless economy: An inquiry into human satisfaction and consumer dissatisfaction*. New York: Oxford University Press.

Seligman, M. E., & Csikszentmihalyi, M. (2000). Positive psychology. An introduction. *American Psychologist*, *55*(1), 5–14.

Shedler, J., Mayman, M., & Manis, M. (1993). The illusion of mental health. *American Psychologist*, *48*(11), 1117–1131.

Sirgy, M. J., Michalos, A. C., Ferris, A. L., Easterlin, R., Patrick, D., & Pavot, W. (2006). The Quality-of-life (QOL) research movement: Past, present, and future. *Social Indicators Research*, *76*, 343–466.

Smith, A. (1776/1977). *An inquiry into the nature and causes of the wealth of nations*. Chicago: University of Chicago Press.

Stiglitz, J., Sen, A., & Fitoussi, J.-A. (2010). *Mismeasuring our lives: Why GDP doesn't add up*. The Report by the Commission on the Measurement of Economic Performance and Social Progress. New York: The New Press.

U.S. Bureau of the Census (1981). *Social indicators III*. Washington, DC: U.S. Government Printing Office.

U.S. Office of Management and Budget (1974). *Social indicators, 1973*. Washington, DC: U.S. Government Printing Office.

U.S. Office of Management and Budget (1976). *Social indicators, 1976*. Washington, DC: U.S. Government Printing Office.

Weber, M. (1930). *The Protestant ethic and the spirit of capitalism*. London: Routledge Classics.

Wilson, W. (1967). Correlates of avowed happiness. *Psychological Bulletin*, *67*, 284–306.

Further Reading

Bok, S. (2010). *Exploring happiness: From Aristotle to brain science*. New Haven and London: Yale University Press. An interesting look at the history of the philosophy of happiness according to key themes, as well as an up-to-date description of current scientific developments.

Diener, E., Oishi, S., & Lucas, R. (2009). Subjective well-being: The science of happiness and life satisfaction. In C. R. Snyder & S. J. Lopez (Eds.), *Oxford handbook of positive psychology* (pp. 63–73). Oxford: Oxford University Press. Written by leading wellbeing psychologists, this introduces some of the key concepts and their historical origins.

Haybron, D. (2008). Philosophy and the science of subjective well-being. In M. Eid & R. Larsen (Eds.), *The science of subjective well-being* (pp. 17–43).

New York: The Guildford Press. An in-depth analysis of the philosophy of wellbeing and how this relates to modern scientific concepts.

MacKerron, G. (2011). Happiness economics from 35,000 feet. *Journal of Economic Surveys, 26*, 705–735. A useful summary of some of the economic approaches to studying wellbeing, this also includes as a description of the key findings from wellbeing economics.

McMahon, D. M. (2006). *The pursuit of happiness: A history from the Greeks to the Present*. London, U.K.: Penguin Books. An invaluable and comprehensive history of happiness in western philosophy—a key text for readers who wish to get an overview of the subject.

Sirgy, M. J., Michalos, A. C., Ferris, A. L., Easterlin, R., Patrick, D., & Pavot, W. (2006). The Quality-of-life (QOL) research movement: past, present, and future. *Social Indicators Research, 76*, 343–466. This comprehensive paper traces the history of research in social indicators and quality of life from the perspectives of several disciplines: philosophy, sociology, economics, subjective wellbeing, health-related quality of life, marketing and organizational psychology.

3

Income and Wellbeing

A Selective Review

Brendan Kennelly
NUI Galway, Ireland

Introduction

One of the most fundamental questions about wellbeing is the relationship
between it and income. This issue can be explored at several levels. What
role does income play in determining individual wellbeing? What is the
relationship over time and across countries between aggregate measures of
income and aggregate measures of wellbeing? Can the impact of income
on wellbeing be distinguished from other factors such as health or social
relationships or work?

An issue may be fundamental, but this sometimes does not prevent it
from being ignored by researchers for long periods of time. It is a reasonable
summary of a great deal of economic analysis in the twentieth century that
the relationship between income and wellbeing was taken to be unworthy
of much investigation. Blanchflower and Oswald (2011) recall how difficult
it was for them to interest fellow economists in their work on subjective
wellbeing in the early 1990s. To paraphrase John Rawls, more income was
assumed to be something that all rational individuals wanted. There seemed
to be little desire to question this assumption and generations of economics
students began their study of microeconomics by accepting this analysis
as given. As Stutzer and Frey (2012) have said, doubting that income
and happiness were close correlates constituted an important challenge to
traditional economics.

The Economics of Wellbeing: Wellbeing: A Complete Reference Guide, Volume V.
Edited by David McDaid and Cary L. Cooper.
© 2014 John Wiley & Sons, Ltd. Published 2014 by John Wiley & Sons, Inc.
DOI: 10.1002/9781118539415.wbwell03

The public policy implications of the standard approach in economics were clear: governments should try to maximize aggregate income and/or maximize economic growth. What was true for a society would also apply to individuals and, strange as it may now seem, many people in the Western world seemed to survive reasonably well without the multitude of self-help and advice books that have appeared in recent years and purport to tell people how to be "really" happy or fulfilled. Further evidence for the primary importance of economic factors in peoples' lives came from studies of voting behavior which found strong relationships between economic conditions and voting intentions (Price & Sanders, 1995).

A cursory examination of what economists and others have been doing in the past 20 years easily finds that much has changed. It has become the norm for people writing about wellbeing and economics to begin by referring to how many papers have been published on this topic. So, on February 21, 2013 a search on Google Scholar for the words "economics" and "happiness" produced 264,000 results. Narrowing the search down to papers published since 2012 produced 14,100 results. The main search engine for economics research is EconLit, and a search for the word "happiness" on that engine produced 1,666 results. If other relevant terms such as "life satisfaction" or "subjective wellbeing" were used on these search engines, the number of results would increase significantly.

My aim in this chapter is twofold. First, I want to explore whether this burst of intellectual effort has changed what we think we know about the relationship between subjective wellbeing and income. There is an enormous literature on this issue, so my review will be selective rather than comprehensive. Second, I want to think about the public policy implications arising from recent research on this issue. I shall divide the chapter into three subsections on within-country studies, time-series studies, and cross-country studies and draw together what I think are the most important findings in the concluding section.

Subjective Wellbeing

Happiness economics or the economics of happiness are the names most often given to the rapidly growing subfield of economics that analyzes the determinants of subjective wellbeing (for recent overviews, see MacKerron, 2011 and Stutzer & Frey, 2012). One of the issues that I think is particularly important is that subjective wellbeing, happiness, satisfaction with life, life evaluation, and experienced wellbeing are terms that sound so alike to many people that they are used interchangeably. Yet, as Deaton, Diener, Kahneman, Stone, and others have argued, there is a fundamental difference between concepts that measure experienced wellbeing and concepts that measure life evaluation. I think this is a fundamental point and one that is easily understood, if you simply consider whether it is possible to be experiencing happiness at the moment, or to have experienced it in the past year, while at the same time being dissatisfied with your life as a whole (I believe the answer is that it is). I think it is also possible to imagine that you could be quite satisfied with your life as a whole, but be in a moment or a period where you are feeling unhappy. It is, of course, possible to say that your "overall happiness" is itself a function of how happy you are currently and how satisfied you are with your life as a whole. But such a claim simply leads to ever more circular reasoning and confusion. Another issue is that in evaluating your life you might ask how happy you are with your life, and, if you did, it is possible that the distinction between life evaluation and experienced happiness would become blurred once again.

I prefer an approach that assumes that a general concept, subjective wellbeing, exists and that explores the different ways in which this concept can be captured, although Deaton and Stone warn about the dangers of even using subjective wellbeing as an overarching concept (Deaton & Stone, 2013).

There is one other issue that has to be noted at the outset—namely, that the measures of subjective wellbeing are by their very nature bounded—an issue that has been discussed at length by some commentators (Johns & Ormerod, 2007). If I state in 2009 that I am very satisfied with my life (where "very satisfied" is the highest possible answer) then what do I say in 2010 if you ask me again and I think my life has got better? The lower the number of possible answers to a subjective wellbeing question, the greater is this problem. Given that income measured at an individual level is essentially a continuous variable, then relating it to a variable with as few as three possible outcomes is a major problem (McCloskey, 2012), although many researchers have claimed that this does not pose a serious issue to empirical analysis.

Income and Happiness

It is reasonable to trace the beginning of the happiness economics field to the publication of Richard Easterlin's first paper on this topic in 1974 (Easterlin, 1974). When he wrote the paper in the early 1970s, there was very limited data on happiness. Easterlin examined the available evidence on the relationship between income and happiness in three areas—within a country at a point in time, within a country over time, and across countries.

Within a country Easterlin found clear evidence of a positive relationship between income and happiness. From today's perspective his conclusion might be questioned because of the limited analysis that he conducted. The data was taken from a poll of 1,517 people in the United States in 1970. They were asked whether they were very happy, fairly happy, or not very happy. Respondents were classified into one of six income categories, and Easterlin found that the proportion of people who said they were very happy was considerably higher in high-income groups than in low-income groups.

This basic finding has been replicated in many studies since then. For example, Sacks, Stevenson, and Wolfers (2010) analyzed the relationship between life evaluation and income in the 25 most populous countries in the world in a Gallup poll in 2010 and found that in all of them there was a clear positive relationship between life satisfaction and income with no sign of satiation. Life satisfaction in that poll was measured using a Cantril ladder-of-life question in which people are asked to think of a ladder with 10 steps, where the top step represents the best possible life and the bottom step represents the worst possible life, and asked on which step of the ladder they personally stand at the present time.

Many analysts in this field use the terms happiness and life satisfaction interchangeably and use whatever data is available to them, but Kahneman and Deaton (2010) have argued that it is important to distinguish between emotional wellbeing (also known as hedonic wellbeing or experienced happiness) and life evaluation. Emotional wellbeing refers to the feelings that people experience as they live their lives, whereas life evaluation refers to the judgments that individuals make when they think about their lives. They analyzed responses from more than 450,000 residents in the United States who were surveyed by Gallup in 2008 and 2009 (Gallup began to survey 1,000 people in the United States every day in January 2008). The respondents were asked questions about emotional wellbeing and life evaluation. Deaton and Kahneman argued that income should be measured in logs so that they could focus on whether a percentage change in income has the same impact on subjective wellbeing at different levels of income.

They found that the log of income is positively correlated with life evaluation over the whole range of incomes in their sample, but that this does not hold for their measures of experienced wellbeing. Measures of emotional wellbeing reached a satiation point about an annual income of

US$75,000—beyond that there is no improvement in any of three measures of emotional wellbeing. They noted that about one third of households in the United States had income higher than $75,000 in 2008. They left open the question as to whether it would be more appropriate for public policy to focus on emotional wellbeing or life evaluation if a society decided that it should include subjective wellbeing as a policy objective. Kahneman interprets these results as providing strong evidence that life satisfaction and experienced wellbeing are different concepts. However, many researchers in this field continue to use these measures interchangeably without reflecting on this claim.

However, while the Cantril ladder has become widely accepted as the best possible measure of the life evaluation question, there are problems with it as well. The biggest problem is the inclusion of the word "possible" before life in the question that it presents to respondents (the highest rung on the ladder is the best possible life). This might be interpreted by people in such a way that, in evaluating their lives, they might first consider what is possible and then think about how close to that possibility they think they are. But how do we determine what that possible life is? How many of us have lowered our hopes and expectations in such a way that we might reasonably respond that, though we are high up on the ladder of possible life, we are also dissatisfied in view of what life might have been?

Deaton and Stone (2013) note that many researchers have reported that, while individual income has a positive effective on subjective wellbeing, country or local income has a negative effect. This finding has been interpreted usually as evidence of a relative income effect and has sometimes been used to argue for extra taxes on high incomes or on items associated with high incomes such as luxury goods (Clark, 2011; Frank, 2012). The problem with this claim is that Deaton and Stone find no evidence for it when they analyze more than 1,000,000 responses to life evaluation questions put in the daily Gallup polls in the United States. They find no evidence that the positive effects of income on life evaluation are offset by negative effects from the average income in various areas such as zipcode or county. Indeed the coefficient on zipcode suggests that the average response to the Cantril ladder question is *positively* relative to average income in a zipcode area. This is particularly important as, if a relative income effect exists, one would be more likely to find it in a small geographical area such as a zipcode.

These results do not hold when experienced happiness is used as a measure for subjective wellbeing. For example, the average level of happiness in a state is negatively associated with the average income of a state. The results for experienced happiness could be interpreted as providing support to the relative income hypothesis (Deaton & Stone, 2013). However, they suggest that a hypothesis that is consistent for both measures of subjective wellbeing is that when individuals are asked life evaluation questions they think about their permanent income, which is proxied by the income in their local area, whereas when people are asked about their experienced happiness they think about their current transitory income.

It is reasonable to think that the relative income hypothesis would be more likely to be found in the life evaluation sphere (in thinking about my life as a whole I might think about the people around me) than the experienced happiness question (in answering a question such as "Was I happy yesterday?" I am more likely to think about my own emotional experience than about the income of people in my area).

The positive relationship between subjective wellbeing and individual income has been analyzed using other large data sets as well. Blanchflower and Oswald (2011) ran a regression on 48,000 observations from the United States collected in General Social Surveys between 1972 and 2008. Subjective wellbeing is measured by responses to the following question: "Taken all together, how would you say things are these days—would you say that you are very happy, pretty happy, or not too happy?" Thus there are only three possible answers, two of them indicating a positive level of happiness and one indicating a negative level. Also the question seems to me to be an unfortunate hybrid of a life evaluation question and an experienced happiness question. Respondents are asked to think about life generally (taken all together), but also about their current situation (how things are *these days*), and asked to think about evaluating their life by focusing on how happy they are. Blanchflower and Oswald find that income has a positive significant effect on their measure of subjective wellbeing with this data. They do a similar analysis with a much larger data set from the Behavioral Response Factor Surveillance System (BRFSS) which surveyed over 360,000 people in the United States in 2009. Two subjective wellbeing questions were asked. The first asked people "in general, how satisfied are you with your life?" The second asked people "thinking about your mental health, which includes stress, depression, and problems with emotions, for how many days during the past 30 days was your mental health not good?" Income has a strong effect on both measures, a finding that remains even when a large number of other variables are controlled for.

Income, Wellbeing, and the Easterlin Paradox

As I mentioned earlier, the happiness economics field can be traced back to the publication of Richard Easterlin's paper in 1974. Easterlin also looked at cross-country and time-series evidence on happiness and what he found there has subsequently become known as the Easterlin Paradox (as we will see, some researchers think that the Paradox doesn't exist). Easterlin looked at the available cross-country evidence and concluded that he could not find a clear positive relationship between income and happiness across countries. He also looked at time-series evidence for happiness in the United States and did not find evidence of an increase in happiness over a period when national income had grown considerably. Easterlin was cautious in his initial analysis and simply concluded that, if income and happiness were correlated, the relationship between them over time was not as obvious as in the within-country cross-sectional data, which clearly showed that, at any moment in time, people with higher incomes were on average happier than people with lower incomes. He explained these results by arguing that people had interdependent preference functions so that happiness varies directly with one's own income and inversely with the incomes of others.

In 1975, Moses Abramovitz gave a public lecture entitled *Economic growth and its discontents* at the University of Edinburgh; this followed on from an initial exchange with Tibor Scitovosky and Alex Inkeles in 1973 (Abramovitz, Scitovsky, & Inkeles, 1973). The lecture focused on possible explanations for what Abramovitz termed the contradictions that Easterlin had found in his 1974 paper. Abramovitz referred to these contradictions as the Easterlin Paradox (Abramovitz, 1979) and the term has remained in use ever since.

From the beginning there has been confusion as to whether the Paradox refers only to the contradiction between the point-in-time evidence and the time-series evidence or whether it also includes the contradiction between the within-country evidence at a point in time and the cross-sectional evidence from different countries. Abramovitz included both issues when he coined and defined the term Easterlin Paradox. Subsequent writers have differed on this issue. Some, including Easterlin himself, refer solely to the difference between point-in-time evidence and time-series evidence when discussing the Paradox, whereas others such as Sacks, Stevenson, and Wolfers (2012) prefer the broader definition.

When Easterlin revisited the relationship between income and happiness 20 years after his original paper on the topic, he had no hesitation in concluding that the evidence accumulated between the early 1970s and the early 1990s was sufficiently clear that he gave an emphatic "no" when answering the question "Will raising the income of all raise the happiness of all?" (Easterlin, 1995). In this paper he argued that the theory was supported by time-series evidence from the United States, Japan, and nine European countries.

In more recent papers Easterlin has argued that the available evidence continues to support his original finding. For example, Easterlin and Angelescu (2010) examined time-series evidence on happiness and growth in 37 countries. The analysis covered 17 developed countries, 11 transition countries, and 9 developing countries. They measured happiness by responses to an overall life satisfaction question: "All things considered, how satisfied are you with your life as a whole these days?" The time span varied from 12 years in some countries to as many as 34 in the United States.

There are a number of data issues that they discuss at the outset of the paper and these are worth noting as other authors have disagreed with how Easterlin and his coauthors have handled some of these data issues. For example, the geographic coverage of the surveys in some countries changed over time and they tried to minimize the effects of these changes by constructing time series that cover the same population at different dates. This means that their data covers less than 100% of the population, but they claim that the data typically covers the more literate and urbanized section of the population, which are more likely to be experiencing the income benefits of economic growth.

They also delete certain Eurobarometer data where the life satisfaction question was preceded by a question on satisfaction with finances. That omission seems particularly problematic. It seems fairly reasonable that, in thinking about whether you are satisfied with your life, how satisfied you are with your finances might play a role in your thoughts. If including a question on satisfaction with finances introduces a downward bias to subsequent questions on satisfaction with life, does that not suggest that it is actually a good thing if surveys on subjective wellbeing first of all ask people how satisfied they are with major areas of their life (finances being one; work, health, family being others) and then ask them to give a judgment on their overall evaluation of life?

The issue of what data should or should not be used to test the relationship between income and happiness has continued to be a controversial issue.

For example, Easterlin has used data from annual Latinobarometer surveys in 17 Latin American countries covering the period 1994 to 2006. Instead of using data on life satisfaction he uses data on financial satisfaction because the question has been the same throughout this time period. The question asks "How would you define, in general, the current economic situation of yourself and your family? Would you say that is very bad, bad, regular, good, or very good?" Easterlin argues that responses to this question should be more closely tied to economic growth than those on life satisfaction, but finds that there is no evidence of a positive correlation between increases in financial satisfaction and economic growth (Easterlin, 2013a).

Easterlin has also used China as an exemplar of a country that has experienced rapid economic growth over a long period of time without experiencing increases in subjective wellbeing. Deaton and Stone (2013) criticize the Chinese data as being of "dubious comparability."

The Easterlin Paradox was accepted by most (though not all) researchers in this area as an established statistical finding until recently. In 2008 Stevenson and Wolfers published a paper that claimed that Easterlin was wrong and argued that there was in fact a positive relationship between satisfaction with life and national income (Stevenson & Wolfers, 2008). They claimed that this relationship existed both in cross-country comparisons and in time-series analysis of individual countries and argued that both findings cast serious doubt on whether the Easterlin Paradox existed at all. I shall deal with their analysis of the time-series evidence in this section and look at the cross-country comparisons later. Stevenson and Wolfers have extended their analysis in a series of recent papers with Daniel Sacks (Sacks et al., 2010, 2012) and I will rely on their most recent research in what follows.

Japan has often been regarded as an exemplar for the hypothesis that an increase in gross domestic product (GDP) does not necessarily imply an increase in subjective wellbeing. Easterlin discussed it at some length and included a graph that showed that subjective wellbeing in Japan had remained essentially the same between 1958 and 1986 even though per capita GDP had increased fivefold in that time period (Easterlin, 1995). Stevenson and Wolfers (2008) have pointed out that the questions and responses in different Japanese surveys are not directly comparable with each other. For example, in 1964 the top response changed from "Although I am not innumerably [sic] satisfied with my life, I am generally satisfied with life now" to "Completely satisfied" and the percentage of people selecting the top category fell from 18% to 4%. When changes in the questionnaire were taken into account, Stevenson and Wolfers (2008) found that subjective wellbeing did increase in Japan during periods when the increase in per capital GDP was highest. Easterlin has not mentioned the case of Japan in recent papers (Easterlin 2013a, 2013b).

The Eurobarometer survey has measured satisfaction with life in nine European countries since 1973. The life satisfaction question asks, "On the whole, are you very satisfied, fairly satisfied, not very satisfied, or not at all satisfied with the life you lead?" It is a peculiar way of asking the question as, on the positive side of the spectrum, there is no possible answer to balance the "not at all satisfied" answer on the negative side. Similarly, if a person was fairly dissatisfied he or she might wonder which of the negative answers to choose. Sacks, Stevenson, and Wolfers (2012) regress life satisfaction in each country against real GDP per capita with data from 1973 to 2009 and find that, in all but one case (Belgium), there is a positive relationship between these variables. In seven cases the correlation between the life satisfaction variable and GDP per capita is significantly different from zero.

Note there are at least two ways of analyzing long-run data on a variable such as subjective wellbeing. One is to treat each country as a separate case and examine how a consistently defined measure of subjective wellbeing has changed over time as a country's per capita GDP or economic growth has changed. This yields about 50 observations for each of the nine countries that have been part of the Eurobarometer series since 1973 (the Eurobarometer survey is generally conducted twice a year). This is the approach favoured by Sacks et al. An alternative is to think of each country as a single data point comprising the average change in life satisfaction and the average change in per capita GDP. This is the approach favoured by Easterlin (2013b) who claims that this approach shows no correlation between economic growth and life satisfaction. Consider Ireland, for example. Sacks et al. find a significant positive correlation between life satisfaction and per capital GDP between 1973 and 2009 while Easterlin's single observation for Ireland is one with a relatively small increase in life satisfaction and a very high growth rate in GDP per capita. So depending on your approach Ireland either illustrates that life satisfaction tends to move in line with GDP per capita or is a good example of how a long period of relatively high economic growth is a associated with a small increase in satisfaction with life.

The recent debate between Sacks and colleagues and Easterlin has centered on data issues such as how long does a time series have to be in order for us to be able to make inferences about the long-run relationship between economic variables and subjective wellbeing and which surveys should be included or excluded because of questions over the representativeness of the sample or over the way in which subjective wellbeing is measured. Observing the debate is a little like watching a tennis match with claim and counterclaim being served and volleyed back and forth.

Eventually we may have consistent, high-quality data that will allow us to do better analyses. The Gallup organization is conducting annual surveys in over 160 countries that include questions on life evaluation (measured by the Cantril scale) and on experienced emotional wellbeing (measured by both positive and negative feelings). This dataset promises to be analysed intensely, and Diener et al. have used the data from the surveys conducted between 2005 and 2011 in recent papers (Diener, Kahneman, Tov, & Arora, 2010; Diener, Tay, & Oishi, 2013). It is very unlikely that Easterlin and others would regard 7 years as a long enough time period, but the results from Diener and colleagues are striking nonetheless. They found that household income was positively associated over time with both measures of subjective wellbeing while GDP per capita was associated with changes in life evaluation but not with experienced happiness. Rising income had about the same effects on subjective wellbeing in poor and wealthy countries (Diener et al., 2013, pp. 273–274). They argue that household income is a better indicator of the standard of living than GDP per capita. The 2005–2011 time period is, of course, not a representative 7-year period, and it is unclear whether relationships that might be found across the world during a time of severe recession would continue to hold in more "normal" economic times.

Almost everybody accepts that subjective wellbeing in the United States has not increased in the past 30 years, even though the economy has generally expanded during that time. Sacks et al. (2012) argue that the United States remains a "paradoxical counter-example" (an interesting use of the word paradoxical!) and that the increase in inequality in the United States might be the underlying factor why subjective wellbeing has not increased as the economy has expanded. For Easterlin, the US is simply another example of his general point.

One issue that I think should get more attention is why the long run might matter more than the short run. Individuals care both about the short run and long run and, as the cliché goes, the important point is to get a balance between short-term and long-term goals. Political parties that go to the polls with platforms saying we will promote your long-term but not your short-term wellbeing tend not to do very well.

Cross-Country Analysis of Income and Wellbeing

The third kind of empirical studies are cross-country studies. These have generated a great deal of interest from academics and the general public. For the latter, it has become a kind of a parlor game to wonder why your own country is where it is on league tables and to wonder whether the evidence from surveys does or does not match national stereotypes. As for academics—as we have seen, some of them think that the cross-country evidence can help us understand whether the Easterlin Paradox holds, although Easterlin himself thinks that cross-country evidence cannot do so.

The effect of income on subjective wellbeing in cross-country studies seems to depend in part on how subjective wellbeing is measured. There seems to be general agreement among researchers that at a point in time the average life evaluation score for a country will be positively correlated with average income. For example, Sacks et al. (2012) find a strong positive correlation between average life satisfaction and per capita GDP for 2010 using Gallup data. The slope of the estimated relationship is 0.34. This is similar to what many others such have found (Fleche, Smith, & Sorsa, 2011; Helliwell, 2008).

However, it is less clear whether there is a cross-country correlation between income and measures of experienced daily happiness. Deaton and Stone (2013) did not find such a relationship between happiness and per capita GDP and note some surprising results, such as that Italy and Denmark were unhappier on average than Mozambique, Sudan, and Rwanda. Denmark is a particularly odd result because it has often been near or at the top in happiness league tables. Fleche and colleagues (2011) pointed out that the average score for Denmark in the World Values Survey is the highest among 32 countries based on different waves of the survey between 1984 and 2008.

Implications and Discussion

The main points that I have learned from my selective review of the relationship between income and wellbeing are the following:

1. There are serious methodological issues with the bounded nature of all measures of subjective wellbeing. Forty-three percent of people in the

American Institute of Public Opinion (AIPO) poll conducted in the United States in December 1970 described themselves as very happy, the highest possible response available on the survey. What could they say the following year or 5 years later if they were asked again about their happiness and they regarded themselves as happier than they were in December 1970? If they were happier in subsequent years due solely or in part to higher income, then a simple regression of happiness and income would not have been able to pick up an effect.

2. Every measure of subjective wellbeing needs to be considered on its own merits. It is now reasonably clear that measures evaluating life and measures of experienced affective emotions are not the same. The carefree use of the word happiness has become an obstacle to progress in this area.

3. Within a country at a point in time there seems to be a reasonably stable positive relationship between income and measures evaluating life. The higher a person's income the more likely it is that the person will evaluate her or his life in a very positive way.

4. Within a country at a point in time there is a positive relationship between income and measures of experienced wellbeing up to some income level. Beyond that income level more income is not associated with higher levels of experienced wellbeing.

5. Over time the evidence is mixed and fiercely contested. The method-ological issues referred to earlier are central to this issue and I cannot see how they are ever going to be overcome unless somebody discovers an Edgeworthian hedonimeter (Edgeworth, 1881), an instrument to measure utility or happiness proposed by Francis Edgeworth, or some corresponding method for measuring life evaluation on an unbounded scale.

6. People in higher-income countries generally evaluate their lives in a more positive way than people in poorer countries. That relationship does not hold for measures of experienced wellbeing. I tend to agree with Deaton and Stone (2013) who argue that a measure of hedonic wellbeing that shows that the average Dane or Italian is worse off than the average person from Mozambique, Sudan or Rwanda is basically meaningless.

Overall, I am not persuaded that the explicit or implicit focus on income as a policy goal should be changed. The factors that lead any individual at any point in time to be more or less happy in an experiential sense or to be more or less satisfied with how life has gone are so mysterious, so trivial, so profound, and so specific to each individual that we are less likely to do harm if we simply accept that more income is probably better for most individuals and that individuals themselves are best positioned to decide whether or not they are exceptions to this general pattern. When there is so much uncertainty about a possible public policy objective doing nothing seems like a good idea.

References

Abramovitz, M. (1979). Economic growth and its discontents. In M. J. Boskin (Ed.), *Economics and human welfare: Essays in honour of Tibor Scitovsky* (pp. 1–22). New York: Academic Press.

Abramovitz, M., Scitovsky, T., & Inkeles, A. (1973). Economic growth and its discontents. *Bulletin of the American Academy of Arts*, *27*(1), 11–27.

Blanchflower, D. G., & Oswald, A. J. (2011). International happiness: A new view on the measure of performance. *Academy of Management Perspectives*, *25*(6), 6–22.

Clark, A. E. (2011). Income and happiness: Getting the debate straight. *Applied Research in the Quality of Life*, *6*, 253–263.

Deaton, A., & Stone, A. A. (2013). Two happiness puzzles. *American Economic Review*, *103*(3), 291–297.

Diener, E., Kahneman, D., Tov, W., & Arora, R. (2010). Income's association with judgments of life versus feelings. In E. Diener, D. Kahneman, & J. F. Helliwell (Eds.), *International differences in wellbeing* (pp. 3–15). Oxford: Oxford University Press.

Diener, E., Tay, L., & Oishi, S. (2013). Rising income and the subjective wellbeing of nations. *Journal of Personality and Social Psychology*, *104*, 267–276.

Easterlin, R. (1974). Does economic growth improve the human lot? Some empirical evidence. In P. A. David & M. W. Reder (Eds.), *Nations and households in economic growth: Essays in honor of Moses Abramovitz* (pp. 89–125). New York: Academic Press.

Easterlin, R. (1995). Will raising the incomes of all increase the happiness of all? *Journal of Economic Behaviour and Organization*, *27*, 35–47.

Easterlin, R. (2013a). *Happiness and economic growth: The evidence* (IZA Discussion Paper Number 7187). Bonn: IZA.

Easterlin, R. (2013b). Happiness, growth and public policy. *Economic Inquiry*, *51*, 1–15.

Easterlin, R., & Angelescu, L. (2010). Happiness and growth the world over: Time series evidence on the happiness–income paradox. In R. Easterlin (Ed.), *Happiness, growth, and the life cycle* (pp. 111–152). Oxford: Oxford University Press.

Edgeworth, F. (1881). *Mathematical psychics: An essay on the application of mathematics to the moral sciences*. New York: Augustus M. Kelly.

Fleche, S., Smith, C., & Sorsa, P. (2011). *Exploring determinants of subjective wellbeing in OECD countries: Evidence from the World Value Survey* (OECD Economics Department Working Papers no. 921). Paris: OECD.

Frank, R. H. (2012). The Easterlin Paradox revisited. *Emotion, 12*(6), 1188–1191.

Helliwell, J. F. (2008). *Life satisfaction and the quality of development* (NBER Working Paper No. 14507). Cambridge, MA: National Bureau of Economic Research.

Johns, H., & Ormerod, P. (2007). *Happiness, economics and public policy*. London: The Institute of Economic Affairs.

Kahneman, D., & Deaton, A. A. (2010). High income improves evaluation of life but not emotional wellbeing. *Proceedings of the National Academy of Sciences of the United States of America, 107*(38), 16489–16493.

MacKerron, G. (2011). Happiness economics from 35,000 feet. *Journal of Economic Surveys, 26*, 705–735.

McCloskey, D. (2012). Happyism: The creepy new economics of peasure. *New Republic*, June 8. http://www.newrepublic.com/article/politics/magazine/103952/happyism-deirdre-mccloskey-economics-happiness#.

Price, S., & Sanders, D. (1995). Economic expectations and voting intentions in the UK, 1979–1987: A pooled cross-section approach. *Political Studies, 43*, 451–471.

Sacks, D. W., Stevenson, B., & Wolfers, J. (2010). *Subjective wellbeing, income, economic development, and growth* (NBER Working Paper no. 16441). Cambridge, MA: National Bureau of Economic Research.

Sacks, D. W., Stevenson, B., & Wolfers, J. (2012). The new stylized facts about income and subjective wellbeing. *Emotion, 12*(6), 1181–1187.

Stevenson, B., & Wolfers, J. (2008). Economic growth and subjective wellbeing: Reassessing the Easterlin Paradox. *Brookings Papers on Economic Activity, 39*, 1–87.

Stutzer, A., & Frey, B. (2012). *Recent developments in the economics of happiness: A selective overview* (IZA Discussion Paper no. Number 7078). Bonn: IZA.

Further Reading

The paper by George MacKerron cited above is a comprehensive introduction to theoretical and empirical work in this area.

New papers by Easterlin and by Sacks, Stevenson, and Wolfers are published regularly. Many of their newest papers can be found as discussion papers on the IZA web site, http://www.iza.org/en/webcontent/publications/papers.

The New Economics Foundation has published a very useful review on wellbeing evidence for policy. See http://www.neweconomics.org/publications.

4

Does Money Buy Me Love?
Testing Alternative Measures of National Wellbeing

Arthur Grimes
Motu Economic and Public Policy Research, New Zealand

Les Oxley
University of Waikato, New Zealand

Nicholas Tarrant
GT Research and Consulting, New Zealand

Introduction

Although material prosperity in most nations, including New Zealand, has increased over the past 50 years, many people suffer from uncertainties and anxieties, social and economic divisions are widening, and concern is growing about environmental degradation. Life satisfaction and happiness have not changed much in many developed countries despite decades of rising gross domestic product (GDP) per capita (Easterlin, 1974; Helliwell, Layard, & Sachs, 2012; Layard, 2011). Nevertheless, policy makers in most countries do aim to improve living standards sustainably into the future. Two questions then arise: Are policy makers' current behaviors sustainably increasing wellbeing?; and How would they know that this is the case? In order to answer these questions, policy makers and researchers typically use one or more aggregate measures of wellbeing and/or sustainability as inputs

The Economics of Wellbeing: Wellbeing: A Complete Reference Guide, Volume V.
Edited by David McDaid and Cary L. Cooper.
© 2014 John Wiley & Sons, Ltd. Published 2014 by John Wiley & Sons, Inc.
DOI: 10.1002/9781118539415.wbwell04

into their evaluations of whether policies and outcomes are on a desirable track.

Many measures of aggregate wellbeing and sustainability exist. We compile a range of existing aggregate wellbeing measures including: material measures such as GDP per capita (GDP(pc)), surveyed measures such as life satisfaction, and composite measures such as the Human Development Index (HDI), covering the Organisation for Economic Co-operation and Development (OECD) and a wider range of countries. We describe the relationships between alternative wellbeing measures and describe how New Zealand fares relative to other countries across these measures. We then test the predictive power of wellbeing and sustainability measures for an objective (revealed preference) indicator of how people value countries' relative attractiveness. The objective indicator that we adopt is a long history (50 years) of net migration outcomes across developed countries, indicating people's preferred (re)location choices.

As of 2010, New Zealand was ranked third globally on the HDI, sixth by Gallup for surveyed happiness, but only thirty-third on GDP(pc). Furthermore, in 2005, New Zealand ranked fourth worst out of 25 developed countries on a measure of Ecological Footprint (EcoFprint), a well-known sustainability metric. These measures cast a very different light on New Zealand's broad social, economic, and sustainability performance. Given these differences, which measure(s) should policy makers and researchers pay heed to?

Following Waring (Waring, 1989), Stiglitz and colleagues argue that "What we measure affects what we do; and if our measurements are flawed, decisions may be distorted" (Stiglitz, Sen, & Fitoussi, 2009). They argue that work is required to improve measures of sustainable economic performance and social progress incorporating, inter alia, inequality as well as average performance outcomes. In this chapter we do not create new indices of wellbeing, sustainability, or inequality, but instead use well-known existing measures to explore the information content of alternative indices.

The power of competing aggregate indices to predict objective outcomes valued by people has received little comparative testing. Such objective outcomes might include mental and physical health outcomes, anthropometric status (e.g., stature), and observed life choices designed to improve an individual's or household's wellbeing. In this chapter, we concentrate on this last aspect. We use net migration over 50 years—divided into 10 5-year windows—as a summary revealed-preference indicator of national wellbeing, as observed by potential and actual migrants. In our tests, this variable is our dependent variable, observed (as a panel) for the initial 24 OECD countries over 50 years.

We explain migration outcomes using a range of well-known aggregate wellbeing indicators. Our data include long series on GDP(pc) and also gross national income per capita (GNI(pc)), population, male and female life expectancy, measures of life satisfaction, inequality, the HDI, EcoFprint, and degrees of globalization. Our key contribution is to demonstrate that multiple wellbeing measures are required to explain migration outcomes. None of the above measures is sufficient by itself to explain the choices that people make to establish what they perceive as a better life for themselves, their families, and their descendants.

The initial part of our study is descriptive. First, we look at the relationships between key wellbeing and sustainability measures across a large range of countries, then examine how New Zealand compares with other countries according to these performance measures. The second part of the study presents tests of the predictive power of alternative measures for net international migration outcomes.

The results are relevant for policy makers in New Zealand and elsewhere. While there is increased interest amongst officials in New Zealand in examining broad measures of wellbeing (Gleisner, Llewellyn-Fowler, & McAlister, 2011), some narrower GDP targets have been mooted (Cullen, 2005; Key, 2010). This narrower approach contrasts with the policy of the U.K. Prime Minister, David Cameron, who has argued for the need to focus not just on GDP, but on general wellbeing (Cameron, 2010), and the U.K. government has established a national forum to measure wellbeing. Our study informs such work by providing tests of a range of wellbeing and sustainability measures to establish whether indices that incorporate factors beyond those captured by purely material-based measures, have predictive content. If they do, then these measures—or at least the factors within them—need to be included in evaluating the desirability of policy choices.

Prior Studies and Conceptual Model

To evaluate aggregate wellbeing outcomes—and despite difficulties of aggregation over individuals (Blackorby & Donaldson, 1990), aggregate indicators inevitably play a role in guiding policy makers and researchers—there exists a range of national wellbeing measures from material measures, such as GDP(pc) and GNI(pc), to surveyed happiness and life satisfaction (Layard, 2011), to composite measures such as the HDI (United Nations Development Program, 2010), and sustainability measures such as Genuine Savings (Hamilton & Clemens, 1999; Hamilton & Withagen, 2007; World Bank, 1997) and EcoFprint (World Wildlife Fund, 2008). Each of these measures has some theoretical underpinning that justifies its use as an indicator of wellbeing and/or sustainability for a country.

In recent years, there has been a plethora of composite indices, in addition to the HDI, created to proxy aggregate country wellbeing and/or sustainability. Such indices include the New Economics Foundation (NEF) Happy Planet Index (HPI), the OECD's Better Life Index (OECD-BLI) and the Yale Center for Environmental Law and Policy's Environmental Performance Index (EPI). These indicators generally have a less well-developed theoretical underpinning than the measures outlined above.

For sustainability, a long-term economic indicator is Genuine Savings, derived from a formal model of how wellbeing can be sustained over time. It focuses on changes in an economy's capabilities (stocks), which constitute the degree to which current generations pass on opportunities to future generations to maintain their wellbeing. The theory assumes some substitutability between capital assets—produced, natural, human, and social. In contrast, EcoFprint privileges natural capital above all other forms and is based on the implied desirability of national self-sufficiency. In practice, there are too few country estimates of Genuine Savings to enable its use in cross-country panel regressions. By contrast, a 25-country panel exists (covering 1960–2005) for EcoFprint. Despite its limitations in terms of economic theory, we utilize the EcoFprint measure as one (albeit potentially flawed) indicator of sustainability.

In their overarching study, Stiglitz and colleagues say that work is required to: obtain better aggregate measures of economic performance; shift the emphasis from measuring economic production to measuring people's wellbeing; adopt better measures of sustainability; and increase the focus on inequality measures (Stiglitz et al., 2009). It can be argued that national measures may be insufficient where worldviews differ for groups within a country. For example, in New Zealand, indigenous experts have argued that additional wellbeing measures may be applicable for the Māori that may not be applicable for the Pākehā (New Zealanders of European descent) (Durie, 2006). While potentially an important issue worthy of further study, data limitations mean that we concentrate solely on national measures of wellbeing and sustainability in this chapter.

To understand whether measured increases in wellbeing are sustainable, one must have some metric against which to test the predictive power of alternative indices. As yet, there have been few such studies other than those of Ferreira and colleagues (Ferreira, Hamilton, & Vincent, 2008; Ferreira & Vincent, 2005). None of these studies examines the impact of alternative measures of wellbeing or sustainability on migration choices.

Modern economic geography, built around the concept of adjustment towards spatial equilibrium, recognizes that migration is an equilibrating mechanism that operates when one region has greater expected utility for residents than does another region. The spatial equilibrium concept has been summarized as assuming that the utility level of individuals in any region i, $U(G_T{}^i, G_N{}^i, \theta^i)$, is determined by their consumption of traded goods ($G_T{}^i$), non-traded goods ($G_N{}^i$) and local amenities (θ^i) (Glaeser & Gottlieb, 2009). Given the individual's budget constraint and the assumptions that traded goods prices follow the law of one price and that non-earned income is unaffected by location, utility can be expressed by the indirect utility function, $V(Y^i, P^i, \theta^i)$, where Y^i is locally earned wage income and P^i is the price of nontraded goods (including housing services). Both Y^i and P^i are endogenous and so reflect the population and productive characteristics of a region. In spatial equilibrium:

$$V(Y^i, P^i, \theta^i) = \bar{U} \tag{4.1}$$

where $\bar{U}$ is the (equal) level of utility that would be obtained by locating in any other region. Where $V(Y^i, P^i, \theta^i) \neq \bar{U}$, we can postulate a migration function such as:

$$dL/dt = M(V - \bar{U}) \tag{4.2}$$

where L is population in region i, t represents time, and $M_V > 0$ (Grimes, 2013). For instance, ceteris paribus, if a spatial equilibrium initially exists but then local amenities in i decline (contributing to a reduction in wellbeing), there will be outmigration from region i even though relative incomes have not initially altered. Indeed, to restore spatial equilibrium, the migration mechanism must eventually induce either an offsetting rise in local incomes (Y^i) or a reduction in local living costs (P^i). This theoretical basis demonstrates that incomes cannot, in general, be expected to be a sufficient statistic to describe absolute or relative regional (or national) wellbeing.

At the individual level, following previous work (Dustmann, 2003; McCann, Poot, & Sanderson, 2010), we can model prospective migrants as forward-looking optimizers under conditions of uncertainty. An individual, j, has the option of living in the domestic (d) or foreign (f) country. She has an age-related (a) single-period indirect utility function (U^a) defined over wages (w_t) and non-pecuniary amenities (n_t) received in the country in which she resides in period t, and has an age-related value function (V^a) conditional on country location [where $y_t = 1$ (resp. 0) denotes living in the foreign (resp. domestic) country; so $|\Delta y_t| = 1$ represents migration to or from the domestic country]; δ is the individual's rate of time preference. Each location switch incurs a fixed cost, F^j (which, for expositional simplicity, is assumed to be the only parameter that varies across individuals). An individual migrates (from d to f) if and only if:

$$[U^a(w_t^f, n_t^f) - U^a(w_t^d, n_t^d) + \delta E_t(V^a_{t+1}|y_t = 1) - E_t(V^a_{t+1}|y_t = 0)]$$
$$> F^j(|\Delta y_{t-1}|)$$
$$(4.3)$$

Decision-making in accordance with (equation 4.3) yields a range of possible outcomes. If the individual values wages highly early in life $\partial U^{a'}/\partial w > \partial U^{a''}/\partial w$ where $a' < a''$ (i.e., where the person is younger) and values non-pecuniary amenities more in later life (i.e., $\partial U^{a'}/\partial n < \partial U^{a''}/\partial n$) then, depending on the size of F^j, it may be optimal for the individual to migrate from a high-amenity (domestic) country to a high-wage (foreign) country early in life, and later migrate back to the domestic country despite incurring two fixed migration costs. If the individual considers that current domestic nonpecuniary amenities are not sustainable, this may lower $E_t(V^a_{t+1}|y_t = 0)$ favoring emigration today. This framework provides a conceptual basis, consistent with adjustment towards spatial equilibrium, to test how residents at different life-stages value current and future (sustainable) pecuniary and nonpecuniary benefits. In the current study, we aggregate across all age groups, but the framework signals potential extensions that disaggregate migration decisions by age (and potentially also by different ethnicities or other social groups with differing F^j or differing utility functions).

To operationalize the test implicit in (equation 4.3), we require data on migration choices, measures of contemporaneous pecuniary and nonpecuniary wellbeing affecting U^a, and a measure of sustainability affecting V^a. We describe our data corresponding to these facets in the next section.

We denote net migration to country i in year t as M_{it}, and material, surveyed, composite, and sustainability measures in country i at time t as G_{it}, N_{it}, H_{it}, S_{it} respectively. The global value in t for each of these measures is denoted G_{*t}, N_{*t}, H_{*t}, S_{*t} respectively. Following the framework outlined in (equation 4.3), we assume that: each of G_{it}, N_{it} and H_{it} affects $U^a(w_t^d, n_t^d)$; each of G_{*t}, N_{*t} and H_{*t} affects $U^a(w_t^f, n_t^f)$; S_{it} affects $E_t(V^a_{t+1} \mid y_t = 0)$; and S_{*t} affects $E_t(V^a_{t+1} \mid y_t = 1)$. We can then test significance of each of the arguments in the regression:

$$M_{it} = \alpha_0 + \alpha_1(G_{it} - G_{*t}) + \alpha_2(N_{it} - N_{*t}) + \alpha_3(H_{it} - H_{*t})$$
$$+ \alpha_4(S_{it} - S_{*t}) + \mu_{it} \quad (4.4)$$

where $\mu_{it} = \varepsilon_{it} + \lambda_i + \lambda'_t$.

λ_i is a country-fixed effect to account for constant, unobserved country-specific wellbeing or sustainability factors; λ'_t is a time-fixed effect that captures global influences on migration decisions (e.g., security concerns that affect F^j) affecting migration for all countries in time t equally; ε_{it} is the residual.

In our panel regression, we can replace all of the foreign variables with time-fixed effects, λ''_t, since these variables are common to all countries. We can then estimate the equation:

$$M_{it} = \alpha_0 + \alpha_1 G_{it} + \alpha_2 N_{it} + \alpha_3 H_{it} + \alpha_4 S_{it} + \mu_{it} \quad (4.5)$$

where $\mu_{it} = \varepsilon_{it} + \lambda_t + \lambda_i$; and $\lambda_t = \lambda'_t + \lambda''_t$

Equation (4.5) is estimated as a panel regression with a number of measures included to proxy each of G, N, H, and S. In interpreting the results, it should be noted that, ceteris paribus, the likelihood of migration will be higher (lower) for individuals with low (high) F^j. Thus regression results based on (equation 4.5) can most reliably be taken as tests of wellbeing factors that are taken into account by migration-prone (low F^j) individuals rather than by those who may be resistant to migration even where conditions are better abroad than at home. We henceforth refer to the former group as potential migrants.

Wellbeing and Sustainability Data

There is a wide range of alternative wellbeing and sustainability measures. We analyze relationships amongst them to examine the extent to which differing measures provide materially different information. Initially we do so using a 2010 (or latest available) cross-sectional country snapshot for 14 measures

Table 4.1. Cross-Sectional Correlation Coefficients (Full Sample. 2010 or Most Recent Prior Data).

	GNI (pc)	GDP (pc)	Life Exp	Fem/ Male	HDI	EPI	Eco Fprint	Eco- Glob	Soc- Glob	LS- HPI	OECD- BLI	LS- Mean	LS- Sdev	Gini
GNI(pc)	1													
GDP(pc)	0.91	1												
Life Exp	0.58	0.60	1											
Fem/Male	0.09	0.20	0.31	1										
HDI	0.71	0.73	0.90	0.33	1									
EPI	0.53	0.57	0.40	0.05	0.47	1								
EcoFprint	0.59	0.59	−0.02	−0.29	0.14	0.11	1							
Eco-Glob	0.67	0.71	0.56	0.23	0.69	0.49	0.31	1						
Soc-Glob	0.81	0.82	0.69	0.31	0.79	0.61	0.18	0.78	1					
LS-HPI	0.43	0.49	0.07	−0.68	0.19	0.39	0.42	0.49	0.44	1				
OECD-BLI	0.80	0.85	0.32	−0.54	0.44	0.65	0.52	0.35	0.66	0.71	1			
LS-Mean	0.33	0.39	0.36	−0.05	0.34	0.27	−0.22	0.37	0.41	0.14	0.28	1		

| LS-Sdev | −0.43 | −0.54 | −0.27 | −0.02 | −0.25 | −0.35 | 0.17 | −0.32 | −0.43 | −0.37 | −0.49 | −0.58 | 1 | |
| Gini | −0.38 | −0.38 | −0.23 | −0.17 | −0.26 | −0.22 | −0.19 | −0.32 | −4.40 | −0.31 | −0.47 | 0.05 | 0.15 | 1 |

GNI(pc) is gross national income per capita in PPP terms, current dollars (source: World Bank).

GDP(pc) is gross domestic product per capita in PPP terms, 1990 U.S.dollars (source: Maddison, 2006).

LifeExp is average of female and male life expectancy at birth (source: World Bank).

Fem/Male is ratio of female to male life expectancy at birth (source: World Bank).

HDI is the Human Development Index, updated definition (source: UNDP).

EPI is the Environmental Performance Index (source: Yale Center for Environmental Law and Policy, Yale University).

EcoFprint is Ecological Footprint used by New Economics Foundation (NEF) for Happy Planet Index, version 1 (source: WWF).

Eco-Glob is the Economic Globalisation index (source: Dreher, 2006, updated in Dreher et al, 2008).

Soc-Glob is the Social Globalization index (source: Dreher (2006), updated in Dreher et al. (2008).

LS-HPI is Life Satisfaction modeled by Abdallah et al. (2008) for the NEF Happy Planet Index, version 1 (source: NEF).

OECD-BLI is the OECD's (equal-weighted) Better Life Index (source: OECD).

LS-Mean is the mean life satisfaction score from the World Values Survey (source: WVS).

LS-Sdev is the standard deviation of life satisfaction (source: WVS).

Gini is the Gini coefficient of income inequality (source: CIA Factbook; and OECD).

GDPgrowth is the growth rate of GDP(pc) over the most recent decade (not included in Table 4.1).

(Table 4.1). These measures cover material wellbeing, surveyed wellbeing, inequality indicators, composite measures, sustainability measures, objective wellbeing measures, and two indices of the international connectedness of countries (though these latter indices may be interpreted as contextual variables rather than wellbeing indicators per se).

The main objective wellbeing measure is life expectancy at birth (LifeExp). We supplement this measure with the ratio of female to male life expectancy (Fem/Male). A low value of this ratio may be an indicator of discrimination against females or of poor primary health-care systems that result in high maternal mortality rates. The two connectedness indicators are measures of economic globalization (Eco-Glob) and social globalization (Soc-Glob) (Dreher, 2006; Dreher, Gaston, & Martens, 2008).

Two material wellbeing measures are reported. The first is GNI per capita at purchasing power parity (PPP). The second is GDP per capita at PPP. Because GNI relates to the incomes of residents whereas GDP relates to production within a country (for which some returns may accrue to foreigners), we consider that GNI is the better indicator of material wellbeing for a country's residents.

Surveyed wellbeing includes two measures of life satisfaction. The first is LS-Mean, a country's Mean Life Satisfaction in its most recent World Values Survey (WVS). Prior values (used in the panel regressions) rely on interpolated values between surveys for each country; the first surveyed value is extended back to the start of the sample for each country, while the latest surveyed value is extended forward to the end of the sample. The second measure is LS-HPI, a Life Satisfaction measure compiled by the New Economics Foundation (NEF) for its Happy Planet Index (for 25 OECD countries). It is available for every fifth year over the period 1960–2005. This series is based on WVS (where available) but also uses modeled data based on other life satisfaction surveys and on other series (e.g., from UNDP's Human Development Report) to extend the data back for each country to 1960. The series' construction is detailed by Abdallah and colleagues (Abdallah, Thompson, & Marks 2008). Importantly, for our panel regressions, no stock or flow measure of migration is used in the modeling of LS-HPI; nor are income variables included in its modeling. Because of its modeled component, LS-HPI, though based on life satisfaction measures, is not necessarily consistent with the WVS measure.

One inequality measure is derived from the World Values Survey. It is the standard deviation of responses within a country to the WVS Life Satisfaction question (denoted LS-Sdev), which is interpolated/extrapolated as for LS-Mean. A high score for this measure indicates greater inequality of life satisfaction within a country. The second inequality measure is a standard Gini coefficient (expressed as a percentage) relating to income inequality (Gini). The CIA Factbook measure is used in our descriptive work as this source provides data for a wide range of countries. The latest available measure (provided it dates from at least 1995) is used. In our panel regression analysis, we use the OECD Gini measure which is available every fifth year for the period 1980–2010. A high value for either Gini measure denotes greater inequality of income.

Two composite measures are reported. The first is the (updated definition of the) UNDP's Human Development Index (HDI) for 2010. Data has been compiled for every fifth year over the period 1980–2010. The second is the OECD's equally weighted Better Life Index (OECD-BLI), just for 2010. Other composite indices now abound (e.g., the Legatum Prosperity Index and Genuine Progress Indicators) but the HDI and OECD-BLI are the most commonly cited internationally comparable composite indices. In addition, the New Economic Foundation (NEF) Happy Planet Index (HPI) is a composite measure, but we include its three component measures (LifeExp, LS-HPI, and EcoFprint) directly (albeit in an unrestricted functional form, unlike the restricted form of the HPI).

Finally, we report two environmental sustainability measures. The first is the NEF's EcoFprint measure, in turn sourced from World Wildlife Fund (WWF, 2008). These data are available for every fifth year for the period 1960–2005 from NEF for 25 OECD countries. A high EcoFprint score indicates a greater degree of unsustainable development according to the theoretical underpinning of this measure (an EcoFprint greater than one indicates that a country requires more than its current land area to support itself). The second measure is a composite index of environmental outcomes, the Environmental Performance Indicator (EPI) compiled by the Yale Center for Environmental Law and Policy. The 2010 series is used here. A high EPI score indicates that a country is performing well in terms of its environmental outcomes.

We provide a scatterplot for 2010 (or using the latest available prior data) of GNI(pc) against each of the other series to assess: (a) the difference in information content in each series relative to information on average material wellbeing; and (b) how the nature of the relationship changes according to country wealth. These scatterplots are shown as Figures 4.1 to 4.13; each figure also reports the simple correlation coefficient (r) between the two series. In some cases, it is clear from the graph that the correlation coefficient

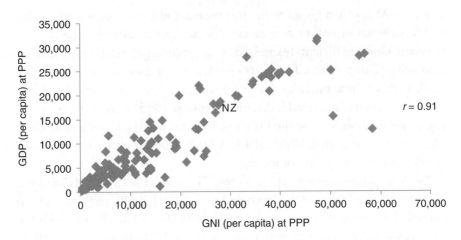

Figure 4.1. GNI (per capita) and GDP (per capita).

would be higher if a different functional form were used for the correlation but, for purposes of consistency, the simple linear relationship is shown in each case.

From Figure 4.1, the two material measures contain very similar snapshot information ($r = 0.91$) and so either GDP(pc) or GNI(pc) can be used as a snapshot measure of material resources for a country. (The two major outliers in the southeast of the graph are oil/gas producers, Kuwait and the United Arab Emirates.) We note that trends in the two series could diverge over time for a country running a persistent current account surplus (deficit), thereby building up foreign assets (liabilities) creating a growing wedge between production and incomes in a country. We subsequently analyze correlations of indicators over the full sample period.

Life expectancy (Figure 4.2) increases sharply up to a per capita income level of US$10,000 p.a. (in 2010 US$); but thereafter there is little further increase in mean life expectancy at birth as countries become richer. The female/male life expectancy graph (Figure 4.3) shows a complex relationship. There is a clear positive relationship between this ratio and income for poor to medium-income countries (up to a GNI(pc) level of around $20,000). Above this level, the ratio drops back to a stable level independent of income. Some of the countries with the highest ratio of female to male life expectancy are former Soviet countries where the high ratio is due to low male life expectancy associated, inter alia, with alcohol abuse. Countries with low levels of the ratio generally reflect high female mortality rates in very low-income countries (e.g., Bangladesh) and/or reflect the incidence of AIDS (Botswana, Lesotho, Swaziland).

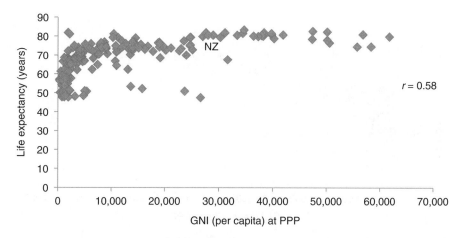

Figure 4.2. GNI (per capita) and Life Expectancy.

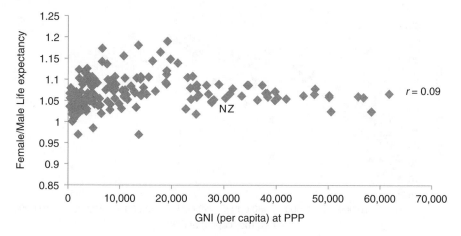

Figure 4.3. GNI (per capita) and Female/Male Life Expectancy Ratio.

Figures 4.4 and 4.5 indicate that richer countries are more highly connected to the rest of the world than poorer countries, in terms of both economic and social linkages. Each of the correlations is strong ($r = 0.67$ for economic globalization and 0.81 for social globalization respectively). In both cases, the relationship may be approximated as a logarithmic relationship, with globalization increasing as a country becomes richer but at a reduced rate. We stress that none of these graphs indicates causality in either direction, so we cannot conclude that higher income causes greater international connectedness or vice versa, or whether a third factor is responsible for the observed relationships.

61

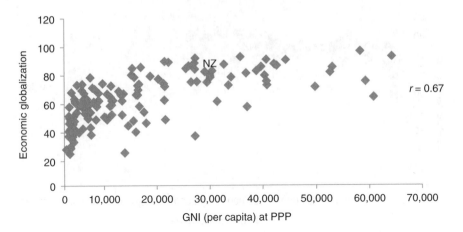

Figure 4.4. GNI (per capita) and Economic Globalization.

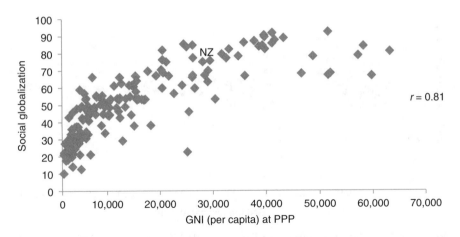

Figure 4.5. GNI (per capita) and Social Globalization.

The two life satisfaction series are graphed in Figures 4.6 and 4.7. Figure 4.6 provides the NEF's HPI modeled measure of life satisfaction for 25 OECD countries, while Figure 4.7 uses WVS data. There is a moderately strong positive relationship between the NEF's measure and average incomes ($r = .43$). For the WVS measure ($r = .33$), the positive relationship is evident up to a mean income of around $45,000, but not beyond that level. The dispersion of life satisfaction outcomes across countries appears to diminish as mean incomes rise towards $45,000. This may indicate that nonincome elements, which vary significantly across countries, are more important for

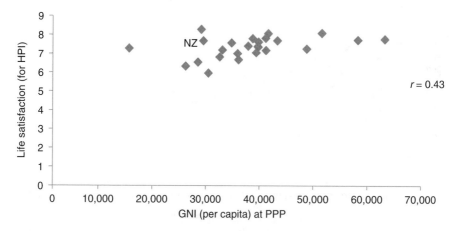

Figure 4.6. GNI (per capita) and Life Satisfaction (HPI).

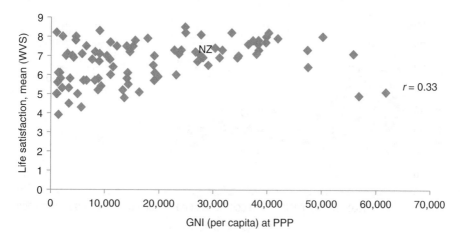

Figure 4.7. GNI (per capita) and Life Satisfaction, Mean (WVS).

life satisfaction outcomes in countries that are, on average, poorer than in richer countries.

Inequality (standard deviation) of life satisfaction is also moderately related to mean country income (Figure 4.8). Life satisfaction inequality tends to fall as countries become richer ($r = -.43$). Income inequality too tends to fall as countries become richer (Figure 4.9). Thus, wealthier countries tend to have lower Gini coefficients ($r = -.38$). Nevertheless there remains a considerable degree of dispersion around this relationship at all income levels.

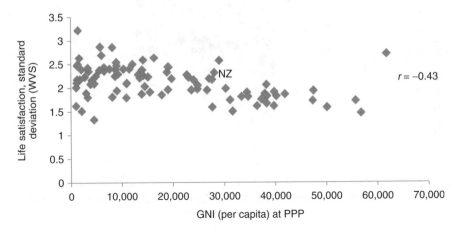

Figure 4.8. GNI (per capita) and Life Satisfaction, Standard Deviation (WVS).

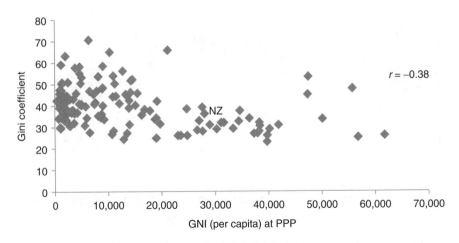

Figure 4.9. GNI (per capita) and Gini Coefficient.

Figures 4.10 and 4.11 indicate that higher incomes are closely related to the two reported composite indices of human wellbeing, the HDI ($r = .71$) and the OECD-BLI ($r = .80$). The high correlation of income with each of these series suggests that neither measure adds a large amount of extra information on wellbeing relative to the GNI(pc) series. However, the shape of the relationship does change as income changes, so potentially providing some extra information. In the case of the HDI, the positive relationship with GNI(pc) is apparent up to a mean income of around $30,000, whereas the positive relationship extends to a cut-off of around $40,000 for the

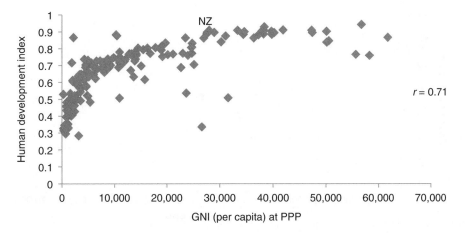

Figure 4.10. GNI (per capita) and UNDP Human Development Index.

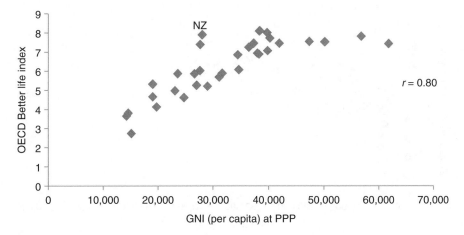

Figure 4.11. GNI (per capita) and OECD Better Life Index.

OECD-BLI. Above these cut-off points, the indicated level of wellbeing appears broadly constant as income rises further.

The two sustainability indicators provide quite different pictures of environmental outcomes from each other. According to the EcoFprint measure (Figure 4.12), richer OECD countries, on average, have a higher ecological footprint than less wealthy countries ($r = .59$) and, accordingly, have less sustainable economies. By contrast, the EPI measure (Figure 4.13) indicates that wealthier countries have better overall environmental records than less well-off countries ($r = .53$). The EPI measure covers 131 countries

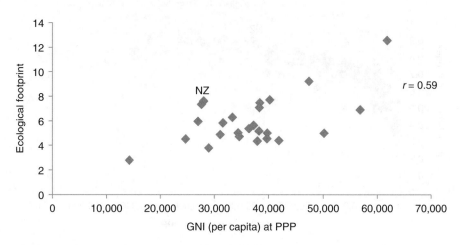

Figure 4.12. GNI (per capita) and Ecological Footprint.

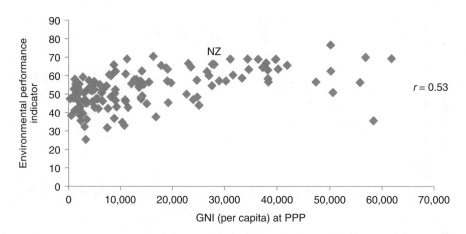

Figure 4.13. GNI (per capita) and Yale Environmental Performance Indicator.

compared with the 25 country EcoFprint series. Figure 4.14 presents a scatterplot for these two series against each other, but covers only the 25 countries for which both measures exist. The correlation coefficient is low ($r=.11$) but, to the extent that there is a correlation, the data suggest that countries with better environmental performance (EPI) have higher ecological footprints and hence are less sustainable according to that measure. Thus the sustainability indicators present an inconsistent picture of environmental performance.

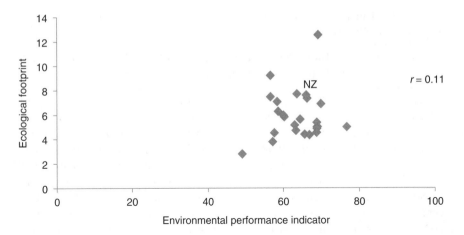

Figure 4.14. Environmental Performance Indicator and Ecological Footprint.

A full complement of cross-sectional correlation coefficients between all 14 series (using their 2010 or most recently available prior values) is shown in Table 4.1. In general, the inequality measures are negatively correlated with other wellbeing measures while almost all other wellbeing measures (other than EcoFprint and the female/male life expectancy ratio) are positively related to one another. Thus alternative measures show some consistency in broad wellbeing outcomes for countries. Nevertheless, the fact that many correlations are well below 1 indicates that alternative measures contain additional information relative to other measures.

Table 4.2 provides panel correlation coefficients measured over two separate time periods for wellbeing and sustainability series for which we have time series of data. (The panel correlation coefficient is the square root of the R^2 statistic for a panel regression of one variable on the other plus a constant, with the sign given by the sign of the regression coefficient in the panel regression.) Each of the ten series is measured every 5 years through to 2005, beginning either in 1960 or 1980. We use data in the form in which it appears in our tests in the previous section; thus we use log(GDP(pc)) and restrict our attention to the initial 24 OECD countries for which we have almost complete data. The bottom left portion of the table presents the correlation coefficients for the full 1960–2005 period for variables that have data covering this full period; the upper right portion presents coefficients for the 1980–2005 period. For reasons of space, we omit log((GNI(pc)); its correlation with log(GDP(pc)) is 0.90 over 1980–2005, and each of these variables has similar correlations with each of the other variables. Also for

Table 4.2. Panel Correlation Coefficients (OECD24. Bottom Left: 1960–2005; Top Right: 1980–2005).

	log (GDP)*	Life Exp	Fem/ Male	Eco Fprint	LS-HPI	LS-Mean	LS-Sdev	Gini	HDI
log(GDP)*	–	0.80	−0.10	0.41	0.50	0.22	−0.64	−0.22	0.81
LifeExp	0.84	–	−0.24	−0.04	0.09	0.13	−0.47	0.10	0.73
Fem/Male	0.05	−0.16	–	−0.06	−0.19	−0.02	0.04	−0.11	−0.25
EcoFprint	0.45	0.20	0.08	–	0.52	−0.27	−0.04	−0.21	0.25
LS-HPI	0.54	0.33	−0.05	0.52	–	0.24	−0.40	−0.56	0.38
LS-Mean	n.a.	n.a.	n.a.	n.a.	n.a.	–	−0.29	0.01	0.13
LS-Sdev	n.a.	n.a.	n.a.	n.a.	n.a.	n.a.	–	0.29	−0.41
Gini	n.a.	n.a.	n.a.	n.a.	n.a.	n.a.	n.a.	–	−0.07
HDI	n.a.	n.a.	n.a.	n.a.	n.a.	n.a.	n.a.	n.a.	–

*Per capita. $|r| > .16$ is significant at the 1% level (full sample).
Variables are defined below Table 4.1.

reasons of space, we likewise omit the variables used as control variables in the following section. The Gini coefficient used in Table 4.2 (and subsequently) is the OECD measure.

The table shows that log(GDP(pc)) is highly positively correlated ($|r| > 0.70$) with both LifeExp and HDI, which, in turn, are highly positively correlated with each other (as expected, given that LifeEx*p* is a component of the HDI). HDI, therefore, adds little to log(GDP(pc)) in measuring differences in cross-country wellbeing. log(GDP(pc)) is moderately positively correlated ($0.40 < |r| < 0.70$) with LS-HPI and it has a positive but small correlation with LS-Mean. Consistent with the cross-section, EcoFprint is moderately positively correlated with both log(GDP(pc)) and LS-HPI; hence countries that are supposedly ecologically unsustainable tend to be richer and have higher life satisfaction than other countries.

Inequality is unequivocally negatively correlated with most other measures of wellbeing. For instance, LS-Sdev is moderately negatively correlated with each of log(GDP(pc)), LifeExp, LS-HPI, and HDI; while Gini is moderately negatively correlated with LS-HPI. Thus, in an associative sense, inequality is reduced in countries with higher incomes and higher life satisfaction. Again, no causality can be attributed in either direction for any of these correlations.

Before presenting tests of the predictive power of the various indicators, we describe how New Zealand (NZ) fares in relation to the indicators that have been presented. Each of Figures 4.1 to 4.14 indicates the point corresponding to New Zealand. Per capita GNI and GDP for the country is moderately high in relation to the full sample (Figure 4.1). However, for the "OECD" sample (which, in these figures, corresponds to countries in the NEF-sourced indicators, being the initial 24 members of the OECD [excluding Turkey] plus Mexico and Korea), New Zealand has the fifth lowest level of GNI(pc) even after PPP adjustments (Figure 4.6). Other than Mexico, New Zealand's GNI(pc) is barely above that of any of the other OECD countries, and is less than half that of the wealthiest countries.

On some other measures, but by no means all, New Zealand fares better. Table 4.3 provides actual and percentile rankings of New Zealand's performance according to each measure (using 2010 or the most recent available prior data), both relative to the full sample and relative to the 24 earliest OECD members. New Zealand was the 24th country to join the OECD (in 1973). All 24 countries (with the possible exception of Turkey, a founder member of the OECD) can be considered to have been "rich" countries at the start of our data sample (1960). Thus, comparisons of outcomes post-1960 do not suffer from a selection bias that would occur

Table 4.3. New Zealand Indicator Rankings (Full Sample and 24 OECD Countries; 2010 or Most Recent Prior Data).

Indicator	Full sample ranking	Full sample percentile	OECD24 country ranking	OECD24 country percentile
GNI(pc)	28/182	15	22/24	92
GDP(pc)	25/189	13	19/21	90
LifeExp	19/193	10	12/24	50
Fem/Male	132/194	68	21/24	88
HDI	5/187	3	5/24	21
EPI	14/131	11	11/24	46
EcoFprint	22/25	88	20/23	87
Eco-Glob	21/144	15	10/24	42
Soc-Glob	30/198	15	20/24	83
LS-HPI	9/25	36	9/23	39
OECD-BLI	4/33	12	4/23	17
LS-Mean	48/94	51	18/24	75
LS-Sdev	65/94	69	22/24	92
Gini	51/135	38	21/24	88

A low ranking and a low percentile imply a comparatively high level of wellbeing.
Variables are defined below Table 4.1.

if subsequent joining member nations of the OECD were included in the "OECD" sample (De Long, 1988).

The samples for each measure differ, since data availability differs across series. In each case, a lower absolute and/or percentile ranking signifies greater wellbeing; for instance, a percentile ranking of 1% for the Gini coefficient indicates that that country has extremely equal income distribution relative to other countries. For New Zealand, the female/male life expectancy ratio is not relevant since that ratio appears to have information content only for countries that are considerably poorer than New Zealand; hence this measure is not discussed further below.

Based on the full samples, New Zealand ranks in the top third of countries for eight of the 13 indicators. It falls out of the top third of countries for the two inequality measures (69th and 38th percentiles for LS-Sdev and Gini respectively) for EcoFprint (88th percentile) and for the two life satisfaction measures (36th and 51st percentiles for LS-HPI and LS-Mean respectively). We note, however, that New Zealand performs highly on the "competing" Gallup Survey of Happiness (for which the country ranked sixth globally in 2010).

For the original OECD (OECD24) countries, New Zealand's rankings are less positive. It ranks in the top third of countries on only two of the thirteen measures: UNDP's HDI (21st percentile) and OECD- BLI (17th percentile). Each of these is a composite index reflecting its constructors' views of what constitutes greater wellbeing. New Zealand ranks in the bottom third of countries on seven of the 13 measures: the two income measures, the two inequality measures, mean life satisfaction (WVS measure), ecological footprint, and social globalization (though the last of these may be considered a contextual variable rather than an explicit measure of wellbeing). New Zealand ranks in the middle third of this sample for life expectancy, EPI, life satisfaction (HPI measure) and economic globalization.

Tables 4.4 and 4.5 track New Zealand's absolute and percentile rankings within the OECD24 for the nine variables covered in Table 4.2, plus log(GNI(pc)) for 1960, 1980, and 2005. All data are available for the last two of these periods; 1960 data are available for five variables. Again, a low (resp. high) percentile ranking denotes a beneficial (resp. detrimental) relative outcome. Figure 4.15 provides this percentile information visually.

The deterioration in New Zealand outcomes is clearly evident from Figure 4.15. In 1960, New Zealand ranked highly on per capita income,

Table 4.4. New Zealand's Absolute Rankings (within OECD24).

	1960	1980	2005
log(GDP(pc))	3/22	17/22	18/22
log(GNI(pc))	–	18/24	22/24
LifeExp	9/24	18/24	11/24
Fem/Male	14/24	19/24	23/24
EcoFprint	23/23	16/23	20/23
LS-HPI	15/23	15/23	9/23
LS-Mean	–	21/24	20/24
LS-Sdev	–	24/24	22/24
Gini	–	10/23	20/23
HDI	–	5/23	4/24

A low absolute ranking implies a comparatively high level of wellbeing.
Variables are defined below Table 4.1.

Table 4.5. New Zealand's Percentile Rankings (within OECD24).

	1960	1980	2005
log(GDP(pc))	14	77	82
log(GNI(pc))	–	75	92
LifeExp	38	75	46
Fem/Male	58	79	96
EcoFprint	100	70	87
LS-HPI	65	65	39
LS-Mean	–	88	83
LS-Sdev	–	100	92
Gini	–	43	87
HDI	–	22	17

A low percentile ranking implies a comparatively high level of wellbeing.
Variables are defined below Table 4.1.

moderately on life expectancy and life satisfaction, and poorly only on ecological footprint. By 1980, New Zealand ranked in the bottom quartile for six of the ten measures, and, by 2005, New Zealand ranked in the bottom quintile for seven of the ten measures. Nevertheless, it still ranked in the top quartile on the HDI and ranked in the second quartile on life expectancy and life satisfaction.

New Zealand's highly variable rankings—from high rankings for the composite wellbeing indicators (HDI and OECD-BLI) to very low

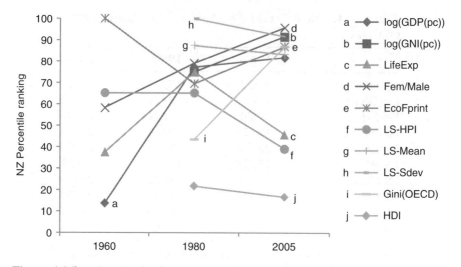

Figure 4.15. New Zealand's Percentile Rankings (within OECD24). A low percentile ranking implies a comparatively high level of wellbeing.

(developed-country) rankings on material wellbeing, inequality, and ecological footprint, with only moderate rankings on life satisfaction measures—leaves open a major question: Which of the factors taken into account by each of these measures actually matter to individuals? It is to this question that we now turn.

Wellbeing, Sustainability, and International Migration

In order to test the predictive content of the available indicators, we estimate an international migration relationship based on equation (4.5). Specifically, we have sourced data from the World Bank (and, in turn, from the United Nations Population Division) on the net total of migrants during the period; that is, the total number of immigrants less the total number of emigrants, including both citizens and noncitizens. Data are estimates for successive 5-year periods. To derive estimates of net migration, the UN Population Division takes into account the past migration history of a country or area, the migration policy of a country, and influxes of refugees. The data to calculate these official estimates come from a variety of sources, including border statistics, administrative records, surveys, and censuses. When no official estimates can be made because of insufficient data, net migration is derived through the balance equation, which is the difference between overall population growth and the natural increase in population.

Each data point is therefore a 5-year sum of net migration for each country. The first observation covers 1961–1965 (labeled 1965 in our database) and the last covers 2006–2010 (labeled 2010). Estimates are made for each of 216 countries for 10 periods (covering 50 years). We express the 5-yearly net migration flow (NMig) as a ratio of the population (Pop) at the end of the previous period (e.g., the 2010 figure is the 2006–2010 migration flow divided by population in 2005). Population estimates are also sourced from the World Bank. Thus, including country (i) and period (t) subscripts, our dependent variable is $NMig_{it}/Pop_{it-1}$.

The explanatory variables are the variables that appear in Tables 4.4 and 4.5 plus the two globalization variables (Eco-Glob and Soc-Glob) and an additional variable, the prior decade's growth rate in (PPP-adjusted) GDP per capita, GDPgrowth (i.e., the 1960 observation for GDPgrowth$_{it}$ is country i's GDP growth per capita between 1950 and 1960). All explanatory variables are entered with a lag (t−1) to avoid issues of endogeneity arising from current migration flows impacting on the values of the explanatory variables. Data is available for the full 50-year time period for: GDP(pc)—which we enter in logarithmic form, LifeExp, Fem/Male and GDPgrowth. Data is available for the shorter 30-year timespan for each of these variables plus: log(GNI(pc)), HDI, EcoFprint, Eco-Glob, Soc-Glob, LS-HPI, LS-Mean, LS-Sdev and Gini; all variables are defined below Table 4.1. log(GNI(pc)) is our preferred per capita income measure, so we use this variable for the 1985–2010 estimates, and use log(GDP(pc)) for the 1965–2010 estimates for which log(GNI(pc)) is unavailable.

Some of the series are available only for OECD countries while, for variables available more widely, data quality issues are of greater concern for non-OECD than for OECD countries. We also expect that migration flows are less restricted between OECD countries than from non-OECD countries to OECD countries. For these reasons, we restrict our migration estimates to OECD countries, and further restrict our analysis to the 24 OECD countries as at 1973 to avoid sample selection bias (De Long, 1988).

The base equations for 1965–2010 and 1985–2010 respectively, are shown as equations (4.6) and (4.7):

$$NMig_{it}/Pop_{it-1} = \alpha_0 + \alpha_1 \log\left(GDP(pc)\right)_{it-1} + \lambda_t + \lambda_i + \varepsilon_{it} \qquad (4.6)$$

$$NMig_{it}/Pop_{it-1} = \alpha_0 + \alpha_1 \log\left(GNI(pc)\right)_{it-1} + \lambda_t + \lambda_i + \varepsilon_{it} \qquad (4.7)$$

Each base equation includes both time and country fixed effects. As discussed with reference to equations (4.4) and (4.5), the inclusion of time-fixed effects proxies both for global conditions impacting on migration flows and for international norms for each of the explanatory variables. Thus, for instance, the per capita GDP and GNI terms in equations (4.6) and (4.7) are implicitly expressed relative to the OECD average level for those variables for each year. The country-fixed effects proxy for country-specific characteristics and immigration policies that have a consistent effect over time.

Equations (4.6) and (4.7) model the impacts on net migration of average material wellbeing factors (and/or factors highly correlated with material wellbeing) as proxied by national accounts data. If migrants are driven to improve their lives solely by material concerns and/or by any factors highly correlated with material concerns (plus any constant differentials accounted for by the country-fixed-effect terms), then no other terms should be significant when added to equations (4.6) or (4.7). We test this hypothesis by adding other wellbeing and sustainability terms to these equations and testing for their significance. In doing so, we wish to test whether the added variables have significant explanatory power over and above the income terms in predicting migration flows. Our test is, therefore, a stringent one. The added term has to be significant at the 5% level in an equation that includes itself plus the income term. If the variable is highly correlated with income it might be significant in a migration equation when entered by itself but may not be significant once the income term is included. Thus, any equation containing significant added terms unequivocally adds extra information to explain migration flows that is not contained in the base income variable.

Table 4.6 provides results for these tests for each of the two time periods. All potentially included variables are listed. The equation that includes solely the income term is shown together with any equations that include an added term that passes the 5% significance test.

The (lagged) income variable is significant at the 1% level in each case. This result is clear evidence that migration flows respond to the relative material wellbeing of countries (or to factors positively correlated with material well-being). Over each period we find also that the HPI Life Satisfaction measure as modeled by Abdallah and colleagues adds further information over and above material wellbeing (Abdallah et al., 2008). Thus potential migrants respond positively to the factors within LS-HPI that are uncorrelated with either log(GDP(pc)) or log(GNI(pc)). This series, therefore, captures

Table 4.6. OECD24 Equations for Net Migration(t)/Population($t-1$).

Explanatory variables ($t-1$)	[1]	[2]	[1]	[2]
	1965–2010		**1985–2010**	
log(GDP(pc))	0.0408**	0.0336**		
log(GNI(pc))			0.0386**	0.0495**
GDPgrowth				
LifeExp				
Fem/Male				
EcoFprint				
LS-HPI		0.0096**		0.0245**
LS-Mean>				
LS-Sdev>				
Gini>				
HDI>				
Eco-Glob>				
Soc-Glob>				
Countries	22	21	24	23
Observations	220	210	144	138
R^2	0.5150	0.5215	0.6116	0.6580
s.e.e.	0.0132	0.0132	0.0117	0.0110
D.W.	1.50	1.52	1.70	1.89

Variables are defined below Table 4.1.
> Indicates that this explanatory variable is available only for the 1985–2010 analysis.
Coefficient significant at 1% (**), 5% (*).
Dependent variable (22-country) mean: 1965–2010 = 0.0099; standard deviation = 0.0175.
Dependent variable (24-country) mean: 1985–2010 = 0.0148; standard deviation = 0.0168.
s.e.e. is the equation standard error.
D.W. is the Durbin-Watson test for auto-correlation.
Equation shown only if added variable is significant at 5% given the inclusion of log(GDP(pc)) or log(GNI(pc)).
All equations include (unreported) constant-term, country-fixed effects, and period-fixed effects.

significant non-income-related factors that affect individuals' revealed preference decisions to improve their life outcomes through migration. No other variable is significant in the equations related to Table 4.6.

The country-fixed effects capture the impacts of migration restrictions and migration preferences (together represented by the fixed-cost term, F^j, in equation (4.3)) that remain constant over time. However, migration restrictions and preferences may vary over time in response to changing economic and social circumstances of countries. To capture this possibility, we extend the base equation to include three control variables that may themselves explain, or be correlated with, changes in migration restrictions and/or migration preferences within a country. The three variables are: $GDPgrowth_{it-1}$, $Eco\text{-}Glob_{it-1}$, and $Soc\text{-}Glob_{it-1}$.

The first of these variables is included on the basis that a country that has had recent strong GDP growth may relax its immigration restrictions owing to the requirements for a growing workforce. The economic and social globalization variables are measures of a country's integration with the global economy and society which, in turn, may be associated with its immigration policies. Neither variable includes migration flows directly, but the social globalization measure includes the stock of migrants within a country. Migration studies show that new migrants tend to move to areas where there is already a stock of people from their home country in residence. Thus the variable helps to pick up social factors, as well as migration policies, that affect the tendency of a country to attract migrants separate from wellbeing and sustainability factors. These three additional variables are included solely as control variables in an extended equation and so we do not interpret their coefficients.

Table 4.7 provides results for this extended specification for each of the two time periods. As for Table 4.6, all potentially included variables are again listed, and the equation that includes solely the income term (in addition to the unreported control variables and time- and country-fixed effects) is shown. Any equation that includes an added term that passes the 5% significance test is also shown. For the full period, the income term is again consistently significant as is the HPI-based life satisfaction measure (LS-HPI), each at the 1% level.

Over the shorter period, the income measure is again significant, but so too are three extra variables when included by themselves together with log(GNI(pc)). The first of these is LS-HPI as before. The second is the standard deviation in the WVS measure of life satisfaction (LS-Sdev), with its coefficient indicating that net inward migration flows are lower for countries with higher inequality of life satisfaction. Third, the ecological footprint variable (EcoFprint) is significant, but positive. Taken at face value, this result implies that potential migrants favor (re)location in countries that have an unsustainable economic structure (when viewed in ecological terms). As already shown, however, a country's ecological footprint has little or no relationship with its current environmental outcomes (i.e., with Yale's EPI measure). Instead, it may be the case that countries that are currently

Table 4.7. OECD24 Equations for Net Migration(t)/Population($t-1$) with Added Controls.

	[1]	[2]	[1]	[2]	[3]	[4]	[5]
	1965–2010		1985–2010				
log(GDP(pc))	0.0406**	0.0313**					
log(GNIpc))			0.0277*	0.0515**	0.0386*	0.0304*	0.0440**
LifeExp							
Fem/Male							
EcoFprint				0.0044*			0.0034
LS-HPI		0.0122**			0.0208*		0.0164*
LS-Mean>							
LS-Sdev>						−0.0251*	−0.0060
Gini>							
HDI>							
Countries	22	21	22	21	21	22	21
Observations	220	210	132	126	126	132	126
R^2	0.5216	0.5383	0.5781	0.6103	0.6125	0.5942	0.6285
s.e.e.	0.0131	0.0130	0.0111	0.0107	0.0107	0.0110	0.0106
D.W.	1.53	1.59	1.65	1.85	1.81	1.76	1.90

Variables are defined below Table 4.1.
> Indicates that this explanatory variable is available only for the 1985–2010 analysis.
Coefficient significant at 1% (**), 5% (*).
Dependent variable (22-country) mean: 1965–2010 = 0.0099; standard deviation = 0.0175.
Dependent variable (22-country) mean: 1985–2010 = 0.0137; standard deviation = 0.0150.
s.e.e. is the equation standard error.
D.W. is the Durbin-Watson test for auto-correlation.
Equation shown only if added variable is significant at 5% given the inclusion of log(GDP(pc)) or log(GNI(pc)).
All equations include (unreported) constant term, country-fixed effects and period-fixed effects.
1965–2010 equations also include lagged GDP growth.
1985–2010 equations also include lagged GDP growth, lagged economic globalization and lagged social globalization index.

exploiting large resource endowments have positive short-term economic prospects that attract migrants.

When the three additional variables are included together (column [5] in Table 4.7), LS-HPI remains significant ($p = .050$), but neither EcoFprint ($p = .070$) nor LS-Sdev ($p = .665$) is significant. When LS-Sdev is dropped from this extended equation, EcoFprint remains positive but is just insignificant ($p = .052$), while LS-HPI remains significant (not shown in Table 4.4). Each equation that includes LS-HPI has a much higher Durbin-Watson (D.W.) statistic than do those equations that only have income as an explanatory variable, and there is no evidence of auto-correlation for the 1985–2010 equations that incorporate LS-HPI.

Overall, the results indicate a robust finding that the HPI-based life satisfaction measure, LS-HPI, as modeled previously by Abdallah and colleagues, is significant across all specifications across both time periods. This result indicates that migrants respond to more than just material wellbeing, proxied by $\log(GDP(pc))$ or $\log(GNI(pc))$. Thus non-income-related factors contributing to life satisfaction are important determinants of migration decisions. The results also unequivocally indicate that material wellbeing is a key determinant of migration decisions. The revealed preference actions of migrants therefore indicate that material wellbeing, and life satisfaction factors beyond those that are correlated with purely material outcomes, are both important factors for potential migrants seeking to improve their life outcomes.

Summary and Conclusions

Many measures of aggregate wellbeing and sustainability exist for multiple countries. These include measures of material wellbeing, surveyed wellbeing measures, composite wellbeing measures, and ecologically based sustainability measures. The alternative measures have greater or lesser degrees of theoretical underpinning and may have differing objectives from one another. A small number of objective indicators of wellbeing also exist, including life expectancy. We argue that revealed preference indicators such as migration choices—where the choices are made so as to improve life outcomes now and into the future—are also objective indicators of wellbeing.

Most wellbeing and sustainability indicators are positively correlated with one another. Inequality measures are also correlated: countries that register higher wellbeing on most wellbeing indicators having lower inequality (both of life satisfaction and of incomes). One indicator that has a counter-intuitive relationship with others (based on ecological theory) is EcoFprint, the ecological footprint measure calculated by the World Wildlife Fund. Countries with a high EcoFprint tend to have high measures of wellbeing according to other indices and, more surprisingly, have (on average) slightly higher scores for Yale's Environmental Performance Index, *EPI*, for contemporary environmental outcomes.

In examining one country, New Zealand, we find that alternative measures of wellbeing and sustainability can give substantively different indications of how well the country is faring. For instance, within the OECD, New

Zealand fares poorly on material income measures, only moderately on life satisfaction measures (albeit highly on one happiness measure), and fares well on two composite measures of wellbeing. It performs moderately well on one environmental indicator (EPI) but not on the other (EcoFprint).

Given these diverse indications, we test the information content of a range of indicators for predicting migration outcomes over a 50-year time period for the 24 initial OECD countries. Each indicator must have sufficient coverage across countries and across time (at least 30 years) to be included in our tests. These tests deliver a strikingly consistent result across two separate time periods and across two alternative specifications. We find that both material wellbeing (GDP(pc) or GNI(pc)) and life satisfaction (LS-HPI as previously modeled by Abdallah et al. (2008), which is based, in turn, on life satisfaction survey results) are significant determinants of migration decisions. Thus, a measure of material wellbeing such as GDP, while being an important predictor of migration, is an insufficient index for measuring aggregate wellbeing for potential migrants. A broader measure of life satisfaction (that includes a component that is uncorrelated with material wellbeing factors) must also be included in the definition of aggregate wellbeing for these individuals.

Our results provide empirical evidence for the observation that policy makers face an explicit welfare trade-off in cases where a prospective policy increases per capita incomes but decreases some other facet(s) of life satisfaction. Where such a trade-off occurs, a typical economic impact report or monetary cost-benefit analysis (that does not monetize intangible values contributing to life satisfaction) will provide an insufficient yardstick to determine whether a policy should be adopted (Layard, 2011). A broader analysis that includes the value placed on general life satisfaction is required. Our results are consistent with the conventional wisdom that extra money (income) does improve wellbeing, but they also demonstrate that (per capita) incomes should not be the sole basis for assessing the merits of alternative public policies.

Acknowledgment

This chapter was prepared with funding from the Morgan Foundation and from the Royal Society of New Zealand Marsden Fund programme (MEP1201) on "Testing the validity and robustness of national wellbeing and sustainability measures." We gratefully acknowledge both sources of funding. The authors thank Robert MacCulloch, Susan Guthrie, Gareth

Morgan, Motu colleagues, and participants at the International Wellbeing Conference, Wellington (June 2012) and the New Zealand Association of Economists Conference, Palmerston North (June 2012) for helpful comments on an earlier draft. However sole responsibility for the analysis rests with the authors.

References

Abdallah, S., Thompson, S., & Marks, N. (2008). Estimating worldwide life satisfaction. *Ecological Economics*, *65*, 35–47.

Blackorby, C., & Donaldson, D. (1990). A review article: The case against the use of sum of compensating variations in cost-benefit analysis. *Canadian Journal of Economics*, *23*, 471–494.

Cameron, D. (2010). *Speech on wellbeing*. London: Cabinet Office. Retrieved from https://www.gov.uk/government/speeches/pm-speech-on-wellbeing

Cullen, M. (2005, December 20). *Timetable for business tax review*. Press release. http://taxpolicy.ird.govt.nz/news/2005-12-20-business-tax-review-update#statement.

De Long, J. (1988). Productivity growth, convergence, and welfare: Comment. *American Economic Review*, *78*, 1138–1154.

Dreher, A. (2006). Does globalization affect growth? Empirical evidence from a new index. *Applied Economics*, *38*, 1091–1110.

Dreher, A., Gaston, N., & Martens, P. (2008). *Measuring globalization—Gauging its consequence*. New York: Springer.

Durie, M. (2006). *Measuring Māori wellbeing*. Wellington: New Zealand Treasury.

Dustmann, C. (2003). Return migration, wage differentials, and the optimal migration duration. *European Economic Review*, *47*, 353–367.

Easterlin, R. (1974). Does economic growth improve the human lot? Some empirical evidence. In P. David & M. Reeder (Eds.), *Nations and households in economic growth: Essays in honor of Moses Abromovitz* (pp. 89–125). New York and London: Academic Press.

Ferreira, S., Hamilton, K., & Vincent, J. (2008). Comprehensive wealth & future consumption: Accounting for population growth. *World Bank Economic Review*, *22*, 233–248.

Ferreira, S., & Vincent, J. (2005). Genuine savings: Leading indicator of sustainable development? *Economic Development and Cultural Change*, *53*, 737–754.

Glaeser, E., & Gottlieb, J. (2009). The wealth of cities: Agglomeration economies & spatial equilibrium in the United States. *Journal of Economic Literature*, *47*, 983–1028.

Gleisner, B., Llewellyn-Fowler, M., & McAlister, F. (2011). Working towards higher living standards for New Zealanders. *New Zealand Treasury Paper* no. 11(2). http://www.treasury.govt.nz/publications/research-policy/tp/higherlivingstandards/01.htm.

Grimes, A. (2013). Infrastructure and regional growth. In M. Fischer & P. Nijkamp (Eds.), *Handbook of regional science*. Heidelberg: Springer.

Hamilton, K., & Clemens, M. (1999). Genuine savings rates in developing countries. *World Bank Economic Review, 13,* 333–356.

Hamilton, K., & Withagen, C. (2007). Savings growth and the path of utility. *Canadian Journal of Economics, 40,* 703–713.

Helliwell, J., Layard, R., & Sachs, J. (2012). *World happiness report*. Earth Institute: Columbia University.

Key, J. (2010). Statement to parliament. http://www.voxy.co.nz/politics/speech-john-key-statement-parliament-9-february-2010/5/37739.

Layard, R. (2011). *Happiness: Lessons from a new science* (2nd ed.). London: Penguin.

Maddison, A. (2006). *The world economy* (Vols. 1 & 2). Paris: OECD.

McCann, P., Poot, J., & Sanderson, L. (2010). Migration, relationship capital and international travel: Theory and evidence. *Journal of Economic Geography, 10,* 361–387.

Stiglitz, J., Sen, A., & Fitoussi, J.-P. (2009). *Report by the Commission on the Measurement of Economic Performance and Social Progress*. Paris: OECD.

United Nations Development Programme (UNDP) (2010). The real wealth of nations: Pathways to human development. In UNDP, *Human Development Report 2010*. New York: UNDP.

Waring, M. (1989). *If women counted*. London: Macmillan.

World Bank (1997). *Expanding the measure of wealth: Indicators of sustainable development*. ESD Studies, vol. 17. Washington, DC: World Bank.

World Wildlife Fund (2008). *Living planet report 2008*. Gland, Switzerland: WWF.

Further Readings

Alesina, A., Di Tella, R., & MacCulloch, R., (2004). Inequality and happiness: Are Europeans and Americans different? *Journal of Public Economics, 88,* 2009–2042.

Di Tella, R., & MacCulloch, R. (2007). Gross national happiness as an answer to the Easterlin Paradox? *Journal of Development Economics, 16.* http://www.people.hbs.edu/rditella/papers/WPGNHappiness.pdf.

Di Tella, R., MacCulloch, R., & Oswald, A. (2003). The macroeconomics of happiness. *Review of Economics and Statistics, 85,* 793–809.

Escosura, L. (2010). Improving human development: A long-run view. *Journal of Economic Surveys, 24,* 841–894.

Fleurbaey, M. (2009). Beyond the GDP: The quest for a measure of social welfare. *Journal of Economic Literature, 47,* 1029–1075.

Ranis G. & Stewart F. (2010). *Success and failure in human development, 1970–2007* (Human Development Research Paper 2010/10). http://hdr.undp.org/en/reports/global/hdr2010/papers/HDRP_2010_10.pdf.

Sen, A. (1999). *Development as freedom*. New York: Alfred A. Knopf.

This chapter presents estimates of the IEWB for Australia*, Belgium, Canada*, Denmark, Finland, France, Germany*, Italy, the Netherlands, Norway*, Spain, Sweden*, the United Kingdom* and the United States* between 1995 and 2010.[2] However, because discussion of 14 different countries rapidly becomes very unwieldy, we focus initially on four nations—the United States, Canada, Germany, and Spain. These particular countries are chosen because within both the "Anglo" and "Continental European" welfare state regimes one can observe great variation in the impacts of the Great Recession, and it is interesting to compare countries where the recession has had a large and continuing impact (Spain and the United States) with countries that had largely recovered by 2010 (Germany and Canada). We then compare all 14 countries' experiences.

We pose three questions. First, how has the recession changed the level of wellbeing in different countries, as indicated by the IEWB? Second, did countries have similar or different shocks to the different components of their economic wellbeing in the 2007 to 2010 period? Third, how different is the within-country cyclical relationship between changes in dimensions of economic wellbeing and gross domestic product (GDP) growth or unemployment?

Because we can be sure that some readers of this chapter will not have read our earlier papers, we begin with a brief outline of the methodology of the IEWB, as well as a summary of how the Great Recession differed across countries in its impact on GDP and employment. To set the context for our discussion of cyclical impacts on the IEWB, we then discuss trends of the IEWB in Canada, the United States, Germany, and Spain from 1995 to 2010. The next section then compares the differing impacts of the Great Recession on the components of economic wellbeing during the 2007–2010 period across all 14 countries. The final part of the chapter discusses the sensitivity of different dimensions of wellbeing to year-to-year changes in output and unemployment and we conclude by summarizing possible implications.

The Index of Economic Wellbeing: Motivation and Framework

The IEWB is an intermediate type of index (Osberg & Sharpe, 2005). While broader in conception than GDP per capita, it still aims only at the "economic" dimension of life. The philosophy of the IEWB is that there

Table 5.1. Dimensions of Economic Wellbeing.

Concept	Present	Future
"Typical citizen" or "representative agent"	[A] *Average flow of current income*	[B] *Aggregate accumulation of productive stocks*
Heterogeneity of individual citizens	[C] *Distribution of potential consumption—income inequality and poverty*	[D] *Insecurity of future incomes*

is more to "wellbeing" than economic wellbeing, but there is more to economic wellbeing than GDP per capita, and it is useful to have better measures of the economic wellbeing of society because better measurement may help guide better decisions (Osberg, 1985; Sharpe & Salzman, 2003). The IEWB avoids consideration of broader "quality of life" issues (Di Tella, MacCulloch, & Oswald, 2003) (such as crime rates) on the grounds that too much aggregation of the dissimilar dimensions of social and political wellbeing can obscure understanding. Rather, the IEWB takes a broad view of "economic wellbeing" as "access to the resources needed for material consumption" because the narrow focus of GDP accounting omits consideration of many issues (for example, leisure time, longevity of life, asset stock levels) which are important to the command over resources of individuals. The IEWB is based on four dimensions of economic wellbeing—average current consumption flows, aggregate accumulation for future consumption (i.e. per capita wealth—broadly conceived), income distribution and economic security.

Table 5.1 illustrates our identification of four components of wellbeing, which recognize trends in both average outcomes and in the diversity of outcomes, both now and in the future.

When an average income flow concept, like GDP per capita, is used as a summative index of society's wellbeing, the analyst implicitly is stopping in quadrant [A]. This assumes (a) that the experience of a representative agent can summarize the wellbeing of society and (b) that the measured income flow optimally weights consumption and savings, so that one need not explicitly distinguish between present consumption flows and the accumulation of asset stocks which will enable future consumption flows. However, if society is composed of diverse individuals living in an uncertain world who typically "live in the present, anticipating the future," each individual's estimate

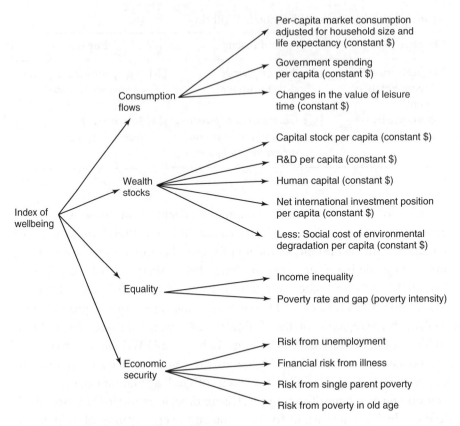

Figure 5.1. Index of Wellbeing Tree.

of societal economic wellbeing will depend on the proportion of national income saved for the future—i.e. both quadrants [A] and [B] matter.

In addition, real societies are not equal. There is a long tradition in economics that "social welfare" depends on both average incomes and the degree of inequality and poverty in the distribution of incomes—quadrant [C]. Putting individual heterogeneity and multiple time periods together, we have quadrant [D]. *Ex ante*, individuals do not know who will be hit by the hazards of economic life. When the future is uncertain, and complete insurance is unobtainable (either privately or through the welfare state), risk-averse individuals will care about the degree to which their economic future is secure.

The four components of the IEWB used in this chapter are made up of a number of variables, as shown in the weighting tree in Figure 5.1.[3]

The consumption component, measured in prices on a per capita basis, includes private consumption, with adjustments for family size and life expectancy, public consumption, and changes in the value of leisure as proxied by changes in working time. The wealth component, measured in prices on a per capita basis, includes estimates of residential and non-residential physical capital, research and development (R & D) capital, human capital, the net international investment position, and environmental degradation, as proxied by the social costs of greenhouse gases.

The equality component of Figure 5.1, measured as an index, includes a measure of income distribution, the Gini coefficient, and poverty intensity (the product of the poverty rate and gap) for all persons. The Gini is given a weight of 0.25 and poverty intensity is weighted 0.75. The economic security component, also measured as an index, consists of four subcomponents: the risk from unemployment; the financial risk from illness; the risk from single-parent poverty; and the risk from poverty in old age. Each subcomponent is weighted by the relative importance of the population affected by the risk.

These four components therefore have a logical rationale and a manageable dimensionality—the IEWB is then calculated as the weighted sum of [A] + [B] + [C] + [D]. However, although we may all agree that these four dimensions of wellbeing are all valuable to some degree, individuals differ in their relative preferences for each component. Some people, for example, consider equality to be more important than environmental preservation or per capita wealth, while others think the opposite. Different individuals often assign differing degrees of relative importance to each dimension of wellbeing. Indeed, each citizen in a democratic society has the right to come to a personal conclusion about the relative weight of each dimension. But because all citizens are occasionally called upon, in a democracy, to exercise choices (e.g., in voting) on issues that affect the collectivity (and some individuals, such as civil servants, make such decisions on a daily basis), they all also have reason sometimes to ask questions of the form

Would public policy X make "society" better off?

A measure of social wellbeing can be useful if some people, at least some of the time, want to answer such questions in an evidence-based way. We can assume that individuals know more about their own preferences and their own life situation than anyone else is likely to, so individuals probably do not need help in calculating the implications for their own personal utility of public policy on any given issue. However, individuals who care about some combination of their own wellbeing and society's wellbeing can be seen as maximizing:

$U_i = \alpha_1$ (own utility) $+ \alpha_2$ (Social Index expressing own estimate of society's wellbeing).

If $\alpha_2 = 0$ for all persons, at all times, then there is no point in constructing the IEWB—or any other social index. We are presuming that for some people, at least some of the time, $\alpha_2 \neq 0$.

In the real world, citizens are frequently called upon to choose between public policies affecting dimensions of life (e.g., education, or health, or the environment) that cannot be measured in directly comparable units. Hence, individuals often have to come to a summative decision—i.e., have a way of "adding it all up"—across domains that are conceptually dissimilar. We argue that the role of people who construct social indices should be one of helping citizens—e.g., as voters in elections and as bureaucrats in policy making—to come to reasonable summative decisions about the level of society's wellbeing. From this perspective, the purpose of index construction should be to help individuals think systematically about public policy, without necessarily presuming that all individuals have the same values. Although it may not be possible to define an *objective* index of societal wellbeing, individuals still have the problem (indeed, the moral responsibility) of coming to a *subjective* evaluation of social states, and they need organized, objective data if they are to do it in a reasonable way.

The Differing Impacts of the Great Recession

Conventional summary statistics on the impacts of the Great Recession do not, to put it mildly, tell a consistent story across countries. In Table 5.2, columns 1 and 2 report the total percentage change in employment and in GDP per capita between 2007 and 2010 in the 14 countries examined.[4] Comparing 2007 and 2010, total employment was up by 5.7% in Australia and down by 9.4% in Spain. Column 1 shows that there is a nearly even split between the eight countries with a net increase in employment over the period among the population aged 15 to 64 and the six countries which have experienced a net decline in employment. Differentials in growth of

Table 5.2. The Varying Impacts of the Great Recession.

	2007 to 2010			
	Change in employment (%)	Change in GDP/capita (%)	Change in unemployment rate	Change in IEWB
Australia	5.7	−0.2	0.8	0.005
Belgium	2.4	1.2	0.8	0.023
Canada	0.6	−2.5	2.0	0.007
Denmark	−3.5	−1.6	3.7	−0.026
Finland	−2.0	−3.5	1.5	0.026
France	0.5	−1.4	1.4	−0.021
Germany	1.8	0.7	−1.6	0.032
Italy	−1.5	−4.8	2.5	−0.002
The Netherlands	0.9	−0.9	1.3	0.011
Norway	1.9	−2.0	1.1	0.054
Spain	−9.4	−5.3	11.8	−0.071
Sweden	−0.3	−2.2	2.4	−0.006
United Kingdom	1.1	−4.5	2.5	−0.001
United States	−5.4	−3.5	5.0	0.012

GDP per capita are not quite as dramatic—as column 3 shows, only in Belgium and Germany was the recovery in employment large enough to produce a net improvement in GDP per capita. But, although one would normally expect the direction of change in employment and growth in GDP per capita to be the same, this is only true in half the countries.

Both Belgium and Germany had more jobs and higher GDP per capita in 2010 than in 2007. There were six other countries with net employment creation (Australia, Canada, France, the Netherlands, Norway, and the United Kingdom) but with negative GDP per capita growth. By contrast, the period was unambiguously bad news in Finland, Italy, Spain, Sweden, and the United States, where both employment and GDP per capita were lower in 2010 than in 2007. Indeed, U.S. employment in 2010 was still 5.4% below its 2007 level and employment in Spain was still down by 9.4%.

Conventional statistics thus reveal large differences, across countries, in the depth and duration of the impacts of the recession which followed the financial crisis of 2008. We turn now to looking at what indices of wellbeing indicate.

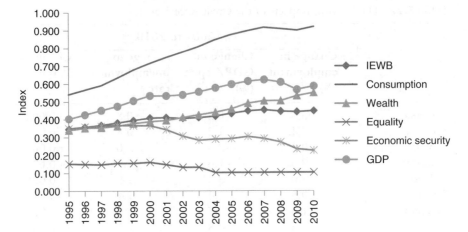

Figure 5.2. Trends in the IEWB, Its Components, & Scaled GDP per Capita, United States, 1995–2010. Data tables corresponding to Figures 5.2 to 5.20 are available from http://www.csls.ca/iwb/articles.asp.

Trends in the IEWB in Canada, Germany, Spain, and the United States 1995 to 2010

Figures 5.2 to 5.5 compare long-run trends in the four components of economic wellbeing, and the IEWB as a whole, with trends in GDP for four illustrative countries, the United States, Canada, Germany, and Spain.[5] For each country, we compare trends in the "base" index with trends in GDP per capita.[6] The four figures show the level in each year of the index of each component of economic wellbeing (i.e., consumption, accumulation, distribution, and economic security), as well as the level of the aggregate IEWB when each component receives equal weight. To facilitate comparisons, we also apply the Linear Scaling methodology to GDP per capita. To keep all our comparisons on a common footing, we use the [Max-Min] range defined by data from the 14 countries for which we construct the IEWB. Figure 5.2 looks at the United States, showing the level of aggregate indices (GDP per capita and the IEWB) and the components of the IEWB [consumption, accumulation (wealth), equality, and economic security]. The U.S. IEWB illustrates how aggregate wellbeing can be driven by diverging trends in the components of wellbeing. If the four components are equally weighted, as in Figure 5.2, the IEWB shows a lower

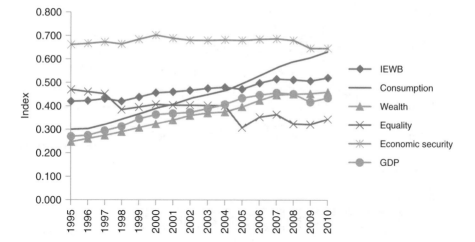

Figure 5.3. Trends in the IEWB, Its Components, & Scaled GDP per Capita, Canada, 1995–2010.

level and a flatter trend over the period than per capita consumption (which rose strongly) and aggregate wealth (a somewhat smaller increase than for consumption). Both market consumption and investment are important components of GDP, and the upward trend in GDP per capita exceeds that in the IEWB. However, compared to the other countries examined here, the United States sits low in the range of observed equality and security, with a downward trend over time. As a consequence, when all four components are weighted equally in the IEWB, the downward trend in equality and security offsets the high level and upward trend of average consumption and aggregate wealth. This implies that the aggregate IEWB is quite flat, especially compared to consumption trends.

A moderate upward trend for the IEWB was observed for Canada (Figure 5.3). One can see in the data both the stronger upward trend in GDP per capita and the deviation downward which marked the recession of 2007–2009. In Canada, the IEWB has been less volatile than GDP because the components of the IEWB are heavily influenced by factors that do not necessarily vary with the business cycle or respond directly to economic growth. For example, security from the risks of uninsured health care costs has declined over time in Canada—but on a secular trend, as, for most people, prescription drug costs are not, for example, covered under Canadian public health insurance and they have risen over time. Looking only at the period discussed in this chapter (1995–2010), one will not be

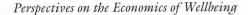

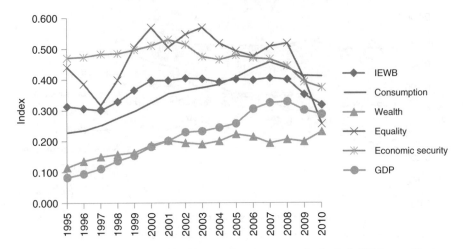

Figure 5.4. Trends in the IEWB, Its Components, & Scaled GDP per Capita, Spain, 1995–2010.

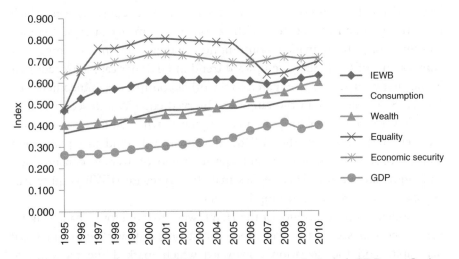

Figure 5.5. Trends in the IEWB, Its Components, & Scaled GDP per Capita, Germany, 1995–2010.

able to observe the impact on equality in Canada of the substantial cuts to social assistance and unemployment insurance made in 1995–1996. Even so, a downward shift in equality in Canada, together with some decline in security offset much of the strong long-run growth in consumption and wealth.[7]

The Great Recession may be a smallish bump in Canadian trends, but it is all too apparent in the Spanish data for 2008–2010 seen in Figure 5.4. Indeed, in Spain between 2007 and 2010, a moderate increase (from 12.9% to 14.4%) in the poverty rate interacts multiplicatively with a large increase in the poverty gap (from 0.242 to 0.355) to cause a large increase in poverty intensity [= (poverty rate)*(average poverty gap)]. Because the IEWB index of equality trends is 0.25 weighted to the Gini index of equivalent income and 0.75 weighted to poverty intensity, the downward dive in the equality component of the IEWB after 2007 is especially notable. The unemployment rate increase (from 8.3% to 20.2%) in Spain also shows up clearly in the economic security component of the IEWB. The wealth and consumption components of the IEWB also declined in the recession, but not to the same degree. Since consumption is a large fraction of GDP, it is not surprising that trends in consumption and GDP are quite similar.

Together, the large declines in equality and economic security in Spain mean that the IEWB fell there by considerably more than the change in GDP per capita. Unlike the pattern observed in Canada (where the IEWB was less volatile), economic wellbeing in Spain changed more in this recession than did GDP per capita. Later in this chapter we will see that within-country year-to-year changes in output and employment often do not significantly affect the IEWB index of equality—presumably because most such changes have historically been marginal impacts on the income distribution. However, the Spanish example of 2007–2010 may be a reminder that sometimes changes in output and employment are more than marginal, with large and multiplicative impacts on equality.

A significant feature of the German data in Figure 5.5 is the strong upward movement of the poverty rate (from 6.7% to 9.5%) and the poverty gap (from 0.174 to 0.219) between 2005 and 2007, that is, *before* the Great Recession. This gives a strong downward push to our equality index prior to the recession. It then improves slightly over the same period during which other countries (e.g., Spain) experienced strong deterioration. Although the recession did produce a slight downward bump in GDP in 2009, it is hard to see in the German data evidence of any impact at all on indicators of economic wellbeing. However, this is partly an issue of idiosyncratic context—the fact that the rate and depth of German poverty had increased so strongly *before* the recession. Obtaining a fuller understanding of German trends over the 2005 to 2007 period is an important objective of our future research.

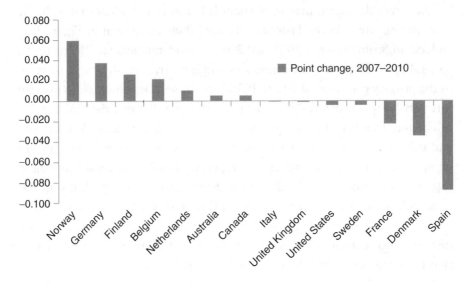

Figure 5.6. Change in Index of Economic Wellbeing, 2007–2010.

Divergences and Commonalities in Economic Wellbeing within Countries: 2007–2010

Figure 5.6 compares the overall movement in economic wellbeing between 2007 and 2010 in the 14 countries examined in this study. Figures 5.7 to 5.10 then compare movements in the four components of wellbeing—average consumption, per capita wealth, equality, and economic security. Although Figure 5.6 indicates a wide divergence across nations in the direction and size of trends in aggregate economic wellbeing, those results on aggregate wellbeing depend crucially on the fact that this figure weights each component of wellbeing equally. Denmark and Spain have done poorly on most dimensions of wellbeing while Norway, Germany, and Finland have done well—but in between the rankings of countries differ widely. If all the components of economic wellbeing had followed similar trends over time, the relative weights placed on each component would not matter much—but that is not the case for most of the countries examined here. Hence, one way of reading the comparisons of Figures 5.7 to 5.10 is to say that they illustrate the importance of the relative weights assigned to each component of economic wellbeing.

As Figure 5.7 illustrates, most nations actually avoided a decrease in per-capita consumption between 2007 and 2010. Spain and the United Kingdom are outliers, with declines of 0.044 and 0.053 index points

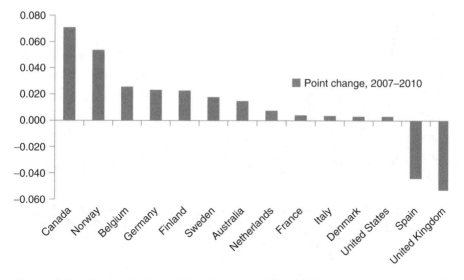

Figure 5.7. Change in Consumption Index, 2007–2010.

respectively. This is about the same as the difference in 2010 between Australia and Belgium in per capita consumption. Hence, an analyst who believed that the most important component in economic wellbeing is the level of per capita consumption, and assigned a high relative weight to that component, would tend to conclude that economic wellbeing had increased over the 2007–2010 period—at least for 12 of the 14 countries.

Figure 5.8 tells an even more positive story for aggregate wealth. Spain did poorly on other dimensions, but the rise in its wealth index (by 0.037) was near the median of country performance. The only nation with a decline over the period 2007 to 2010 was Sweden (a change which was very small −0.009 index points). Hence, an analyst whose values emphasized the importance of aggregate sustainability, and who therefore assigned a large weight to the aggregate accumulation of productive resources, could easily come to the conclusion that 2007–2010 was a period of positive outcomes for almost all countries.

Our measures of consumption per capita and aggregate accumulation extend national income accounting measures in several important ways (e.g., we make allowance for the impact on effective consumption of trends in household size and include environmental stocks and depreciated research and development spending as part of the accumulation of productive assets). Nevertheless, they are heavily influenced by trends in the underlying System of National Accounts (SNA) measures of consumption and investment. They

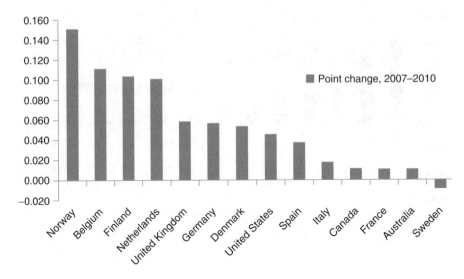

Figure 5.8. Change in Wealth Index, 2007–2010.

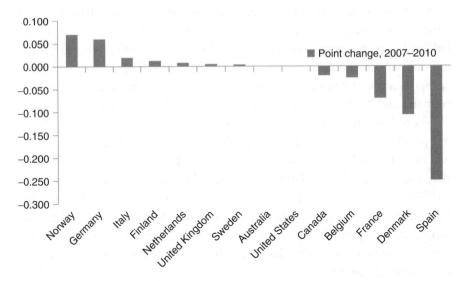

Figure 5.9. Change in Equality Index, 2007–2010.

also share with GDP calculations the fact that they are aggregate measures, which entirely ignore distributional issues and uncertainty about the future.

In constructing the IEWB, we have argued repeatedly for a methodology that does not always and automatically assign a zero weight to distributional and insecurity issues. As Figures 5.9 and 5.10 indicate, when these issues

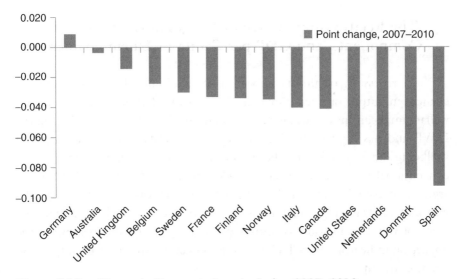

Figure 5.10. Change in Economic Security Index, 2007–2010.

are considered the 2007–2010 period generally looks much less positive than when they are ignored (as in Figures 5.7 and 5.8). Figure 5.9 shows how adverse movements in poverty and inequality were quite significant in several countries (as already discussed, worst in Spain, not just because the poverty rate increased but also because the average depth of poverty grew significantly). Marginal improvements in our equality index in Norway and Germany contrast with declines in Canada, France, Belgium, Denmark, and Sweden. Figure 5.10 shows that our economic security index declined in 13 of 14 countries.

Taken together, Figures 5.6 to 5.10 imply a potential for differing values to drive divergence in assessment of the implications of the Great Recession. Those who favor the view that measures of economic wellbeing should focus on aggregates or averages—such as per capita consumption or wealth—will be likely to assess the 2007 to 2010 period as predominantly positive in almost all of the 14 nations we study. Those who emphasize the importance of equality in the distribution of current income and economic security about future income will be likely to come to the opposite conclusion—and especially so if concerns about greater economic insecurity are considered more relatively important. The weighting of the different dimensions of wellbeing thus matters significantly. Indeed, making more transparent this sensitivity of aggregate measures of wellbeing to the underlying components of wellbeing has always been one of our major objectives in constructing the IEWB.

The Relationship between Changes in the IEWB, Its Components, and GDP per Capita or Unemployment

When a recession occurs its impact is often discussed with reference to changes in output or unemployment. This chapter has been urging that the welfare implications of business cycle variations should be assessed using the IEWB and has argued that business cycle impacts on the components of wellbeing differ significantly. How can one assess the relationship between conventional measures of business cycle impacts and the IEWB? Can one argue that some countries do a better job than others in reducing the volatility of wellbeing—that is, for a given size of shock to unemployment or output, do some countries do better than others in limiting the impact on indicators of wellbeing of business cycle variations in output and unemployment?

Arthur Okun's (1962) estimation of the relationship between changes in GDP and changes in the unemployment rate has attained the status of being labeled "Okun's Law". To assess the relationship between output variability (or unemployment changes) and changes in economic wellbeing, we rely on a similar specification. Specifically, we start by estimating OLS equations of the form:

$$\Delta \text{IEWB} = k_1 + c_1^*(\Delta \text{ unemployment}) \tag{5.1}$$

$$\Delta \text{IEWB} = k_2 + c_2^*(\%\Delta \text{ output}) \tag{5.2}$$

We estimate equations (5.1) and (5.2) by ordinary least squares (OLS) separately for each country—since our data is limited to 15 annual observations for each country, the standard error of these estimates is necessarily large.[8] We discuss first the results for changes in the aggregate IEWB (equally weighted), and then proceed to discuss the results of similar regression estimates of the relationship between changes in the components (wealth accumulation, consumption, equality, and security) of the IEWB and changes in unemployment and output. Each figure presents, for each country and for the pooled sample, bar graph representations of our estimates of coefficients c1 and c2 respectively, with the plus or minus two standard error confidence interval marked (where this interval spans zero, the interpretation is that one cannot reject, at 95% confidence, the hypothesis that the value of the coefficient is really zero).

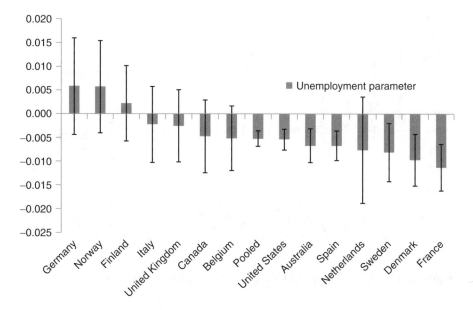

Figure 5.11.   Unemployment Changes & IEWB Changes.

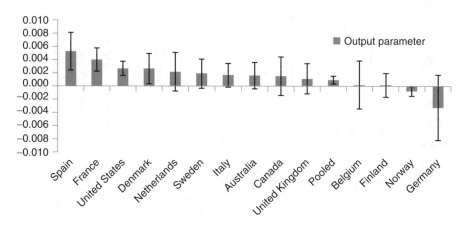

Figure 5.12.   Output Changes & IEWB Changes.

As Figure 5.11 indicates, changes in the unemployment rate do negatively affect the aggregate (equally weighted) IEWB in most countries but only in five countries is this statistically significantly different from zero. Output changes shown in Figure 5.12 are positively correlated—but also often indistinguishable from zero at a 95% level of statistical confidence. Is this a reasonable pattern for a defensible index of economic wellbeing?

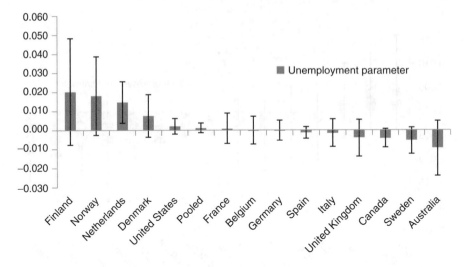

Figure 5.13. Unemployment Changes & Wealth Index Changes.

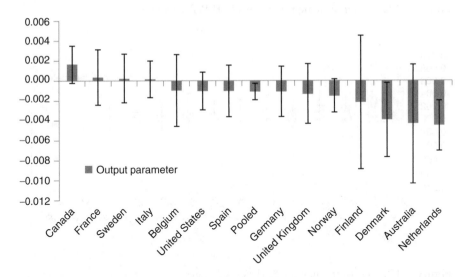

Figure 5.14. GDP Changes & Wealth Index Changes.

To illustrate why aggregate indices of economic wellbeing might not be very sensitive to short-run variations in GDP per capita and unemployment, Figure 5.13 presents the c_1 estimates of the relationship between year-to-year changes in unemployment and the wealth index and Figure 5.14 presents the c_2 estimates of the relationship between year-to-year changes

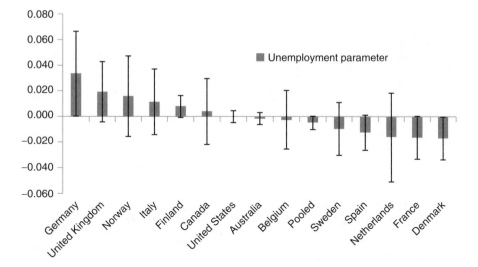

Figure 5.15. Unemployment Changes & Equality Index Changes.

in GDP and the wealth index. Since wealth stocks are built up over many years, it is reasonable to think that they are not likely to be particularly sensitive to year-to-year variations in output or unemployment—as these figures indicate.

Figure 5.15 presents the c_1 estimates of the relationship between year-to-year changes in unemployment and the equality index and Figure 5.16 presents estimates of the c_2 coefficient, linking year-to-year changes in GDP and the equality index. One can sometimes forget that, when the unemployment rate increases from 4% to 6%, one can equally well describe this as the unemployment rate increasing by half or as a decline from 96% to 94% in the percentage of the labor force employed (i.e., a change of 1/48th). In most years, year-to-year changes in output or employment are not large, and measures of inequality within countries are dominated by the continuing inequalities among the vast majority. Figures 5.15 and 5.16 show that year-to-year changes in GDP and unemployment are, for the 1995 to 2010 period as a whole, not strongly related to year-to-year changes in the equality index. However, the 2007–2010 shock to GDP in Spain was strong enough to show up as a statistically significant positive correlation between GDP changes and equality index changes, and our results on in international trends in the IEWB earlier may indicate that non-marginal shocks can interact multiplicatively to produce significantly sized impacts.

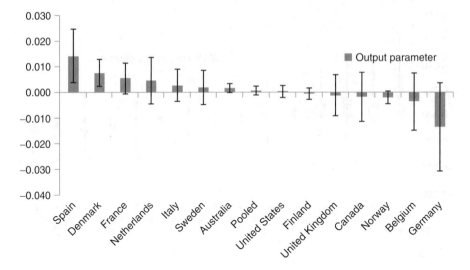

Figure 5.16. GDP Changes & Equality Index Changes.

Since per capita consumption is an annual flow measure, it is reasonable to expect it to respond to year to year changes, and Figures 5.17 and 5.18 indicate that this is normally the case, usually at statistically significant levels.[9] Nevertheless, it is still striking how much countries vary. As Figure 5.18 indicates volatility of GDP movement is far more immediately translated into movement in per capita consumption in the United States, the United Kingdom, and Australia than in Finland, Germany, and Norway—indeed Norway is in the unique position that it seems able to separate GDP movements from aggregate consumption changes nearly completely. One possible explanation for the Norwegian results is that oil price movements will affect Norwegian GDP, but, because oil revenues are deposited in a sovereign wealth fund, consumption implications will be averaged over the price cycle.

The most cyclically sensitive component of the IEWB is the economic security index, as Figures 5.19 and 5.20 illustrate.[10] Unemployment is negatively related to economic security and GDP growth is positively related—no surprise there.

However, if one of the objectives of the welfare state is to improve citizens' sense of economic security by decreasing their exposure to the volatility of GDP movements, then it is interesting that some countries do much better than others. When we estimate the equation:

$$\Delta \text{Economic Security} = k + c_2^*(\%\Delta \text{ Output}) \qquad (5.3)$$

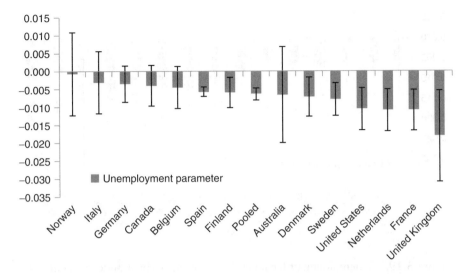

Figure 5.17. Unemployment Changes & Consumption Index Changes.

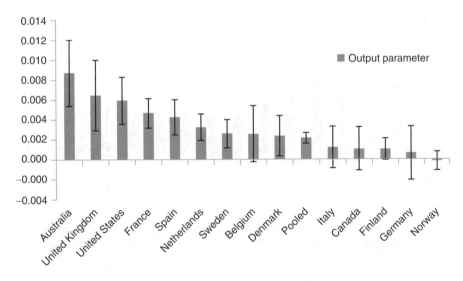

Figure 5.18. GDP Changes & Consumption Index Changes.

our estimate of c_2 is statistically significant (at 95%)—but at very different levels—in almost all countries. France (0.006), Canada (0.005), Netherlands (0.005), Denmark (0.005), and Spain (0.004) are the countries where economic security fluctuates most with variations in GDP growth while economic security in Finland (0.002) and Norway (0.001) is much less

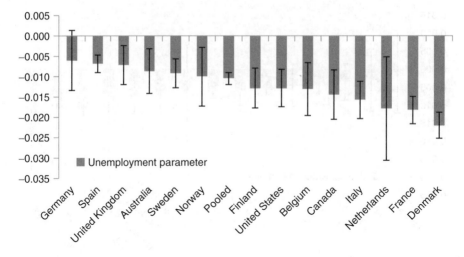

Figure 5.19. Unemployment Changes & Economic Security Index Changes.

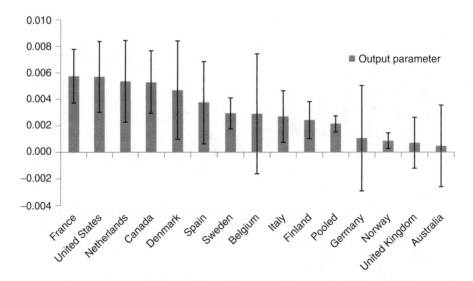

Figure 5.20. GDP Changes & Economic Security Index Changes.

correlated with GDP movements. One way of reading these results is to say that they indicate that these two nations do much better than others in insuring their citizens against the hazards of the business cycle, for any given size of business cycle shock.

Conclusion

The "Great Recession" of 2008 had very different impacts in different countries. Conventional indicators, like unemployment or GDP growth, show that in some countries (e.g., the United States or Spain), it ushered in a prolonged and severe economic downturn, while in other nations (e.g., Australia or Germany) it produced a short negative blip in the data, with few apparent long-term consequences.

This chapter has tried to look at the Great Recession using the lens of the Index of Economic Wellbeing and available data for the period 1995 to 2010 from 14 countries—Australia, Belgium, Canada, Denmark, Finland, France, Germany, Italy, Netherlands, Norway, Spain, Sweden, the United Kingdom and the United States. It has made three main points:

1. Any aggregate index of wellbeing necessarily imposes some weighting of the components of wellbeing. This implies that calculations of trends in aggregate indices can be sensitive to the weighting of components, when trends in those components of wellbeing differ, as was the case across these 14 nations in the 2007–2010 period. In particular, since the 2007–2010 changes in economic security and equality were negative in most of the 14 countries studied while 2007–2010 trends in per capita consumption and aggregate wealth accumulation were more positive, weighting schemes that emphasize security and equality will tend to show more negative impacts of the Great Recession on aggregate wellbeing than weightings which emphasize aggregate consumption or wealth accumulation.

2. Wealth stocks are accumulated over many years and the institutions that determine the distribution of income have great inertia within countries (particularly among that vast majority of the population who retain employment during normal year-to-year fluctuations in output or employment). Hence, in normal times neither of these dimensions of economic wellbeing is very sensitive to year-to-year variations in output or employment within countries. By contrast, annual consumption flows and measures of economic security are much more sensitive. The caveat "in normal times" is necessary because non-marginal shocks and the multiplicative interaction between changes in the poverty rate and the average poverty gap can produce significant cyclical impacts on equality—as the example of Spain 2007–2010 illustrates.

3. Countries differ a lot in the degree to which economic security and consumption flows vary with year to year fluctuations in output and employment. Some countries' institutions are clearly much more effective than others in insulating economic security and average consumption from cyclical volatility, for any given size of shock.

Addendum

Replacement of Luxembourg Income Study (LIS) Poverty and Income Distribution Estimates by Eurostat and National Estimates in the IEWB Database

The estimates of the IEWB used in this chapter for 14 OECD countries (11 EU countries, Canada, the United States, and Australia) for 1995 to 2010 are based on the updated IEWB estimates for OECD countries for the 1980–2010 period recently prepared by the Centre for the Study of Living Standards (CSLS). A major difference between these estimates and our earlier work is that the poverty and income distribution estimates used are no longer based on Luxembourg Income Study (LIS) data but instead now use Eurostat estimates.

The LIS represented a major advance in the availability of consistent micro-data sets for the generation of comparable poverty and income distribution estimates across OECD countries. However, LIS data sets are only available for a small number of years and, for most countries, are not available beyond the mid-2000s. This means that time-series data for LIS countries must often be interpolated between data years, and the LIS cannot be used for analysis of the impact of the Great Recession.

Fortunately, Eurostat has calculated annual estimates up to 2010 in a consistent manner for its members using six of the seven poverty and income distribution variables that the IEWB uses—specifically (using a 50% of median income concept of the poverty line) Eurostat publishes the poverty rate and gap for all persons, the poverty rate and gap for older people, the poverty rate for single-parent households. As well, Eurostat publishes estimates of the Gini coefficient of the inequality of money income. The only variable missing for our purposes is the poverty gap for single-parent households. These data represent a major advance in the availability of internationally comparable data for EU countries. The three non-EU members of our dataset are Canada, the United States, and

Australia. Statistics Canada publishes annual estimates for all six variables we need up to 2010 based on the Survey of Labour and Income Dynamics (SLID) and these estimates have been included in the database. No U.S. statistical agency produces relative poverty estimates comparable to Eurostat estimates of "one half median income" poverty. However, the U.S. Bureau of Census makes available the micro-data sets for the March supplement to the Current Population Survey (CPS), and poverty estimates can be generated from these data sets. The CSLS has used these micro datasets to generate poverty and income distribution estimates comparable to the Eurostat estimates for the 1995–2010 period. These estimates are used in this chapter and are available on the CSLS website.

The Australia Bureau of Statistics also does not appear to produce relative poverty estimates consistent with Eurostat definitions. The estimates for Australia in the paper are based on the LIS, which only goes up to the mid-2000s. Estimates for recent years are assumed unchanged from the most recent LIS numbers.

Notes

1. In previous papers, we relied on the Luxembourg Income Study (LIS) for the data underlying our poverty rate and gap calculations and estimated intervening years (i.e., those not available in LIS) by interpolation. Where possible, this chapter substitutes Eurostat estimates, which are available beginning in 1995 for each year for most European nations. See addendum to chapter for discussion.

2. Osberg and Sharpe (2005) discussed, for the seven countries marked here with an asterisk, the differences between using GDP per capita or the IEWB as a component of the Human Development Index, over the period 1980 to 2001

3. It is important to note that the estimates of the IEWB for OECD countries contain fewer variables than IEWB estimates for Canada and the provinces, because there is greater data available for Canada than for OECD countries. For example, the Canadian estimates include data on certain regrettable expenditures, household production, and natural resources.

4. The onset of the recession in late 2008 implies that 2007 is the last full year's pre-recession data.

5. Our "base" weighting assigns equal weight to each component. Osberg and Sharpe (2005) present similar figures for the United States, the United Kingdom, and Norway, 1980–2001.

6. Linear scaling is used—i.e., each of the four components of economic well-being is assigned an indexed value equal to Value-Min / Max-Min, which represents the relative position of that country, in that year, on the range from

maximum (feasible value) to minimum (feasible value), where both maximum and minimum are set at the actual extremes of the values observed in all countries and all years of the present study, plus (or minus) 10% of the actual observed range.

7. Note that the deficiencies of internationally comparable data prevent us from incorporating the decline in unemployment insurance and employment insurance in Canada over this period. See Osberg (2009) for a fuller discussion.

8. For illustrative purposes we also estimated (1) and (2) jointly for all 14 countries and present those results and the plus or minus two standard error confidence interval—which indicate that the hypothesis of equality of coefficients across countries should generally be rejected, and therefore that pooling of country data would be inappropriate.

9. We stress the limited number of years of data (15) that are available.

10. Since unemployment enters the calculation of the labor market security sub-component of Economic Security, this is partly to be expected—but nothing in IEWB methodology would predict the variability across countries in c_1 and c_2 which we observe.

References

Di Tella, R., MacCulloch, R., & Oswald, A. (2003). The macroeconomics of happiness. *The Review of Economics and Statistics*, *85*(4), 809–827.

Okun, A. M. (1962). Potential GNP: Its measurement and significance. In American Statistical Association (Ed.), *Proceedings of the Business and Economic Statistics Section of the American Statistical Association* (pp. 98–104). Alexandria, VA: American Ststistical Association.

Osberg, L. (1985). The measurement of economic well-being. In D. Laidler (Ed.), *Approaches to economic well-being* (Volume 36, MacDonald Commission) (pp. 49–89). Toronto: University of Toronto Press.

Osberg, L. (2009, May). *Canada's declining social safety net: EI reform and the 2009 budget*. Paper presented to the conference The 2009 federal budget: Challenge, response and retrospect. John Deutsch Institute, Queen's University, Kingston, Ontario.

Osberg, L., & Sharpe, A. (1998). *An index of economic well-being for Canada*. Hull, Québec: Applied Research Branch, Human Resources Development Canada.

Osberg, L., & Sharpe, A. (2002a). An index of economic well-being for selected OECD countries. *Review of Income and Wealth*, *48*(3), 291–316.

Osberg, L., & Sharpe, A. (2002b). International comparisons of trends in economic well-being. *Social Indicators Research*, *58*(1–3), 349–382.

Osberg, L., & Sharpe, A. (2005). How should we measure the "economic" aspects of well-being. *Review of Income and Wealth*, *51*(2), 311–336.

Osberg, L., & Sharpe, A. (2006, July). *New estimates of the Index of Economic Wellbeing for selected OECD countries*. Paper presented at the 7th Conference of the International Society for Quality of Life Studies, Rhodes University, Grahamstown, South Africa.

Sharpe, A., & Salzman, J. (2003, May). *Methodological choices encountered in the construction of composite indicators.* Paper presented to the Annual meeting of the Canadian Economics Association, Carleton University, Ottawa, Ontario.

6

Was the Economic Crisis of 2008 Good for Icelanders?

Impact on Health Behaviors

Tinna Laufey Ásgeirsdóttir

University of Iceland, Iceland

Hope Corman and Kelly Noonan

Rider University and National Bureau of Economic Research, U.S.A.

Þórhildur Ólafsdóttir

University of Iceland, Iceland

Nancy E. Reichman

Robert Wood Johnson Medical School, U.S.A.

Introduction

The seemingly flourishing economy of Iceland suffered a major meltdown that is often pinpointed to the first days of October 2008, when the three largest banks collapsed and became nationalized. In a widely viewed televised address, Prime Minister Geir Haarde announced to the country that: "there is a very real danger, fellow citizens, that the Icelandic economy, in the worst case, could be sucked with the banks into the whirlpool and the result could be national bankruptcy" (Haarde, 2008).[1] The day of this landmark

The Economics of Wellbeing: Wellbeing: A Complete Reference Guide, Volume V.
Edited by David McDaid and Cary L. Cooper.
© 2014 John Wiley & Sons, Ltd. Published 2014 by John Wiley & Sons, Inc.
DOI: 10.1002/9781118539415.wbwell06

speech, October 6, 2008, has widely been viewed as the beginning of the economic crisis in Iceland.[2]

A period of economic and political turmoil followed, leading to uncertainty about the future prospects of the nation. During the following months, hundreds of firms in the country declared bankruptcy. Inhabitants of Iceland, a population of 320,000, who lived in one of the richest countries in the world, were now facing the prospects of unemployment as well as mounting private and national debt. The announcement of the crisis triggered further unforeseen consequences, including a decision by the United Kingdom to invoke anti-terrorism legislation to freeze the assets of one of the three large banks (Landsbanki), emergency funding from the International Monetary Fund, massive protests against the government, and political instability resulting in a cabinet change in February 2009. A sudden and dramatic macro-economic shock of this magnitude and scope affects the entire population, particularly in a small open economy with its own currency and for which exchange rates and prices were suddenly and dramatically altered. Such a shock has the potential to affect multiple domains of wellbeing—financial, psychological, and physical.

A growing literature has focused on the effects of macroeconomic conditions on health in developed countries. Pioneering work by Ruhm found that, although there is considerable evidence that long-term economic growth promotes population health, short-term downturns in economic activity in the United States counterintuitively lead to reduced mortality rates (Ruhm, 2000). That research has spawned a wave of studies investigating the relationships between business cycles and health that has no doubt been fueled in recent years by the Great Recession in the United States and more general global economic decline. Ruhm found that: (1) individuals are less healthy during economic expansions, with the strongest negative effects for those who are of working age, employed, and male; (2) the negative health effects of economic expansions persist or accumulate over time, are larger for acute than chronic ailments, and occur despite a protective effect of income and a possible increase in the use of medical care; and (3) mental health appears to be better during expansions, a pattern opposite from that for physical health (Ruhm, 2003). Similar results have been found in other countries. For example, Gerdtham and Ruhm (2006) found that mortality increased during high employment or strong economic conditions in 23 Organisation for Economic Cooperation and Development countries, and Katikireddi, Niedzwiedz, and Popham (2012) found deteriorations in men's mental health in Britain during recessionary periods. However, Cooper and colleagues found, using data from 13 European Union countries, that unemployment at the individual level was associated with poorer physical and mental health, suggesting that macro-level economic conditions and micro-level economic circumstances affect health through different pathways (Cooper, McCausland, & Theodossiou 2006).

Economic theory and past research point to several mechanisms by which recessions could affect health. At the macro level, recessions could affect health through changes in physical, public service, or social environments. Recessions could enhance health by leading to reductions in air pollution or traffic or increases in social cohesion in times of crisis, but also could compromise health by leading to deteriorations in public service infrastructure (e.g., reductions in health services or essential services such as police and firefighting) or limiting social opportunities due to reductions in facilities or the widespread inability of others to afford them. At the micro level, recessions could affect health through changes in health behaviors (as a response to changes in prices, income, and time constraints, through changes in tastes or time preference, or as a result of changes in environmental factors, such as availability of high-quality health care), exposures to health risks (e.g., a construction worker who becomes unemployed may no longer be working with dangerous machinery), or stress resulting from losing a job, income, and/or wealth. The directional effects for changes in exposures to health risks and stress are clear. For health behaviors, the focus of this chapter, the directional effects would depend on the specific behaviors and pathways.

In considering the effects of macroeconomic fluctuations on health behaviors, studies have generally focused on health-compromising behaviors, such as heavy drinking and smoking. Some have focused on specific subpopulations, such as women of childbearing age (Dehejia & Lleras-Muney, 2004). Many fewer studies have focused on health-promoting behaviors, such as exercise. Although the body of research findings is growing, it is not yet clear whether and how various behaviors are affected. Pacula, in a recent review of the literature on the effects of business cycles on excess alcohol consumption, highlights the empirical challenges involved in isolating business-cycle effects from other confounding factors (Pacula, 2011).

In this study, we use the 2008 economic crisis in Iceland—a severe and unexpected macroeconomic shock—to identify the effects of a macroeconomic downturn on a range of individual health behaviors. We use longitudinal survey data collected in 2007 (during the boom) and 2009 (during the bust) that includes pre- and post-reports of the same health behaviors as well as other relevant variables. We investigate the effects of the crisis on a range of health-compromising behaviors (smoking, heavy drinking, consumption of sugared soft drinks, sweets, and fast food, and indoor tanning) and health-promoting behaviors (consumption of fruit, vegetables, and fish oil, use of dietary supplements, and getting the recommended amount of sleep). We estimate effects for the overall adult population and separately for the working-age population, men, and women.

Across the various health behaviors, the effects of the crisis will depend on the "goods" versus time costs of those behaviors, realized changes in income and time constraints, and crisis-induced changes in relative prices. Overall, we expect that the crisis reduced health behaviors that are goods-intensive, such as cigarette smoking, alcohol consumption, or taking dietary supplements, increased health behaviors that are time-intensive, such as getting the recommended amount of sleep, and reduced health behaviors with higher relative price increases (e.g., heavily imported goods such as alcohol or fruit, since a major effect of the crisis was the devaluation of the Icelandic krona). For behaviors that are both time- and goods-intensive, such as indoor tanning, the expected directionality is ambiguous.

Because we observe information on health behaviors, as well as key hypothesized mechanisms (work hours, real income, financial assets, mortgage debt, and mental health), on the same individuals over time, we are able to investigate mechanisms underlying changes in health behaviors. We are thus able to disentangle—at least to some extent—general effects of the economic downturn overall from those arising from individuals' changes in circumstances that resulted from the shock. In this vein, we infer the role of prices in shaping health behaviors and compute participation elasticities for the various behaviors.

Background

Empirical Literature

The most studied health behaviors as outcomes of macroeconomic fluctuations are alcohol use and abuse.[3] Findings on the effects of the business cycle on problem or heavy drinking remain mixed. For example, three studies using data from the U.S. Behavioral Risk Factor Surveillance System (BRFSS) survey to examine the impact of poor economic conditions on problem drinking have arrived at very different conclusions.[4] Ruhm and Black concluded that problem drinking decreases during recessions

(Ruhm & Black, 2002), while Dee concluded that problem drinking is countercyclical (that is, people drink too much in hard economic times) (Dee, 2001) and Vilaplana and colleagues that drinking is unaffected by the business cycle (Vilaplana, Labeaga, & Jiménez-Martín, 2006). According to Pacula, the discrepancies across studies arise from the use of different empirical specifications, measures of key variables, and choice of control variables (Pacula, 2011). A more recent study (Davalos, Fang, & French, 2012), using the National Epidemiological Survey on Alcohol and Related Conditions, found results consistent with those of Dee—that increases in unemployment rates are positively related to binge drinking. Xu and Kaestner expanded on this line of research in a study of the effects of employment, work hours, and wages on health behaviors, using data on business cycles to identify the key exposures of interest (Xu & Kaestner, 2010). They used the Current Population Survey (CPS) to estimate two-sample instrumental variables (TSIV) models in which work hours and wages were estimated from the CPS and health behaviors were estimated from the BRFSS. The authors found a small but significant negative effect of hours worked on binge drinking of low-wage working-age men, suggesting that binge drinking may be somewhat countercyclical.

Findings for cigarette smoking also are mixed. For example, using 1987–2000 BRFSS data, Ruhm found procyclical effects (i.e., that smoking declines during economic downturns) (Ruhm, 2005). Using 1984–2005 BRFSS data augmented with data from the CPS and applying their TSIV methodology, Xu and Kaestner (2010) found that wages, employment, and hours of work were all positively related to smoking among low-wage men, also providing some evidence that smoking may be procyclical. Charles and DeCicca (2008), using data from the 1997–2001 National Health Interview Surveys, found that the effects of the Metropolitan Statistical Area (MSA) level unemployment rate on men's smoking depend on the man's likelihood of being unemployed. For the 10% of men most vulnerable to unemployment, higher unemployment rates were associated with higher rates of smoking (i.e., smoking appears to be countercyclical). For the 10% of men least vulnerable to unemployment, higher unemployment rates were associated with lower rates of smoking (i.e., smoking appears to be procyclical). For the majority of men, unemployment rates were not associated with smoking.

As far as we know, only two population-based studies have examined the effects of the macroeconomy on dietary behaviors. The first is the seminal study of Ruhm, part of which used BRFSS data from 1987–1995 to investigate the effect of state unemployment rates on daily fruit and vegetable consumption (Ruhm, 2000). He found a countercyclical, but insignificant, effect of state unemployment rates on daily consumption of fruit and vegetables. The other study investigated the effect of business cycles on the consumption of various types of "healthy" and "unhealthy" foods (Dave & Kelly, 2012). Using BRFSS data from 1990–2007, Dave and Kelly found countercyclical (but mostly insignificant) effects for unhealthy foods and significant procyclical effects for healthy foods—that is, a higher risk of unemployment was positively related to consumption of snacks and fast food but negatively associated with consumption of fruit and vegetables. The latter study focused solely on food, examined a broad array of different types of food, and controlled for time-related trends by including indicators for month as well as linear, quadratic, and cubic time trends.

Ásgeirsdóttir and Zoega (2011) used the same data as in the current paper to examine sleep behavior. While that paper is mostly theoretical and the empirical focus was not on the effects of the economic crisis, the authors do report crude results that indicate increased sleep duration in Iceland in 2009, as compared to 2007. Although analyses tailored to our crisis-specific research questions are needed to fully address the economic impact of the collapse on sleep, the findings of Ásgeirsdóttir and Zoega are in accordance with economic theory suggesting that the opportunity cost of sleep—a time-intensive activity—would decrease as labor market opportunities and returns diminish. Another recent study examined physical activity using the American Time Use Survey from 2001–2010 and found that unemployment increases recreational physical activity but reduces overall physical activity as a result of declines in work-related physical activity (Colman & Dave, 2011). The authors also found evidence that strong economic conditions (high rates of employment) reduce sleep, particularly among women.

In their analysis Dave and Kelly (2012) attempted to elucidate specific pathways through which recessions affect health behaviors. In contrast, the bulk of the literature has focused on reduced form effects of business cycles (e.g., most of the articles we have discussed) or has exploited macroeconomic fluctuations to address related questions (e.g., the work of Xu & Kaestner, 2010). A key objective of the Dave and Kelly study was to explore the extent to which individual variations in work status, real family income, food prices, and health insurance coverage affect "healthy food" consumption, holding constant the state unemployment rate (plus an interaction term for the state unemployment rate multiplied by a propensity score for the individual's probability of unemployment). They found that reduced family income and poor mental health appear to be important channels underlying the procyclical nature of "healthy food" consumption. That is, these pathways explained about half of the negative effect of unemployment on "healthy eating," with the other half remaining unexplained.

Economic Crisis in Iceland

The Icelandic banking sector had expanded dramatically in the years preceding its collapse. At the end of June 2008 the combined assets of Iceland's three largest banks (which, as mentioned earlier, collapsed and became nationalized in October 2008) were 14 times larger than the Gross Domestic Product (GDP) of Iceland, making the Icelandic banking system one of the largest in the world in relation to GDP (International Monetary Fund, 2008). According to Nanto (2009, p. 68), the failure of the banks may have been set in motion by the collapse of Lehman Brothers but "at the heart of Iceland's banking crisis is a flawed banking model that is based on an internationally active banking sector that is large relative to the size of the home country's GDP and to the fiscal capacity of the central bank."

The unemployment rate in Iceland increased from 2.3% in the first quarter of 2008 to 7.4% in the fourth quarter of 2010. It peaked in the second quarter of 2009, at 9.1%, with the highest rate among young people 16–24 years old, at 21.9% (Statistics Iceland, 2011). Iceland is one of the world's smallest currency areas, making the krona very vulnerable. The real exchange rate fell by 36% between 2007 and 2009 despite considerable efforts to maintain the value of the krona, the most important action being the imposition of capital controls in late 2008 to hinder the sales of the local currency (Benediktsdottir, Danielsson, & Zoega, 2011). The depreciation in the exchange rate had a significant effect on prices, especially for imported goods. Overall, the Consumer Price Index (CPI) in Iceland increased by 27.3% between November 2007 and November 2009. Thus, everyone, regardless of the effect of the crisis on their individual labor market position, experienced the effects of the crisis through price changes. The prices of domestically produced goods such as fish oil went up by much less than the CPI overall (18.5%), while those for goods that are primarily imported, such as alcohol, tobacco products, and fruit, went up by considerably more than the CPI overall (48.7%, 40.4%, and 91.8%, respectively).[5]

During the crisis, a large share of the populace lost their savings and became burdened with serious debt. When financing their homes, many families had taken loans in foreign currencies to procure lower interest rates and found themselves trapped in negative equity when the Icelandic krona plummeted. Even those who had taken price-indexed Icelandic loans suffered, as the fall of the local currency resulted in considerable inflation.

The economic crisis in Iceland, with its sudden onset and intensity, likely produced shock effects that are distinct from regular business cycle effects. More generally, ambient economic conditions can have many different causes, take on many different forms, and have effects that depend on the specific social and institutional contexts. As such, to understand the effects of economic conditions on health and behaviors it is important to compare results across situations, settings, and outcomes. Each additional study adds new information to the picture being painted by the emerging literature. We are aware of only one published study on health effects of the Icelandic economic crisis. Guðjónsdóttir et al. (2011) found an increase in the total number of visits to the cardiac emergency department in general, and of visits due to ischaemic heart disease in particular, in the days following the address by the Prime Minister. However, this effect was not sustained over time and the authors concluded that it represented a short-term stress reaction.

Contributions of this study

The unique features of the Icelandic economic crisis in terms of a distinct beginning, magnitude, and velocity, along with the opportunity of obtaining unusually comprehensive, individual-level, nationally representative data on the same Icelanders before and after the country's economic downturn, provide a unique opportunity to investigate the effects of a macroeconomic shock on a wide array of health behaviors. The Icelandic economic crisis is a very strong "treatment" in that the nation's economy rapidly went from boom to bust as a result of an unprecedented shock that was unanticipated by most people but affected everyone in some way. As such, the treatment is more distinct than state-to-state differences and/or over-time fluctuations in economic conditions. In addition, we are studying a very short time interval during which the crisis clearly dominated, precluding the need to account for confounding trends—something that has been a persistent methodological challenge in this literature. Furthermore, because about two thirds of Icelanders live in or near Reykjavik, with the rest of the population dispersed across the country in small cities and towns, there is essentially one market involved; the findings, therefore, cannot be confounded by regional migration. Finally, because we observe changes in work hours, income, financial assets, mortgage debt, and mental health with sufficient variation in each, we can directly examine all of those potentially important pathways. Dave and Kelly (2012) were able to explore only some of these factors vis-à-vis food consumption, while Colman and Dave (2011) were able to examine only full-time employment vis-à-vis exercise, and Xu and Kaestner (2010) did not have access to substance abuse measures and potential mediating variables for the same individuals. For all of these reasons, the economic crisis in Iceland presents us with a "clean and well-stocked laboratory" in which to study the effects of a macroeconomic downturn on health behaviors and five potential underlying pathways. Furthermore, being able to adjust for those pathways and observe differential price changes across goods provides a unique opportunity to learn about the potential role of prices when investigating the effects of the macroeconomy on the various health behaviors.

Analytic Framework

We base our analyses on the Grossman-derived demand for health behaviors (Xu & Kaestner, 2010). In this framework, the demand for a health-related input is a function of the price of that input (P_i), the prices of a vector of other health-related inputs (P_j), the prices of a vector of non-health-related goods (P_x), the time inputs for these goods (t_i, t_j, t_x), and other arguments as follows: T_w represents work time, or the time not available to consume; Y represents real income; Z represents personal characteristics including tastes and preferences; and e is the person's health endowment.

$$D_i = (P_i, P_j, P_x, t_i, t_j, t_x, T_w, Y, Z, e) \qquad (6.1)$$

As discussed above, the economic crisis in Iceland affected the real and relative prices of most goods, employment, and real income. Holding constant real income, an increase in the price of any health-related input would be expected to reduce the demand for that input. The relative price increases in Iceland were strongly affected by the devaluation of the krona between 2007 and 2009, such that heavily imported items, such as fruit, had price increases of almost two-fold, while local products, such as fresh haddock and lamb, increased by only 18% and not at all, respectively. All else being equal, the large increases in some prices would reduce demand for those goods, whether those goods are health-promoting (such as fruit) or health-compromising (such as cigarettes). Changes in relative prices may affect substitutions of some goods for others as well. For example, an increase in the price of fresh (and imported) fruit may have reduced the demand for those goods relative to other health-promoting items such as locally produced products (e.g., fish oil).

The effects of the crisis on employment could have affected both time and income constraints. A decrease in work time may have increased the demand for time-intensive health inputs, such as home-cooked meals, relative to that for fast food. Recession-induced decreases in income, through employment or wealth, would be expected to decrease the demand for all but inferior goods, all else being equal. Thus, reductions in income would reduce the consumption of both health-compromising inputs, such as sugared soft drinks or indoor tanning[6] and health-promoting inputs, such as fruit and vegetables. For all of the price and income effects, the magnitudes would be a function of the own price, cross-price, and income elasticities of demand.

The crisis may also have affected health behaviors through changes in health (e). As discussed earlier, there are many pathways other than behaviors through which recessions could affect health, which may, in turn, affect the demand for health-related inputs. For example, the stresses of long hours of work (during the boom) or financial insecurity (during the bust) could have adversely affected mental health, leading to increased consumption of health-compromising inputs such as alcohol or cigarettes.[7] Or, the society-wide shock of the crisis could have affected social cohesion, which could have affected mental or physical health and, in turn, affected health behaviors. There is some empirical evidence linking social cohesion and health behaviors. For example, Patterson and colleagues found smoking to be less prevalent in more socially cohesive neighborhoods (Patterson, Eberly, Ding & Hargreaves, 2004).

In terms of magnitudes, we can only have expectations for behaviors that have been previously studied, and, given the crisis in Iceland was a dramatic shock and occurred in a unique context, we cannot speculate *a priori* how the magnitudes would deviate (or differ) from ranges found in previous studies. We reconcile our estimates, to the extent possible, after presenting our results. For behaviors that have not previously been studied, our estimates will produce important "first" data points.

Data

The data used for this study comes from a health and lifestyle survey "Heilsa og líðan" (Health and Wellbeing) carried out by the Public Health Institute of Iceland in both 2007 and 2009. Questionnaires were mailed on November 1 of each year and almost all were sent back in November or

December of that same year. The survey contained questions about health, illnesses, use of drugs, smoking and drinking, diet, health care, height and weight, accidents, exercise, sleep, quality of life and other lifestyle-related issues, as well as demographics and work-related factors such as work hours and income. A stratified random sample of 9,807 Icelanders, ranging in age from 18 to 79 years of age, was drawn. The net response rate in 2007 was 60.8%. Participants from 2007 who agreed to be contacted again also received the 2009 questionnaire; 69.3% of the 2007 respondents participated in 2009. Due to the stratification in the sampling process, the sample is somewhat older than the adult population of Iceland overall and more likely to live outside the capital region. There were six age groups by two residential groups, forming a total of 12 strata, and all results presented here use sample weights to make the sample nationally representative (Jonsson, Guðlaugsson, Gylfason, & Guðmundsdóttir, 2011).

We focus on 11 different health behaviors as outcomes. The survey included questions about substance use, which we used to create measures of smoking and heavy drinking. Individuals were coded as being a smoker if they answered the question, "Do you smoke?" with a yes. Respondents were asked how often during the past 12 months, if ever, they had consumed at least five alcoholic drinks in one day; that information was used to create a variable for having consumed at least five drinks in one day at least once a month during the past 12 months.[8]

The data also include information on dietary behaviors. Respondents were asked about their consumption of a variety of foods, with the question: "How often do you eat the following categories of food?" We focus on daily (versus less than daily) consumption of fruit or berries and of cooked or raw vegetables as health-promoting behaviors, and daily (versus less than daily) consumption of sugar-containing soft drinks and sweets as health-compromising behaviors. Respondents were also asked about their consumption of fast/prepared foods. We consider weekly (versus less than weekly) consumption of fast food (either at a fast food restaurant or by taking home prepared foods) as a health-compromising behavior. Finally, respondents were asked about consumption of fish liver oil or fish oil capsules and about vitamins, minerals, other food supplements, or health food products, both of which we consider health-promoting behaviors (coded as daily versus less than daily).

The last two behaviors we consider are engaging in indoor tanning at least once in the past year (a health-compromising behavior) and generally receiving 7–9 hours of sleep per night (a health-promoting behavior).

Specifically, respondents were asked how often within the last 12 months they sunbathed with indoor tanning lamps or tanning beds while "scantily dressed in order to receive as much sun or radiation as possible" and "[f]or how many hours a night do you generally sleep?" We coded the former as ever (versus never), and based on the U.S. CDC recommendation of 7–9 hours of sleep per night as optimal from a health perspective (U.S. Centers for Disease Control, 2012), we coded individuals as engaging in a health-promoting level of sleep if they reported generally sleeping between seven and nine hours (versus outside of that range).

In certain models, we include measures of the respondent's sex, age, and education. Education is categorized as the U.S. equivalents of high-school education or less, some college education (but not a 4-year degree), and at least 4 years of college education. The question on educational attainment was improved between waves and asked differently in 2009. Thus, we chose to treat education as time-invariant based first and foremost on the 2009 answers. Given the wide age range of individuals we are examining over a time period of only 2 years, treating educational attainment as time-invariant seems reasonable, particularly for the subanalyses conducted for working-age adults (age 25–64 years). In many analyses, we include time-varying sociodemographic characteristics: marital/cohabitation status, household composition (including other adults and children), and rural residence (an area of fewer than 1,000 inhabitants). Finally, in certain models, we explore specific pathways through which the crisis may have impacted health behaviors. Specifically, we explore the roles of work hours, real income, financial assets, mortgage debt, and mental health.

The measures of labor market activity are based on two questions. In the first, respondents were asked to describe their work arrangements. We coded individuals as not working if they answered, "I do not work." In the second, respondents were asked how many hours they generally spend each week doing paid work. They were given 13 response options, including 0, less than 1 (coded as 1), ten categories ranging from 1–3 hrs to 50–59 hrs, and a top category of 60 hrs or more. We used the mid-points of each of the 1–3 through 50–59 ranges and coded responses of 60 hrs or more as 60.

We measure income using the following question: "In what range do you estimate the total income of all household members (e.g., spouse, children, and parents) in your household (including yourself) to have been generally . . . within the past month or within the past 12 months." The respondents were told that this amount should include "all pre-tax income, such as salaries, overtime, differentials, bonuses, interest and dividends, grants/benefits, and pensions." Icelandic benefits come in multiple forms including child benefits, housing benefits, and interest relief. The benefits generally depend on the individual's labor-market income. In the survey, the response choices for income were in ten categories measured in millions of krona, ranging from "less than 0.9 million krona" and going up to a top category of "more than 18 million krona." Mid-points of the indicated ranges were used, with a top code for the highest category. Individuals living alone were not asked this question. For those individuals, we used the responses to a question on individual income and coded those responses similarly. As discussed earlier, the price level in Iceland rose by about 27% between 2007 and 2009, largely as a result of the crisis. To investigate changes in real income between 2007 and 2009, we standardized to 2009 krona. That is, 2009 real income was equal to 2009 nominal income but 2007 real income was 1.27 times 2007 nominal income.

To measure loss of financial assets, we used questions asked in 2009 about the amounts lost in stocks, private pensions, money market accounts, and other savings as a result of the crisis. For each type of asset, measured in millions of krona, respondents were given eight different response choices ranging from "didn't lose any" to "lost more than 30 million krona." We coded at the mid-points of the different ranges, except for the bottom and top ranges which we coded as zero and 30 million, respectively. To measure changes in mortgage debt, we used information from the following question in the 2009 survey: "How much did your mortgage balance increase since September 2008?" The response choices included "not applicable," "zero or went down," and ranges of percentage increases (e.g., 1–30%, 30–60%, etc.) Because most who responded with a positive range answered in the 1–30% range, we created a dichotomous measure for whether the individual's mortgage debt increased between the two surveys. According to official statistics (Statistics Iceland, 2012), the vast majority of consumer debt was indexed to foreign currencies or the Consumer Price Index, and therefore vulnerable to currency fluctuations. The majority of consumer debt was in mortgages (RSK—Directorate of Internal Revenue, 2012).

We created a measure of "anxiety or poor mental health" based on responses to the following two questions: (1) "Has having any of the following conditions interfered with your daily life in the past 12 months?" One of the response choices was anxiety. (2) "What is your general assessment of your mental health? Do you feel that it is very good, good, fair, or poor?" If the respondent reported that anxiety had interfered with his/her daily life in the past 12 months or that he/she considered his/her mental health to be poor, we coded him/her as having anxiety or poor mental health. Results were insensitive to all alternative measures of mental health that could be created from the data.

Descriptive Analysis

All descriptive statistics and regression estimates are weighted to be nationally representative of the Icelandic population. The top panel of Table 6.1 presents the mean values for the health-compromising behaviors we are studying, for both 2007 and 2009. The second panel presents the corresponding information for the health-promoting behaviors we are studying. The third panel shows means for the time-varying covariates we include in certain models. These are factors, such as the individual's household composition, that could have changed as a result of the crisis. The last panel of Table 6.1 presents means for potential pathways by which the crisis would be expected to affect health behaviors—work hours, real household income, loss in financial assets, increase in mortgage debt, and anxiety or poor mental health. The first set of columns presents means for the full sample (ages 18–79 years), for 2007 and 2009, respectively, and the second set shows corresponding figures for the subsample of individuals of working age (ages 25–64). Asterisks represent statistically significant differences between 2007 and 2009 for a given characteristic. The means for the full and working-age samples are very similar except in terms of the potential mediators. As expected, the working-age population was more likely to be in the labor market, worked more hours, and had higher household income than the full sample. That sample reported losing slightly more assets as a result of the crisis and also had a higher rate of anxiety or poor mental health.

All of the health-compromising behaviors decreased between 2007 and 2009. Most health-promoting behaviors were also lower in 2009 than in 2007, with the two exceptions being daily consumption of fish oil and getting the recommended amount of sleep, both of which increased significantly between 2007 and 2009. The vast majority (over 90%) of respondents who reported amounts of sleep outside the recommended range received too little sleep (result not in table). If all observed changes in health behaviors were due to the economic crisis, the 2009 levels minus the 2007 levels of the various behaviors would represent the average effects of the crisis on those behaviors. The observed differences are consistent with studies finding procyclical effects of health-compromising behaviors such as smoking and alcohol consumption (Ruhm, 2005; Ruhm & Black, 2002), as well as recent

Table 6.1. Sample Means (Weighted).

	Full sample 18–79 years		Working age 25–64 years	
	2007	2009	2007	2009
Health-compromising behaviors				
Currently smokes cigarettes or other tobacco product	.211***	.177	.226***	.188
5+ alcoholic drinks in 1 day at least once a/month (past year)	.223***	.199	.205**	.181
Daily sugared soft drink	.091**	.076	.081***	.064
Daily sweets	.090***	.067	.092***	.067
Weekly fast food	.321***	.271	.318***	.250
Indoor tanning (past year)	.182***	.142	.173***	.128
Health-promoting behaviors				
Daily fruit	.365*	.347	.365	.352
Daily vegetables	.282***	.254	.289**	.264
Daily fish oil	.374***	.405	.358***	.393
Daily vitamins/supplements	.887	.877	.885	.877
Gets recommended sleep (7–9 hrs. per/night)	.732***	.766	.726***	.763
Time-varying covariates				
Married	.544***	.569	.590***	.623
Cohabiting	.201***	.181	.214***	.183
Child in household	.402	.393	.500***	.480
Lives with adult other than partner	.277*	.261	.258	.255
Lives in rural area	.116	.111	.116	.114
Potential mediators				
Hours of work (divided by 10), mean	3.042***	2.769	3.535***	3.273
Real household income (millions of 2009 krona per/year), mean	8.771***	7.077	9.403***	7.617
Loss in financial assets after banks collapsed (millions of krona), mean (reported in 2009)	n/a	2.056	n/a	2.254
Mortgage debt increased after September. 2008 (reported in 2009)	n/a	.629	n/a	.721
Anxiety or poor mental health	.255***	.290	.264***	.302

Notes: *p* values are from *t*-tests for differences in means between 2007 and 2009. Exchange rate was about 123 krona to the U.S. dollar at the end of November 2009. Thus, 1 million krona translates to about US$8,150.

***p < .01; **p < .05; *p < .10.

work which found procyclical effects on consumption of fruit and vegetables (Dave & Kelly, 2012), and work that found countercyclical effects on sleep (Colman & Dave, 2011).

The time-varying covariates that changed significantly between 2007 and 2009 were marital and cohabitation status; marriage increased and cohabitation decreased slightly. In addition, fewer individuals lived with an adult other than a partner in 2009, although this difference is not significant for the working-age population. There were no significant or substantive differences in rates of coresidence with children or rural residence.

Considering variables that represent potential pathways, we find that employment and hours worked fell on average after the crisis. In the full sample, the proportion of adults working fell from .82 to .76 (a drop of 7%; not shown in table), while average work hours dropped from 30.04 to 27.69 (7.8%). Although nominal household income increased somewhat (about 2.5%, not shown in table), real household income decreased substantially (19.3%) as a result of the sharp price increases, discussed earlier, that characterized the Icelandic crisis. On average, respondents reported losing 2.056 million krona in financial assets as a result of the crisis, and 63% reported an increase in mortgage debt. The proportion of individuals reporting anxiety or poor mental health increased from 25.5% in 2007 to 29.0% in 2009. All of these differences are large and statistically significant. We cannot assess significance for the change in financial assets or having an increase in mortgage debt, since we do not know the levels at each of the two time points. Overall, while the outcomes and mediators changed substantially between 2007 in the expected directions, the changes in household composition and area of residence were much more modest.

Methodology

We exploit the shock of the 2008 economic crisis in Iceland to estimate the effects of a macroeconomic downturn on health behaviors. Our primary strategy is to pool the 2007 and 2009 data and estimate individual fixed-effects models, which implicitly control for unobserved time-invariant individual-level characteristics and, more importantly for our study, account for cross-period correlation in standard errors. In these models, we estimate each of the 11 health behaviors, with the key variable of interest being an indicator for 2009 (versus 2007) to capture the effects of the 2008 crisis. We estimate those models without any covariates, with the set of time-varying covariates described earlier, and with both time-varying covariates and potential mediators (work hours, real household income, financial assets, mortgage debt, and mental health) to assess the extent to which changes in those factors appear to explain the effects of the crisis. To assess the potential importance of sample selection as a result of missing data items, we estimate the models with no covariates two different ways—using all possible cases and using our analysis sample, which consists of cases that have non-missing data on all right-hand-side variables (generally about 80% of the "all possible cases" sample)—and compare results. We conduct analyses for the full analysis sample, as well as for subsamples of working-age adults, men, and women. Finally, we consider the potential role of prices in explaining the effects of the crisis on health behaviors and compute participation elasticities for the various behaviors.

We assess robustness of the full-sample estimates to two alternative estimation strategies, both based on pooled 2007 and 2009 observations without controlling for person-specific effects: (1) probit models, and (2) seemingly unrelated regression (SUR) models that simultaneously estimate all 11 behaviors. In both cases, we control for the respondent's age, sex, and education and estimate alternative models that also include the time-varying covariates and both time-varying covariates and mediators.

Most studies on the effects of financial crises have used such before-and-after designs, but with repeat cross-sectional, rather than longitudinal, data. As such, controlling for potential compositional changes in the population represents a key methodological challenge. Our study is unique in that it uses longitudinal data, allowing us to control for person-specific effects as well as relevant time-varying factors. Thus, compositional selection does not complicate our study. However, our study is potentially subject to four other methodological challenges or potential sources of confounding: pre-existing trends in health behaviors, concurrent trends unrelated to the crisis, aging of the sample, and sample attrition. We discuss each of these in turn.

Pre-existing trends.
Given our before-and-after research design, it is necessary to demonstrate that the estimated effects of the crisis are capturing shocks rather than continuations of ongoing long-term trends in health behaviors. Figures 6.1 and 6.2 show trends in alcohol sales, smoking, fruit consumption, and vegetable consumption from approximately 1980 to 2010. The post-crisis period is shaded in dark grey; however, as mentioned earlier, the actual downturn

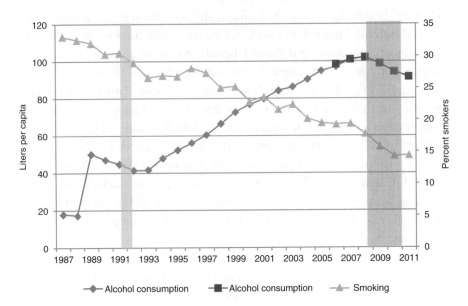

Figure 6.1. Trends in Annual Alcohol Sales in Iceland (liters per capita among individuals age 15+ years) and Percentage of Icelanders Who Smoke Every Day. Statistics Iceland except per capita alcohol sales 2006–2011(squares): Total annual alcohol sales from The State Alcohol and Tobacco Company of Iceland (ÁTVR) 2011 annual report.

began about 6 months earlier than the October 6, 2008 landmark date. A previous recession, during 1991 and 1992, is also shaded for reference. Figure 6.1 shows that alcohol sales had climbed steadily for almost two decades leading up to the 2008 crisis,[9] then declined sharply afterward. This decline is similar to that experienced during the 1991–1992 recession, although in that recession the decline started prior to the economic downturn.[10] From Figure 6.1 we can see that smoking had been declining until about 2004, then started to plateau, and then appeared to resume its decline in 2008.[11] A steeper decline also occurred during the previous recession.[12] Figure 6.2 shows clear long-term upward trends in fruit and vegetable consumption through 2007 and then sudden and sustained drops after the crisis. For these two goods, there were sharp increases in consumption during the boom years preceding the crisis. In addition, there had been no noteworthy downturns in fruit and vegetable consumption during the previous recession. We will consider our estimated effects in light of these baseline trends.

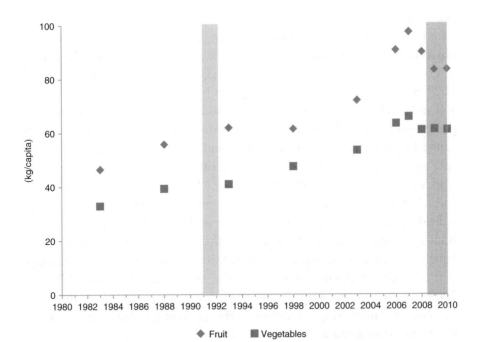

Figure 6.2. Trends in Annual Fruit and Vegetable Consumption in Iceland (kg/capita). Adapted from The Public Health Institute of Iceland. Light shading represents a 1991–1992 recession. Darker shading represents the aftermath of the 2008 crisis.

Concurrent trends.

It is possible that the effects of the crisis reflect other unrelated trends. Given the unique features of the Icelandic economic crisis (the distinct beginning, magnitude, and velocity; the single market; and the shock to most people) and our relatively short observation window of 2 years, it is likely that other trends, if any, paled in comparison. For example, Iceland enacted a smoking ban in restaurants and bars in Iceland on June 1, 2007—5 months prior to the first survey. It is, therefore, theoretically possible that part of the crisis effect for this particular behavior, should we find one, reflects the restaurant smoking ban. However, studies have found that, although smoking bans may impact the quantity of consumption, they do not appear to impact smoking prevalence (Tauras, 2006; Wakefield et al., 2008). Thus, the smoking ban in restaurants and bars in Iceland is not expected to have affected smoking prevalence in the country. In addition, it could not explain the crisis effects for most other behaviors, which were not subject to legislative changes.

Aging of sample.

Given our reliance on longitudinal rather than repeat cross-sectional data, observed crisis effects could theoretically be picking up an aging effect. That is, every single individual in the sample aged two years between 2007 and 2009 and health behaviors can change with age, particularly at very young and old adult ages. We addressed this issue in two ways: (1) estimating pooled probit models (which do not control for person-specific effects or adjust for cross-period correlation in standard errors) and controlling for age; and (2) conducting analyses on the subsample of adults who were of working age (25–64 in 2007), a group for whom 2 years of age should have had relatively small effects on their behaviors. The analyses of working-age individuals are also of substantive interest, as that group is expected to have been particularly affected by the crisis through changes in employment. Finally, the analyses of working-age individuals have the added advantage that educational attainment probably did not change between 2007 and 2009 for the vast majority of this group. As such, using 2009 education (instead of time-varying education in the relevant specifications) becomes much less consequential.

Sample attrition.

As stated earlier, about 30% of those who completed the 2007 survey did not complete the 2009 follow-up survey, and were therefore excluded from our analysis of the effects of the 2008 crisis. Although the sampling weights that were applied adjust for attrition and nonresponse based on gender, age, and residence to produce nationally representative data, there may be some important unaccounted-for differences between stayers and leavers that could bias our estimates. Weighted and unweighted differences between the two groups are presented in Table A6.1 (see Appendix). Respondents who completed the 2009 survey were 7–8 years older, more likely to be female, more likely to live in rural areas, more likely to be married, less likely to be cohabiting, less likely to be living with a child, and much less likely to be living with another adult than those who did not complete the 2009 survey.

Given our focus on health behaviors, we were concerned about differences in health between stayers and leavers. For example, if stayers were healthier than leavers prior to the crisis and responded differently to the crisis, our estimated effects could be either over- or understated. It is reassuring that self-reported health was very similar for stayers and leavers.[13] We were also concerned about sample selection due to emigration, as official statistics indicate that about 5,000 Icelandic citizens (2% of the population) emigrated in 2009 alone (Statistics Iceland, 2013a). For example, if those who did not work because of poor health or worked in occupations associated with poorer health were more likely or less likely to leave the study, our estimated effects could be biased. Again, the differences in means are reassuring. Initial (2007) employment status was very similar for leavers and stayers, and although stayers were more likely than leavers to be in professional occupations and less likely to be in service occupations, there was no difference in attrition for those in skilled or unskilled trades. Overall, it does not appear—based on our comparisons of health/employment factors between stayers and leavers—that sample selection due to emigration or other sources of attrition is an important threat to our inferences about causal effects of the crisis on health behaviors.

Results

Multivariate Analysis

Tables 6.2 and 6.3 present our primary results—weighted fixed-effects estimates of the effects of the crisis on the various health-compromising (Table 6.2) and health-promoting (Table 6.3) behaviors. In the first row of each table, we present estimated effects of the crisis, characterized using an indicator for 2009, when no observations are dropped due to missing right-hand-side variables. The second row presents corresponding estimates for our analysis sample which excludes observations with missing data on right-hand-side variables. For all 11 health behaviors, the estimated effects of the crisis from the restricted sample (second row) fall within one standard error of those from the full sample (top row) and the significance levels are quite similar in the two specifications (standard errors not shown). Thus, our estimates are reasonably robust to the exclusion of observations with missing data on right-hand-side variables.

The estimates in the third row of both Tables 6.2 and 6.3 are from weighted individual fixed-effects models that include our basic set of time-varying covariates. These estimates represent the effects of the crisis holding constant changes in marital and cohabitation status, household composition, and rural residence. Including the time-varying covariates does not appreciably affect the estimated effects of the crisis on health behaviors.[14] The estimated effects of the crisis—the 2009 indicators—are negative and

Table 6.2. Effects of Economic Crisis in Iceland on Health-Compromising Behaviors—Fixed-Effects Models.

	Smoking	Heavy drinking	Daily sugared soft drink	Daily sweets	Weekly fast food	Indoor tanning
Effects of 2009 indicator:						
Full sample (no covariates)	−.033***	−.018**	−.013**	−.020***	−.046***	−.035***
N	7,466	7,526	7,566	7,596	7,688	7,082
Excluding cases with missing data and including:						
No covariates	−.034***	−.024***	−.015**	−.023***	−.050***	−.039***
Time-varying covariates	−.034***	−.025***	−.016***	−.023***	−.048***	−.038***
Time-varying covariates plus mediators	−.031***	−.027*	−.017*	−.005	−.008	−.003
N	5,580	5,586	5,640	5,616	5,676	5,378

Notes: Sample weights are applied. Figures are regression coefficients for effects of the crisis (2009 indicator) relative to 2007. Time-varying covariates are married, cohabiting, lives with adult other than partner, and lives in rural area. Mediators are hours of work, real household income, loss in financial assets, increased mortgage debt, and anxiety or poor mental health.
***$p < .01$; **$p < .05$; *$p < .10$.

Table 6.3. Effects of Economic Crisis in Iceland on Health-Promoting Behaviors—Fixed-Effects Models.

	Daily fruit	Daily vegetables	Daily fish oil	Daily vitamins/ supplements	Recommended sleep
Effects of 2009 indicator:					
Full sample (no covariates)	−.024***	−.022***	.031***	−.011	.034***
N	7,738	7,776	7,618	7,138	7,648
Excluding cases with missing data and including:					
No covariates	−.018*	−.027***	.031***	−.010	.034***
Time-varying covariates	−.018*	−.028***	.032***	−.011	.035***
Time-varying covariates plus mediators	−.029	−.028*	.017	−.016	.042**
N	5,664	5,690	5,600	5,434	5,638

Notes: Sample weights are applied. Figures are regression coefficients for effects of the crisis (2009 indicator) relative to 2007. Time-varying covariates are married, cohabiting, lives with adult other than partner, and lives in rural area. Mediators are hours of work, real household income, loss in financial assets, having an increased mortgage debt, and anxiety or poor mental health.
***$p < .01$; **$p < .05$; *$p < .10$.

significant for all health-compromising behaviors: smoking, heavy drinking, sugared soft drinks, sweets, fast food, and indoor tanning (Table 6.2). The estimates, which range from one to five percentage points, are quite similar to the corresponding mean differences in Table 6.1, underscoring that the crisis was an exogenous shock.

Because alcohol sales were increasing steadily prior to the crisis (Figure 6.1) and might have continued to climb into 2009 had the crisis not occurred, the estimated effects of the crisis on that behavior may be suppressed (that is, we may be underestimating the effects of the crisis). In contrast, because smoking had been trending down before the crisis began (Figure 6.1), we may be overestimating the negative effects of the crisis on smoking. That said, the average reduction in smoking from 2005 to 2007 was about .05 percentage points per year. If the same trend had continued, we would have seen a proportional reduction in smoking, of .1 percentage points for the two years, rather than the observed 3.4 percentage point reduction.

The crisis also reduced certain health-promoting behaviors but increased others (Table 6.3). Specifically, the crisis reduced consumption of fruit and vegetables but increased consumption of fish oil and the likelihood of getting the recommended amount of sleep. It had small and insignificant effects on consumption of vitamins or supplements. As in Table 6.2, we find that the estimated effects are quite similar to the corresponding mean differences in Table 6.1. It is important to note that we could be underestimating the effects of the crisis on fruit and vegetable consumption, as the prerecession increases in consumption of these goods might have continued had the crisis not occurred (Figure 6.2). On the other hand, we would be overestimating the effects of the crisis on consumption of these two goods, if the prerecession increases represented a temporary phenomenon that would not have persisted.

It is useful to compare our estimates to those from the previous literature, most of which focuses on economic conditions in the United States. Overall, the magnitudes of effects for smoking are somewhat larger than what has been found in past research in other contexts, while those for alcohol, fruit, and vegetables are in line with estimates from other studies. As far as we know, there are no comparable estimates for the other behaviors studied.

Ruhm (2005) found that each percentage point increase in the population employed led to a .10–.23 percentage point increase in smoking. The crisis in Iceland led to a 9 percentage point drop in the population employed, which, using Ruhm's estimate, would imply a .9–2.1 percentage point reduction in smoking. We found that the crisis in Iceland led to a 3.4

percentage point reduction in smoking, which is higher than would be implied by the Ruhm study.

Ruhm and Black (2002) found that, for each percentage point increase in unemployment, heavy drinking decreased by .3–.7 percentage points. If we assume that the entire reduction in employment in Iceland was due to individuals becoming unemployed, this range of estimates would suggest a 2.7–6.3 percentage point decrease in heavy drinking in Iceland. Although heavy drinking was defined differently in the Iceland data, our estimated effects of 2–3 percentage points are in the range found by Ruhm and Black.

For fruits and vegetables, Dave and Kelly (2012) found that a 1 percentage point increase in the unemployment rate decreased consumption by about 1%. If we assume that the entire reduction in employment in Iceland was due to individuals becoming unemployed, the estimates of Dave and Kelly suggest that fruit and vegetable consumption would decline by 9%, which is in line with our estimates of 5% and 10% for fruit and vegetables, respectively.

The models in the second and third rows of Tables 6.2 and 6.3 are our main results—the estimated effects of the crisis on health behaviors. The estimates in the fourth rows of Tables 6.2 and 6.3 are from fixed-effects models that include the time-varying covariates plus the five potential mediators of interest: hours of work, real household income, financial assets, having an increase in mortgage debt, and anxiety or poor mental health.[15] The purpose of the mediation analysis is to attempt to disentangle the individual-level versus society-wide effects of the crisis on the various behaviors, rather than to obtain unbiased estimates of the effects of each pathway. For smoking, heavy drinking, and consumption of sugared soft drinks, we find that the inclusion of these individual-level factors in the models scarcely changed the estimated effects of the crisis; since the coefficient of the 2009 indicator decreases by only 9% for smoking and increases slightly for heavy drinking and consumption of soft drinks.[16] This evidence of the small mediating effects of income and unemployment are consistent with findings for heavy drinking (Vilaplana et al., 2006), and are largely consistent with findings from Charles and DeCicca (2008) for smoking among men. For other health-compromising behaviors, specifically sweets, fast-food, and indoor tanning, we find that the inclusion of the mediators virtually eliminates the estimated effects of the crisis.

For health-promoting behaviors (Table 6.3), the mediators reduced the effects of the crisis in only one case—fish oil (by 47%). For the health-compromising behaviors most affected by mediators (sweets, fast food, and tanning), the mediating factor with the greatest impact was increased mortgage debt (see appendix Tables A6.3 and A6.4 for the estimated effects of each of the individual mediators in the models presented in the last rows of Tables 6.2 and 6.3).[17]

Given that, for most of the behaviors, such substantial portions of the effects of the crisis remain unexplained by the most obvious individual pathways and that the shock was so strong and universal, it is likely that the shock operated, at least to some extent, through the broader environment (i.e., through changes that affected everybody, such as price increases).[18]

Alternative Model Specifications

Tables A6.5 and A6.6 in the appendix to this chapter present estimates corresponding to those from the second row of Tables 6.2 and 6.3, but they are marginal effects from pooled probit models that include controls for 2007 age, 2007 age squared, sex, and 2009 education. It is reassuring that the marginal effects from the probit models are quite similar to those from the fixed-effects models, providing a robustness check to our functional form. In addition, these models indicate that, while age is a significant determinant of many of the behaviors, the estimated effects of age are small compared to those of the crisis, suggesting that the estimated effects of the crisis in our fixed-effects models in Tables 6.2 and 6.3 are not substantially confounded by the aging of the sample by 2 years.

As indicated in equation (6.1) earlier, the demand for the different health behaviors may not be independent of one another. To address this possibility, we simultaneously estimated the demand for the six health-compromising behaviors and five health-promoting behaviors using seemingly unrelated regression (SUR) models. These results, based on the pooled 2007 and 2009 data but not accounting for person-specific effects, are presented in Tables A6.7 and A6.8. SUR models and corresponding linear probability models (the latter modeled the behaviors as independent; i.e., the behaviors were estimated as separate equations) were estimated that included only age, sex, and education, and that included age, sex, and education plus time-varying covariates. In all specifications, the linear probability estimates are similar to those from both the corresponding fixed-effects models (from Tables 6.2 and 6.3) and pooled probit models (Tables A6.5 and A6.6). In addition, coefficients from the linear probability and SUR models are almost identical to one another. Thus, estimates in Tables 6.2 and 6.3, Tables A6.5 and A6.6, and Tables A6.7 and A6.8 indicate that our estimates are not sensitive to functional form.

Table 6.4. Effects of Economic Crisis In Iceland on Health-Promoting Behaviors—Fixed-Effects Models for Working-Age Subsample (25–64 Years).

	Daily fruit	Daily vegetables	Daily fish oil	Daily vitamins/ supplements	Recommended sleep
Effects of 2009 indicator with:					
No covariates	−.013	−.025**	.035***	−.007	.037***
Time-varying covariates	−.013	−.025**	.035***	−.008	.037***
Time-varying covariates plus mediators	−.016	−.028	.007	−.018	.043*
N	4,068	4,082	4,024	3,936	4,048

Notes: Sample weights are applied. Figures are regression coefficients for effects of the crisis (2009 indicator) relative to 2007. Time-varying covariates are married, cohabiting, lives with adult other than partner, and lives in rural area. Mediators are hours of work, real income, loss in financial assets, increased mortgage debt, and anxiety or poor mental health.
***$p < .01$; **$p < .05$; *$p < .10$.

In Tables 6.4 and 6.5, we restrict the fixed-effects analyses to individuals of working age—those aged 25–64 years in 2007—the group that should be most affected by changes in employment and for whom 2 years of aging should have minimal effects on health behaviors, on average. The age restriction at the top end is based on the statutory retirement age in Iceland of 67. The results were very similar when we capped the age range at 54 years (results not shown, but available upon request). As expected, the estimated effects of the crisis on health-compromising behaviors were stronger for the working-age population than for the adult population overall. For example, fast food consumption decreased by about 6.7 percentage points (Table 6.5) compared to about 4.8 percentage points for the overall population (Table 6.2). In general, the impacts of the crisis on health-promoting behaviors were somewhat weaker for the working-age population than for the full sample. The only exception was for recommended sleep, for which the effect was greater for the working-age population.

Based on findings of differential effects of economic conditions on health behaviors for males and females (Dave & Kelly, 2012), we estimated models corresponding to those in Tables 6.2 and 6.3 but stratified by gender. These estimates are presented in Table A6.9 (for health-compromising

Table 6.5. Effects of Economic Crisis in Iceland on Health-Compromising Behaviors—Fixed-Effects Models for Working-Age Subsample (25–64 Years).

	Smoking	Heavy drinking	Daily sugared soft drink	Daily sweets	Weekly fast food	Indoor tanning
Effects of 2009 indicator with:						
No covariates	−.038***	−.024**	−.017***	−.025***	−.068***	−.045***
Time-varying covariates	−.039***	−.024**	−.017***	−.024***	−.067***	−.044***
Time-varying covariates plus mediators	−.045***	−.027	−.022**	−.011	−.018	−.008
N	4,050	4,042	4,056	4,038	4,074	3,884

Notes: Sample weights are applied. Figures are regression coefficients for effects of the crisis (2009 indicator) relative to 2007. Time-varying covariates are married, cohabiting, lives with adult other than partner, and lives in rural area. Mediators are hours of work, real income, loss in financial assets, increased mortgage debt, and anxiety or poor mental health.
***$p < .01$; **$p < .05$.

behaviors) and Table A6.10 (for health-promoting behaviors). We found that the crisis had stronger negative (favorable) effects on heavy drinking, soft drink consumption, and fast food consumption for males than for females, while it had stronger negative (favorable) effects on consumption of sweets and indoor tanning for females than for males. The crisis reduced fruit and vegetable consumption more for females than for males. For fish oil consumption, the positive effects of the crisis were much stronger for females than males. In contrast, the beneficial effects of the crisis on sleep were concentrated among males. In additional analyses (not shown) we found that the crisis had a greater impact on individuals who were married than on individuals who were unmarried for soft drinks, fast food, fruit, vegetables, and fish oil, and that the crisis had a greater impact on unmarried individuals than married individuals for binge drinking.

The Role of Prices

As discussed above, much of the impact of the economic shock does not seem to be mediated by individuals' changes in hours of work, real income, financial assets, mortgage debt, or mental health. From this, we infer that there were economy-wide factors at work. An obvious starting point for economy-wide changes that would affect the demand for health-related behaviors is prices, given the importance of price in any demand equation and the large price increases characterizing the Icelandic economic crisis. As indicated earlier, prices increased over 27% between 2007 and 2009 based on Iceland's overall CPI; this compares to a 3.4% in the U.S. CPI over the same 2-year period. In addition, there was substantial variation in price changes across commodities, with price increases ranging from 18.5% for fish oil to over 90% for fruit. Table 6.6 summarizes the nominal price changes (column 1), real price changes (column 2), and participation changes net of mediators (column 3), all calculated in percentage terms, as well as the "participation elasticity" for each of the health-related behaviors that can be purchased in the market (column 4) and the 10% confidence interval for the elasticity estimate. The participation changes were calculated by dividing the coefficients in the bottom row of Tables 6.2 and 6.3, which indicate the effects of the crisis on the behavior net of individual time-varying and mediating factors, by the mean value of the behavior in 2007 from Table 6.1.

If we have adequately accounted for the relevant individual-level mediators, and if price changes were the only society-wide sources of changes in consumption, the figures in column 4 of Table 6.6 would be precise estimates of the participation elasticities of demand for the various behaviors. If other society-wide factors were in play, such as general shifts in tastes or risk preference, however, these calculations would reflect the combined effects of prices and those other factors. For example, President Grimsson speculated that Iceland became even more socially cohesive in the wake of the crisis (Grimsson, 2011). If this is true, and if increased social cohesion led to reductions in health-compromising behaviors (a scenario mentioned earlier), then the figures in column 4 may overestimate the price responsiveness of health-compromising behaviors. As such, we consider those calculations to be preliminary estimates of the participation elasticities of demand for the various health-related behaviors, holding constant the general price level (i.e., prices of all other goods), real income, hours of work, financial assets, mortgage debt, and mental health. Despite this caveat, these calculations provide a useful starting point for examining the price responsiveness of a range of behaviors, many of which have not previously been considered in the literature, on macroeconomic conditions and health. Our expectation is that the elasticities would be within the range of what others have found in other contexts. We can only make comparisons with previous work on

Table 6.6. Price Changes and Participation Elasticities of Various Commodities in Iceland between 2007 and 2009.

Commodity	Nominal price change (%) (1)	Real price change[a] (%) (2)	Participation change net of mediators (%)[b] (3)	"Participation elasticity"[c] (4)	Elasticity range (10% confidence interval) (5)	
					Lower bound	Upper bound
Tobacco	40.4	13.1	−14.8	−1.125	−1.781	−.468
Alcohol	48.7	21.4	−12.3	−.573	−1.131	−.014
Soft drinks	57.1	29.8	−18.9	−.634	−1.248	−.021
Sweets	49.9	22.6	−5.6	−.248	−1.147	−.651
Fast food	23.8	−3.5	2.5	−.714	1.636	−3.064
Indoor tanning (personal services)	38.7	11.4	−1.7	−.147	−1.273	.980
Fruit	91.8	64.5	−7.8	−.121	−.239	−.004
Vegetables	37.8	10.5	−10.0	−.956	−1.911	−.001
Fish oil	18.5	−8.8	4.6	−.522	.337	−1.381
Vitamins and supplements	33.9	6.6	−1.8	−.123	−.580	−.036
Consumer Price Index (CPI)	27.3					

Notes: Price changes are calculated from November of 2007 to November of 2009. Prices for all goods except fast food, fish oil, and vitamins/supplements were obtained from Statistics Iceland (2012). Prices for fish oil, vitamins/supplements and fast food were obtained by personal correspondence with Statistics Iceland.

[a]Real price change is calculated as the nominal price change minus 27.3 (the percentage increase in CPI).

[b]Participation change net of mediators is calculated as the effect of the 2009 indicator, net of all time-varying covariates and mediators (bottom row of Tables 6. 2 and 6.3) divided by the mean value of the behavior during 2007 (from Table 6.1).

[c]Participation elasticity is calculated by dividing column (3) by column (2).

smoking and drinking participation, however, since no relevant estimates are available in the literature for the other health-related behaviors.[19]

We estimate the participation elasticity of heavy drinking to be −0.57, which is a bit higher than the mean of −0.28, but within the range of participation elasticities for heavy drinking found in a recent meta-analysis (Wagenaar, Salois, & Komro 2009). Our estimated smoking participation elasticity of −1.1 is similar to an estimate of an elasticity of −1.0 for non-EU countries in Europe (Gallus, Schiaffino, La Vecchia, Townsend, & Fernandez, 2006).[20] The fact that our elasticities for alcohol and tobacco are of magnitudes that are plausible and consistent with previous studies suggests that those for the less-studied health behaviors are also realistic. From our calculations, we infer that a substantial part of the effects of the crisis in Iceland on health behaviors, particularly vis-à-vis heavy drinking and smoking (for which a comparison to the literature can be made), is likely price-related.

We find an inelastic response to price changes for sugared soft drinks, sweets, indoor tanning, and fast food.[21] For fruit, vitamins/supplements, and fish oil, demand was inelastic, whereas for vegetables the elasticity was approximately unitary.[22]

Conclusion

The 2008 economic crisis in Iceland led to reductions in all the health-compromising behaviors examined—smoking, heavy drinking, consumption of sugared soft drinks, sweets, and fast food, and indoor tanning. It also led to reductions in certain health-promoting behaviors, but increased others. Specifically, the crisis reduced consumption of fruit and vegetables, but increased consumption of fish oil and getting the recommended amount of sleep. Generally, the effects of the crisis on health-compromising behaviors were stronger for the working-age population than for the adult population overall.

Changes in hours of work, real household income, financial assets, mortgage debt, and mental health did not substantially mediate the impact of the crisis on smoking, drinking, or consumption of sugared soft drinks. On the other hand, our mediation analysis points to one specific pathway, increase in mortgage debt, which "explained" virtually all of the effects on some health-compromising behaviors—sweets, fast food, and indoor tanning. For health-promoting behaviors, the five factors representing potential pathways jointly reduced the effects of the crisis only for fish oil. We inferred that broad-based factors—such as prices, which increased over 27% in Iceland between 2007 and 2009—played a large role in the effects of the crisis on health behaviors. We exploited our ability to isolate behavioral changes that are likely due, at least in large part, to price changes, to compute participation elasticities for the various goods. We found mostly inelastic responses to price changes for both health-compromising and health-promoting behaviors.

We investigated the effects of a severe macroeconomic downturn over a short observation period during which few other potentially confounding changes occurred. Previous studies of the effects of macroeconomic conditions on health behaviors have not had this advantage and have rarely been able to examine a broad array of behaviors, control for person-specific effects, consider potential interdependence across behaviors, explore potential individual-level pathways, or consider the potential role of price changes. As such, this study—which does all of these things—makes an important contribution to the literature on the effects of macroeconomic conditions on health behaviors and health. However, the results cannot necessarily be generalized to macroeconomic downturns in general or even to other economic crises such as those recently experienced by Ireland, Greece, and Spain. In terms of the latter, additional research is necessary to ascertain the extent to which individuals' behavioral responses to economic crises vary by context. For example, the effects of economic crises on health behaviors may be very different in countries such as Greece and Spain than in Iceland, because of the relatively strong system of social support in Iceland.

Acknowledgments

This chapter is reprinted from *Economics and Human Biology*, doi 10.1016/j.ehb.2013.03.005, Ásgeirsdóttir, T. L., Corman, H., Noonan, K., Ólafsdóttir, Þ., & Reichman, N. E., Was the economic crisis of 2008 good for Icelanders? Impact on health behaviors, Copyright (2013), with permission from Elsevier.

The authors are grateful to the University of Iceland Research Fund, The Icelandic Research Fund, the Edda Center of Excellence, Princeton University's Center for Health and Wellbeing, and the Rider University Davis Fellowship for financial support; to David Bishai, Dhaval Dave, Partha Deb, Michael Grossman, Ruoding Tan, and the participants in the NBER Spring

2012 Health Economics Workshop for helpful comments; and to Tatána Čepková, Oliver Joszt, and Norma Lamo for excellent research assistance.

Notes

1. See http://www.forsaetisraduneyti.is/radherra/raedurGHH/nr/3034 for a transcript of the speech.
2. As the currency had begun to devalue in the spring of 2008, signaling a possible burst in the economic bubble, some might say that attributing the crisis to a single day is overly simplistic. Source: http://www.cb.is/exchange-rate/.
3. Although light or moderate alcohol use is not necessarily a health-compromising behavior, some studies use overall consumption as a proxy for problem drinking.
4. These papers serve as examples. See Pacula (2011) and Xu and Kaestner (2010) for more extensive literature reviews.
5. Price changes are calculated from November of 2007 to November of 2009. See notes to Table 6.6 in the appendix for data sources.
6. According to the CDC, indoor tanning has been linked with skin cancers (including melanoma, the deadliest type) and cancers of the eye (U.S. Centers for Disease Control, 2013).
7. For example, one study found that, holding income constant, greater financial insecurity is related to a greater probability of continuing to smoke (Barnes & Smith, 2009), and another that job loss is associated with more problem drinking, especially for individuals who are prone to be heavy drinkers (Deb, Gallo, Ayyagari, Fletcher, & Sinclair, 2011)
8. Having five or more drinks on one day is slightly different than the U.S. Centers for Disease Control's definition of "binge drinking," which is drinking five or more drinks in one sitting. Source: http://www.cdc.gov/alcohol/fact-sheets/binge-drinking.htm.
9. The figures shown pertain to any type of alcoholic beverage. The sale of beer was legalized in Iceland on March 1, 1989 and, as such, some of the increase in liters per capita could reflect the substitution of beer (which would require more liters to be purchased to consume a given amount of alcohol) for other types of alcohol.
10. We defined recession as a year with negative GDP growth (Statistics Iceland, 2013b).
11. Between 2001 and 2004, before the boom or the crisis, daily smoking decreased from 22.9% of the population to 19.8%—over 3 percentage points. Between 2004 and 2007, during the boom, daily smoking decreased from 19.8% to 19.0%—a decline of less than one percentage point. In the subsequent years, from 2007 to 2010, daily smoking fell to 14.2% of the population.
12. The general decline likely reflected the aging of the population and (possibly) a lower incidence of smoking initiation in smaller younger cohorts.

13. Although in the unweighted analyses, leavers were somewhat less likely to have good or very good health (.713 versus .745), the magnitude and significance of the difference were greatly reduced when applying weights. Thus, the weights seem to account for this important difference between leavers and stayers

14. Unweighted analyses not shown produced similar results.

15. In order for a factor to mediate the effect of the crisis on other outcomes, it must itself be affected by the crisis. We thus considered the effects of the crisis on potential mediating factors of interest—work hours, real income, financial assets, mortgage debt, and mental health. Results are available in Table A6.2. Considering each of the potential mediators as an outcome, we estimated unadjusted fixed-effects models and fixed-effects models that included the set of time-varying covariates. We found Icelanders worked 2.7 fewer hours, experienced a 1.68 million krona drop in real household income (expressed in 2009 krona), experienced a 2.06 million krona drop in financial assets, were about 63 percentage points more likely to have an increase in mortgage debt, and were about 3 percentage points (about 12%) more likely to report anxiety or poor mental health as a result of the crisis. Both sets of fixed-effects estimates were very similar to those from corresponding mean differences in Table 6.1. Neither time-invariant factors nor observed time-varying factors have any bearing on our estimated effects of the crisis on these potential mediating factors.

16. An example of calculations follows: For smoking, the impact of the crisis was estimated as being 3.4 percentage points when we did not include the mediators, and decreased by .3 percentage points (to 3.1) when we did include the mediators. Thus, inclusion of the mediators reduced the estimated effect by .3/3.4 or 9%.

17. We also ran models that added in the mediators individually and found that they were generally not significant. One exception was increased mortgage debt, which consistently has a strong negative association with sweets, fast food, and tanning.

18. Estimates are insensitive to alternative definitions of the outcomes and mediating variables

19. Dave & Kelly (2012), in their investigation of the effects of business cycles on "healthy" eating, were unable to assess price effects due to the weak correlation between food prices and unemployment, as well as noise in their price data).

20. Given that smoking prevalence had been experiencing a downward trend and alcohol sales an upward trend in Iceland (Figures 6.1 and 6.2), it is possible that the elasticity for smoking is somewhat overestimated and that for heavy drinking is underestimated.

21. Note that we were unable to get precise prices of the latter two behaviors. Rather, we proxy their prices with personal services (tanning) or catering (fast food).

22. If the (unobserved) pre-crisis trends were upward, as for fruit and vegetable consumption (Figure 6.2), the elasticities for other health-promoting behaviors (vitamins/supplements and fish oil) may be underestimated. However, as discussed earlier, it is possible that the crisis caused these behaviors to revert to their pre-boom trends, and that our estimated effects of the crisis on these behaviors are somewhat upwardly biased.

References

Ásgeirsdóttir, T. L., & Zoega, G. (2011). On the economics of sleeping. *Mind and Society, 10*(2), 149–164.

Barnes, M. G., & Smith, T. G. (2009). Tobacco use as response to economic insecurity: Evidence from the National Longitudinal Survey of Youth. *The B.E. Journal of Economic Analysis & Policy, 9*(1), article 47. http://www.business.otago.ac.nz/econ/Personal/ts_files/smoke.pdf.

Benediktsdottir, S., Danielsson, J., & Zoega, G. (2011). Lessons from a collapse of a financial system. *Economic Policy, 26*(66), 183–235.

Charles, K. K., & DeCicca, P. (2008). Local labor market fluctuations and health: Is there a connection and for whom? *Journal of Health Economics, 27*(6), 1532–1550.

Colman, G. J., & Dave, D. M. (2011). *Exercise, physical activity, and exertion over the business cycle* (National Bureau of Economic Research, working paper 17406). http://www.nber.org/papers/w17406.

Cooper, D., McCausland, W. D., & Theodossiou, I. (2006). The health hazards of unemployment and poor education: The socioeconomic determinants of health duration in the European Union. *Economics and Human Biology 4*(3), 273–297.

Davalos, M. E., Fang, H., & French, M. T. (2012). Easing the pain of an economic downturn: Macroeconomic conditions and excessive alcohol consumption. *Health Economics, 21*(11), 1318–1335.

Dave, D. M., & Kelly, I. R. (2012). How does the business cycle affect eating habits? *Social Science Medicine, 74*(2), 254–262.

Deb, P., Gallo, W., Ayyagari, P., Fletcher, J. M., & Sindelar, J. L. (2011). *Job loss: Eat, drink and try to be merry?* (National Bureau of Economic Research, working paper 15122). Retrieved from http://www.nber.org/papers/w15122

Dee, T. S. (2001). Alcohol abuse and economic conditions: Evidence from repeated cross-sections of individual-level data. *Health Economics, 10*(3), 257–270.

Dehejia, R., & Lleras-Muney, A. (2004). Booms, busts and babies' health. *Quarterly Journal of Economics, 119*(3), 1091–1130.

Gallus, S., Schiaffino, A., La Vecchia, C., Townsend, J., & Fernandez, E. (2006). Price and cigarette consumption in Europe. *Tobacco Control, 15*(2), 114–119.

Gerdtham, U. G., & Ruhm, C. J. (2006). Deaths rise in good economic times: Evidence from the OECD. *Economics and Human Biology, 4*(3), 298–316.

Grimsson, O. R. (2011). *Interview with President of Iceland aired on the Swedish public TV2 network news on November 28, 2011.* http://politicalvelcraft. org/2011/12/11/iceland-president-on-crisis-we-allowed-the-banks-to-fail-and-in-the-end-we-were-blessed-with-our-own-currency/

Guðjónsdóttir, G. R., Kristjansson, M., Olafsson, O., Arnar, D. O., Getz, L., Sigurethsson, J. A., . . . Valdimarsdottir, U. (2012). Immediate surge in female visits to the cardiac emergency department following the economic collapse in Iceland: An observational study. *Emergency Medicine Journal, 29*(9), 694–698.

Haarde, G. H. (2008). *Address to the nation by H.E. Geir H. Haarde, Prime Minister of Iceland, October 6.* Rekjavik: Prime Minister's Office. http://eng.forsaetisraduneyti.is/news-and-articles/nr/3035.

International Monetary Fund (2008). *Iceland: Request for standby arrangement— Staff report* (IMF country report 08/362). http://www.imf.org/external/ pubs/ft/scr/2008/cr08362.pdf.

Jonsson, S. H., Guðlaugsson, J. O., Gylfason, H. F., & Guðmundsdóttir, D. G. (2011). Heilsa og Líðan Íslendinga 2007: Framkvæmdaskýrsla [The health and wellbeing of Icelanders 2007: Project report]. Reykjavík: Lýðheilsustöð.

Katikireddi, S. V., Niedzwiedz, C. L., & Popham, F. (2012). Trends in population mental health before and after the 2008 recession: A repeat cross-sectional analysis of the 1991–2010 Health Surveys of England. *British Medical Journal Open, 2*(5), e001790.

Nanto, D. K. (2009). *The global financial crisis: Analysis and policy implications.* Washington, DC: Congressional Research Services. Retrieved from www.fas.org/sgp/crs/misc/RL34742.pdf

Pacula, R. L. (2011). Substance use and recessions: What can be learned from economic analyses of alcohol? *Interantional Journal of Drug Policy, 22*(5), 326–334.

Patterson, J. M., Eberly, L. E., Ding, Y., & Hargreaves, M. (2004). Associations of smoking prevalence with individual and area level social cohesion. *Journal of Epidemiology and Community Health, 58*(8), 692–697.

RSK (Directorate of Internal Revenue) (2012). *Directorate website.* http:// www.rsk.is/fagadilar/stadtolur-skatta/alagning-einstaklinga/nr/267.

Ruhm, C. J. (2000). Are recessions good for your health? *Quarterly Journal of Economics, 115*(2), 617–650.

Ruhm, C. J. (2003). Good times make you sick. *Journal of Health Economics, 22*(4), 637–658.

Ruhm, C. J. (2005). Healthy living in hard times. *Journal of Health Economics, 24*(2), 341–363.

Ruhm, C. J., & Black, W. E. (2002). Does drinking really decrease in bad times? *Journal of Health Economics, 21*(4), 659–678.

Statistics Iceland (2011). *Activity rate, unemployment and labour force by quarters.* http://www.statice.is/Statistics/Wages%2C-income-and-labour-market/Labour-market.

Statistics Iceland (2012). *Financial accounts.* Reykjavik: Statistics Iceland.

Statistics Iceland (2013a). *Migration.* http://www.statice.is/Statistics/Population/ Migration.

Statistics Iceland (2013b). *National accounts overview—Gross domestic product and gross national income at constant prices 1980–2011.* Retrieved from http://www.statice.is/Pages/1267

Tauras, J. A. (2006). Smoke-free air laws, cigarette prices, and adult cigarette demand. *Economic Inquiry, 44*(2), 333–342.

U.S. Centers for Disease Control (2012). *Sleep and sleep disorders.* Atlanta: Centers for Disease Control. http://www.cdc.gov/Features/Sleep/.

U.S. Centers for Disease Control (2013). *Indoor tanning.* http://www.cdc.gov/ cancer/skin/basic_info/indoor_tanning.html.

Vilaplana, C., Labeaga, J. M., & Jiménez-Martín, S. (2006). *Further evidence about alcohol consumption and the business cycle* (Working paper). Madrid: Fundación de estudios de economia aplicada. http://www.fedea.es/ pub/papers/2006/dt2006-06.pdf.

Wagenaar, A. C., Salois, M. J., & Komro, K. A. (2009). Effects of beverage alcohol price and tax levels on drinking: A meta-analysis of 1003 estimates from 112 studies. *Addiction, 104*(2), 179–190.

Wakefield, M. A., Durkin, S., Spittal, M. J., Siahpush, M., Scollo, M., Simpson, J. A., . . . Hill, D. (2008). Impact of tobacco control policies and mass media campaigns on monthly adult smoking prevalence. *American Journal of Public Health, 98*(8), 1443–1450.

Xu, X., & Kaestner, R. (2010). *The business cycle and health behaviors* (National Bureau of Economic Research, working paper 15737). http://www.nber.org/ papers/w15737.pdf.

Appendix

Table A6.1 Characteristics of Full 2007 Sample (Ages 18–79 Years), by Attrition Status.

Sample Characteristics (measured in 2007)	Weighted		Unweighted	
	Leavers (did not complete 2009 interview)	Stayers (completed 2009 interview)	Leavers (did not complete 2009 interview)	Stayers (completed 2009 interview)
Age	39.13 ***	46.87	45.38 ***	53.16
Male	.531 ***	.489	.472	.466
Married	.401 ***	.558	.481 ***	.624
Cohabiting	.231 ***	.183	.191 ***	.141
Child in household	.411 **	.376	.367 ***	.302
Lives with adult other than partner	.375 ***	.273	.315 ***	.228
Lives in rural area	.109*	.126	.159*	.177
Good or very good health status	.780	.788	.713 **	.745
Working	.785	.795	.714	.711
Occupation				
Professional	.425 ***	.491	.393 ***	.441
Clerical	.083	.076	.088	.079
Service	.178 ***	.125	.164 ***	.122
Farm/fish	.046	.056	.075	.079
Skilled trade	.190	.181	.187	.192
Unskilled trade	.079	.071	.093	.087

Notes: p values are from t-tests for differences in means between leavers and stayers: ***$p < .01$; **$p < .05$; *$p < .10$.

Table A6.2 Effects of Economic Crisis In Iceland on Hours Of Work, Real Household Income, Loss in Fnancial Assets, Increased Mortgage Debt, and Anxiety or Poor Mental Health.—Fixed-Effects Models ($N = 5,770$).

	Hours of work (divided by 10)		Real household income		Loss in financial assets		Mortgage debt increased		Anxiety or poor mental heath	
2009 indicator	−.273	−.277	−1.694	−1.683	2.056	2.059	.629	.625	.034	.034
Time-varying covariates	No	Yes	No	Yes	No	Yes	No	Yes	No	Yes

Notes: Sample weights are applied. Figures are regression coefficients for effects of the crisis (2009 indicator) relative to 2007. Time-varying covariates are married, cohabiting, lives with adult other than partner, and lives in rural area. All coefficients of 2009 crisis are statistically significant at $p < .01$.

Table A6.3 Estimated Effects of Mediators on Health-Compromising Behaviors—Fixed-Effects Models.

	Smoking	Heavy drinking	Daily sugared soft drink	Daily sweets	Weekly fast food	Indoor tanning
Hours of work (divided by 10)	.007*	.004	.006**	.002	.008	.001
Real household income (millions of 2009 krona/year)	.001	.004	−.000	.002	.002	.003
Loss in financial assets (millions of krona)	.000	−.001	−.000	−.000	−.002*	.000
Mortgage debt increased	−.000	.019	.006	−.020	−.075***	−.048***
Anxiety or poor mental health	−.003	−.002	−.015	.010	.008	.024
N	5,580	5,586	5,640	5,616	5,676	5,378

Notes: Sample weights are applied. Figures presented are regression coefficients of the mediators from the models in the last row of Table 6.2. That is, for each behavior, all mediators are included in the same model that also controls for time-varying covariates (married, cohabiting, lives with adult other than partner, and lives in rural area).
****p < .01; **p < .05; *p < .10.

Table A6.4 Estimated Effects of Mediators on Health-Promoting Behaviors—Fixed-Effects Models.

	Daily fruit	Daily vegetables	Daily fish oil	Daily Vitamins/ Supplements	Recommended sleep
Hours of work (divided by 10)	.001	.006	–.006	.000	.004
Real household income (millions of 2009 krona/year)	–.005	.002	–.003	.002	–.001
Loss in financial assets (millions of krona)	–.001	.003**	.002	.000	–.002
Mortgage debt increased	.008	–.001	.010	.013	–.003
Anxiety or poor mental health	–.007	–.029	–.028	–.001	–.049**
N	5,664	5,690	5,600	5,434	5,638

Notes: Sample weights are applied. Figures presented are regression coefficients of the mediators from the models in the last row of Table 6.3. That is, for each behavior, all mediators are included in the same model that also controls for 2009 indicator and time-varying covariates (married, cohabiting, lives with adult other than partner, and lives in rural area).

**p < .05.

Table A6.5 Pooled Probit Results—Effects of Economic Crisis in Iceland on Health-Compromising Behaviors.

	Smoking	Heavy drinking	Daily sugared soft drink	Daily sweets	Weekly fast food	Indoor tanning
	ME	ME	ME	ME	ME	ME
2009 indicator	−.033***	−.026***	−.011***	−.023***	−.057***	−.039***
Age	.011***	−.012***	−.005***	−.001	−.014***	−.005*
Age squared	<−.001***	<.000***	<.000	<−.000	<−.000	<−.000
Male	−.019	.186***	.046***	.000	.170***	−.092***
High school or less	.169***	.012	.041**	−.022	−.019	.119***
Some college	.079***	.001	.009	−.009	.018	.077***
Undergraduate degree	.005	−.022	−.024	−.001	.016	.026
N	5,384	5,384	5,438	5,416	5,474	5,200

Notes: Sample weights are applied. "2009 indicator" captures the effect of the crisis (that is, it is relative to 2007).

***$p < .01$; **$p < .05$.

Table A6.6 Pooled Probit Results—Effects of Economic Crisis in Iceland on Health-Promoting Behaviors.

	Daily fruit	Daily vegetable	Daily fish oil	Daily vitamins/ supplements	Recommended sleep
	ME	ME	ME	ME	ME
2009 indicator	−.018	−.030***	.036***	−.012	.035***
Age	.006*	.010***	.003	−.005**	−.001
Age squared	<−.000	<−.000*	<.000**	<.000	<.000
Male	−.234***	−.153***	−.052***	.106***	−.031*
High school or less	−.093***	−.123***	−.106***	.003	−.098***
Some college	−.048	−.064**	−.056*	−.010	−.065**
Undergraduate degree	−.031	−.008	−.039	−.028	−.008
N	5,460	5,486	5,402	5,236	5,442

Notes: Sample weights are applied. "2009 indicator" captures the effect of the crisis (that is, it is relative to 2007).
***$p < .01$; **$p < .05$; *$p < .10$.

Table A6.7 Effects of Economic Crisis in Iceland on Health-Compromising Behaviors—Seemingly Unrelated Regression (SUR) and Linear Probability Estimates.

	Smoking	Heavy drinking	Daily sugared soft drink	Daily sweets	Weekly fast food	Indoor tanning
SUR						
Basic covariates	−.031**	−.025*	−.013	−.024**	−.053***	−.039***
Basic and time-varying covariates	−.028**	−.024*	−.013	−.023**	−.051***	−.038***
Linear probability						
Basic covariates	−.031**	−.025*	−.013	−.024**	−.053***	−.039***
Basic and time-varying covariates	−.028**	−.024*	−.013	−.023**	−.051***	−.038***
N	4,364	4,364	4,364	4,364	4,364	4,364

Notes: Estimates are regression coefficients for the 2009 indicator (effects of the crisis) relative to 2007. Sample weights are applied in models with basic covariates. Basic covariates = age, age squared, gender, and education (high school, some college, college degree). Time-varying covariates are married, cohabiting, lives with adult other than partner, and lives in rural area.
***$p < .01$; **$p < .05$; *$p < .10$.

Table A6.8 Effects of Economic Crisis in Iceland on Health-Promoting Behaviors—Seemingly Unrelated Regression (SUR) and Linear Probability Estimates.

	Daily fruit	Daily vegetables	Daily fish oil	Daily vitamins/ supplements	Recommended sleep
SUR					
Basic covariates	−.016	−.029**	.035**	−.013	.032**
Basic and time-varying covariates	−.017	−.030**	.036**	−.013	.031**
Linear probability					
Basic covariates	−.016	−.029**	.035**	−.013	.032**
Basic and time-varying covariates	−.017	−.030**	.036**	−.013	.031**
N	4,364	4,364	4,364	4,364	4,364

Notes: Estimates are regression coefficients for the 2009 indicator (effects of the crisis) relative to 2007. Sample weights are applied in models with basic covariates. Basic covariates = age, age squared, gender, and education (high school, some college, college degree). Time-varying covariates are married, cohabiting, lives with adult other than partner, and lives in rural area.
** $p < .05$.

Table A6.9 Effects of Economic Crisis in Iceland on Health-Compromising Behaviors—Fixed-Effects Models, Stratified by Gender.

Effects of 2009 indicator:	Smoking	Heavy drinking	Daily sugared soft drink	Daily sweets	Weekly fast food	Indoor tanning
Males						
No time-varying covariates	-.033***	-.037***	-.024**	-.014	-.065***	-.025***
Time-varying covariates	-.034***	-.037***	-.028***	-.016*	-.063***	-.023***
N	2,722	2,740	2,764	2,748	2,784	2,634
Females						
No time-varying covariates	-.034***	-.011	-.006	-.032***	-.033***	-.055***
Time-varying covariates	-.035***	-.012	-.005	-.030***	-.034***	-.054***
N	2,858	2,846	2,876	2,868	2,892	2,744

Notes: Sample weights are applied. Figures are regression coefficients for effects of the crisis (2009 indicator) relative to 2007. Time-varying covariates are married, cohabiting, lives with adult other than partner, and lives in rural area.
****$p < .01$; **$p < .05$; *$p < .10$.

Table A6.10 Effects of Economic Crisis in Iceland on Health-Promoting Behaviors—Fixed-Effects Models, Stratified by Gender.

Effects of 2009 indicator:	Daily fruit	Daily vegetables	Daily fish oil	Daily vitamins/supplements	Recommended sleep
Males					
No time-varying covariates	−.010	−.022*	.013	−.012	.063***
Time-varying covariates	−.009	−.024*	.013	−.013	.063***
N	2,778	2,790	2,766	2,684	2,758
Females					
No time-varying covariates	−.028*	−.032**	.050***	−.007	.004
Time-varying covariates	−.026*	−.032**	.053***	−.009	.004
N	2,886	2,900	2,834	2,750	2,880

Notes: Sample weights are applied. Figures are regression coefficients for effects of the crisis (2009 indicator) relative to 2007. Time-varying covariates are married, cohabiting, lives with adult other than partner, and lives in rural area.

$***p < .01$; $**p < .05$; $*p < .10$.

7

Mental Health

The New Frontier for Labor Economics[1]

Richard Layard

London School of Economics and Political Science, U.K.

Mental health is a key dimension of all our lives. Yet, when the present welfare state was being designed, this was far from people's minds. In his famous report on welfare reform in Britain, William Beveridge identified as the main problems of society five great giants that needed to be slain: they were poverty, unemployment, poor education, bad housing, and disease (by which he meant, of course, physical disease) (Beveridge, 1942; Timmins, 2001).

Over the 70 years since his report, most advanced countries have made huge strides on all of these fronts, except at times unemployment. But there is still widespread misery—and what surveys we have of happiness and misery suggest things have changed little since Beveridge wrote. So what did he and his fellow reformers miss?

They overlooked the human factor—the problems that come from inside ourselves (and not mainly from externals). It is because of the human factor that, despite unparalleled prosperity and mostly high employment, we now observe more family conflict, less trust, and more crime, than when Beveridge wrote. And this, in turn, helps to explain the need that so many people feel for a new metric to measure the progress of society.

The Economics of Wellbeing: Wellbeing: A Complete Reference Guide, Volume V.
Edited by David McDaid and Cary L. Cooper.
© 2014 John Wiley & Sons, Ltd. Published 2014 by John Wiley & Sons, Inc.
DOI: 10.1002/9781118539415.wbwell07

Wellbeing

We have never of course had a single metric before—nobody really believed that gross domestic product (GDP) was an adequate measure of how our society was doing. What is new is that a proper metric is now available—the metric of wellbeing. Questions like "Overall, how satisfied are you with your life nowadays?" have been asked for decades and they have become increasingly validated (Layard, 2010). Increasingly, we are able to predict and explain people's replies to the question. We can also use their replies to predict other things like their life expectancy. And, most important, we have found areas in the brain where the objective electrical activity is well correlated with the subjective self-report (Davidson, Jackson, & Kalin 2000; Layard, 2010). So we should accept these self-reports as a valid proxy for what we care about.

In many countries these measures show no upward trend in wellbeing, as, for example, in the United States and West Germany (see Figures 7.1 and 7.2). There are other countries where wellbeing has increased, but it is clear that economic growth has not brought the increase in life satisfaction that many people would have expected from the huge improvement in living standards that we have experienced and the huge improvements in education, health, and housing since the 1950s. And, incidentally, the main explanation is not inequality, since life satisfaction did not rise even when inequality was falling in the 1950s and 1960s. So, what is the problem?

Many factors are involved, social and personal. This chapter concentrates on one factor only—our failure to grapple with the problem of mental illness.

Mental Health

How do we know this matters? Table 7.1 shows a simple equation to explain life satisfaction among British men aged 34 in 2004. This equation includes all the most powerful explanatory variables available and shows for each of them their β statistics, that is, the partial correlation coefficient for each variable, holding the other variables constant. The most powerful variable is the mental malaise of the individual 8 years earlier.[2] It is more than twice as powerful as the person's income at the time when they were 34. Even if we measure mental malaise 18 years earlier, it still has almost as much

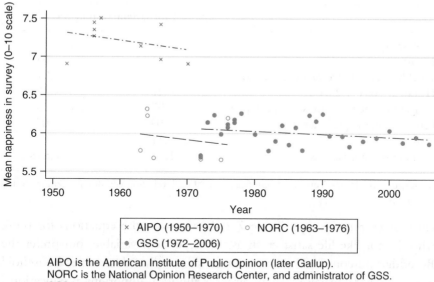

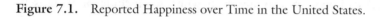

AIPO is the American Institute of Public Opinion (later Gallup).
NORC is the National Opinion Research Center, and administrator of GSS.
GSS is the General Social Survey.
Original question asked on a 3-point scale.

Figure 7.1. Reported Happiness over Time in the United States.

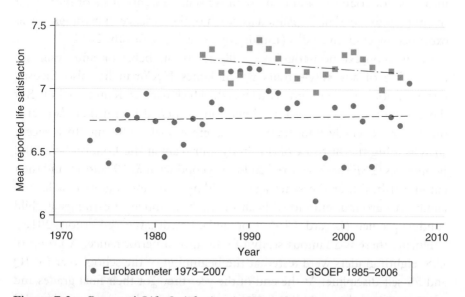

Figure 7.2. Reported Life Satisfaction in West Germany. Adapted from Eurobarometer and German Socioeconomic Panel.

Table 7.1. Determinants of Life Satisfaction (Males Born in 1970).

	Life satisfaction at 34	
Malaise at 26	−.23*	—
Malaise at 16	—	−.08*
Total household income per head (log)	.10*	.11*
Health at 26 (0,1,2,3)	−.10*	−.17*
Educational qualifications (0,1,2,3,4,5)	.07*	.08*
Parental income per head (log)	.03	.03
R square	.11	.07
Number of observations	1,508	1,508

Regressions by James Vernoit. *Significance at 95% level. Source: British Cohort Study β-statistics

effect as current income. Table 7.2 shows two more equations for those who do not like life satisfaction as the dependent variable, but prefer the Beveridge outcomes. The first column shows what determines household income. Mental malaise 8 years earlier is almost as important as educational qualifications. The second column explains self-reported health, and again previous malaise shows up strongly even when we include previous self-reported health. If we focus on earnings as the outcome, a striking Swedish study followed up people who did military service, at which time they were measured for cognitive and non-cognitive skills. Twenty years or more later the non-cognitive skills explained as much of the variance of earnings as was explained by cognitive skills (Lundborg, Nilsson, & Rooth, 2011).

In this context non-cognitive skills focus on behavior and resilience in the face of adversity—traits which James Heckman has also focused our attention on (Almlund, Duckworth, Heckman, & Kautz, 2011). But there is another, more inward, dimension of mental health that also turns out to be extremely important. This is emotional wellbeing. In a recent analysis using the British Cohort Study, our team at the London School of Economics (LSE) has measured children's conduct at 5, 10, and 16 and their emotional health at the same ages. Holding constant cognitive skills and family background, emotional health predicts as much of earnings as child conduct predicts (Layard, Clark, Cornaglia, Powdthavee, & Vernoit, 2013).

Finally, there is a famous study of educational performance. A group of U.S. eighth graders were tested at the beginning of the school year for IQ and for self-discipline. At the end of the year they got their final grades and what explained those grades? Self-discipline explained twice as much as IQ did (Duckworth & Seligman, 2005).

Table 7.2. Determinants of Income and Health (Males Born in 1970).

	Household income per head at 34	Health at 34
Malaise at 26	−0.7*	.14*
Malaise at 16	—	—
Total household income per head (log)	—	.00
Health at 26	.00	.26*
Educational qualifications	.11*	.09*
Parental income per head (log)	.04	.05
R square	.02	.12
Number of observations	1,508	1,508

Regressions by James Vernoit. *Significance at 95% level. Source: British Cohort Study β-statistics.

In the rest of this chapter I will focus on six issues:

1. the scale of mental illness;
2. the costs to the economy and the taxpayer;
3. the cost-effective treatments that exist;
4. the fact that they are rarely available, but could be;
5. prevention;
6. implications for social science.

The Scale of Mental Illness

Before beginning we need a definition of mental illness. People are mentally ill when they experience serious and persistent distress or impairment due to abnormal feelings or behavior that are psychological or neurobiological in origin. So how prevalent is mental illness? We can start with adults, using the U.K. Psychiatric Morbidity Survey, which is a household survey (see Table 7.3).

The survey has been repeated 3 times in 1993, 2000, and 2007. There has been a slight steady increase over the period. This finding is similar to that in some other countries where there have been repeated surveys. When implausible retrospective questionnaires have been used, these usually imply that there has been a substantial increase in—what some people call an

161

Table 7.3. Prevalence of Mental Illness (Adults, U.K.).

Adults	%
Schizophrenia	0.5
Depression	8.5
Anxiety disorders	8.5
Dementia	1.5
Total	19

Source: McManus, Meltzer, Brugha, Bebbington, and Jenkins (2009).

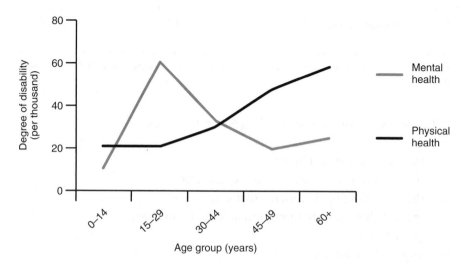

Figure 7.3. Degree of Disability in Each Age Group in Western Europe (Numbers per thousand).

epidemic of—depression. But most psychiatrists do not believe it. Mental health problems have been here since the Stone Age. What is new is that now, for the first time, we have things we can do about them.

To set the scale of mental illness in perspective, we can compare it with the scale of physical ill-health. Here the World Health Organization employs a panel of doctors to gauge the severity of each condition, physical and mental (World Health Organization, 2002). The upshot is remarkable (see Figure 7.3). Mental illness is not only the largest single illness among people of working age. It actually accounts for half of all disability among them—as much as the combined effects of back pain, heart pain, pulmonary problems, diabetes, cancer and all the rest. And this is based on household surveys, not on people claiming benefits.

Economic Costs

Clearly a disease of this magnitude imposes heavy economic costs both on the public finances and on the economy. Table 7.4 shows the rates of people on disability benefit in different countries. In every country these are underestimates. For there is another remarkable fact: of all the people referred to first appointments with a hospital consultant in Britain, only a half have a medically explicable condition (Nimnuan, Hotopf, & Wessely 2001). Some of the others have genuinely inexplicable conditions, but many have conditions that are best explained as psychological in origin.

But numbers on disability benefits only measure a part of the impact of mental illness. First, not all those who can't work get disability benefits. So Table 7.5 shows a measure of the overall employment impact. If you look at the most mentally ill (worst 5%), their employment rate is reduced by a third, and for the next 15% their employment rate is reduced by one fifth. If these people had the same employment rates as everybody else, employment would be 4.4% higher—which is a rough measure of the impact of mental health on GDP via non-employment (given that the relation between mental

Table 7.4. Number of People Claiming Disability Benefits as a Percentage of the Working-Age Population.

	Due to mental illness	All causes
U.K.	2.5	6.1
U.S.A.	2.0	6.6
Average of 6 other OECD countries	2.4	6.4

Source: Organisation for Economic Co-operation and Development (2011).

Table 7.5. Employment Rates for Mentally Ill People As a Percentage of Those for Others.

	Severe disorder (worst 5%)	Moderate disorder (next 15%)
U.K.	65	82
9 other OECD countries	66	87

Source: Organisation for Economic Co-operation and Development (2011).

Table 7.6. Percentage of Days Absent.

	Disorder	No Disorder
U.K.	8.0	2.5
21 European countries	11.2	5.0

Sources: Organisation for Economic Co-operation and Development (2011); Sainsbury Centre for Mental Health (2007).

health and IQ is small) (Singleton, Bumpstead, O'Brien, Lee, & Meltzer, 2001).

But there is also another cost—mentally ill people who are in work take much more time off sick. In fact, half of all days off sick are due to mental illness. This is really expensive for employers. But at the World Economic Forum at Davos in January 2012 there was a meeting of 60 of the world's most enlightened large companies who belong to the Workplace Wellness Alliance. The meeting went on for 90 minutes, and there were presentations about cardio-vascular problems, cancer, diabetes, lung problems, and so on, but no mention of mental illness. People just do not want to discuss it.

In fact, as Table 7.6 shows, another 1% of work hours are lost due to absenteeism and on top of that we have the cost of presenteeism—people whose mind is elsewhere and who underperform even when they are at work. Based on self-reports of underperformance, this may add another 1–2% to the direct output costs of mental illness. All these figures combined suggest an overall output loss close to 7.5% of GDP (see Table 7.7).

Table 7.7. Overall Cost of Mental Illness (U.K.).

At work	% of working hours lost
Nonemployment	4.4
Absenteeism	1.1
Presenteeism	2.0
Total	7.5
Health care	**% of GDP**
Mental health care	1.5
Physical health care	0.8
Total	2.3

There is the cost to the health-care system. Treating mental illness (and providing the related social care) costs roughly 1.5% of GDP in Britain. And on top of this people who have chronic physical conditions cost roughly 50% more in physical health care if they are also mentally ill. That is U.S. evidence and holds constant with the severity of the physical condition. So that means in Britain another cost equal to nearly 1% of GDP (Naylor et al., 2012).[3]

Of all this cost, more than half falls on the taxpayer and the rest on the individuals concerned and on their employers. In total it is no small issue. But these costs say almost nothing about what we should do. That depends on what we can do.

Cost-Effective Treatments

When Beveridge wrote, and until the 1950s, there was little that could be done about mental illness apart from tender, loving care. But in the 1950s spectacular discoveries were made in drugs for schizophrenia, for bipolar disorder, and for depression—and more recently for ADHD (attention deficit hyperactivity disorder).

Since the 1970s there have also been major discoveries in evidence-based methods of psychological therapy. By far the best researched is cognitive behavioral therapy (or CBT), which helps people to reorder their thoughts and thus to manage their feelings and behavior. For anxiety disorders, typical recovery rates are over 50% and are at least as good as with medication. Moreover, in most anxiety cases recovery secured through CBT is permanent, which is not the case with medication. Similarly with depression, recovery rates after 4 months are similar with CBT and with antidepressants, but relapse is much less likely for patients treated with CBT (Roth & Fonagy, 2005).

For these reasons the National Institute for Health and Care Excellence (NICE) in England recommends that all patients with these conditions should be offered the choice of medication or CBT or alternatively certain other evidence-based psychological therapies for specific conditions. The recommendations about psychological therapy are extremely important, because many patients are unwilling to take drugs and because the effects of psychological therapy are, on average, longer lasting.

Therapy is also recommended because it costs so little: about £750 in 2006 money for a course of 10 sessions. And against that we must set the savings that result when successfully treated people return to work (or keep the job they otherwise would have lost). This is where the labor economics comes in. Unfortunately, only a few proper experimental follow-ups have been done with proper control groups (all in the United States). They show that among people treated with CBT some 4% work over the subsequent 25 months (who would not otherwise have done so).[4] So, for every 100 people treated at least 4 x 25 extra months are worked—which makes an average of 1 month per person treated. And what does an extra month's work save the British taxpayer? £750 in 2006 money. So, the net cost to the Exchequer is zero.

At the same time there are likely to be big savings to the National Health Service (NHS) on physical health-care costs. Mentally ill people keep on going to the general practice doctor. But CBT reduces that. A US meta-analysis took all 28 studies that had compared health-care use between people treated with CBT and a randomized control group. In 26 of the 28 studies the reduction in health care use over the subsequent 24 months was large enough to cover the costs of the CBT (Chiles, Lambert, & Hatch 1999). These were among the reasons why NICE had no hesitation some 8 years ago in recommending that all patients suffering from anxiety or depression should be offered psychological therapy. But for many years these recommendations were not carried out.

Undertreatment

The undertreatment of mental illness is a worldwide phenomenon (see Table 7.8). These treatment rates compare with rates of well over 75% for most physical conditions. There are at least three reasons.

1. People and their relations are ashamed to admit there is a problem. But this stigma is greatly compounded by causes 2 and 3.
2. People do not realize that mental health problems can be treated—there is a long time lag.
3. The facilities are simply not available. This has certainly been the binding constraint. In 2009 the majority of people treated for depression or anxiety had waited for over 6 months in England (MIND, 2010)—while for physical conditions the upper limit was 18 weeks. Only 15% of GPs said they could get patients the psychological help they needed.[5]

Table 7.8. Under treatment (Percentage of Mentally Ill People in Any Form of Treatment).

% of all ill people who are in treatment		% of people on disability benefits who are in treatment
Adults		
U.K.	25	50
U.S.A.	28	46
Europe	25	
Children		
U.K.	25	

Sources: Lepine, Gastpar, Mendlewicz, and Tylee (1997), McManus et al. (2009), Organisation for Economic Co-operation and Development (2011).

This is a case of simple discrimination, and it reflects the long-standing resistance in Western society to taking the inner life seriously, as compared with things we can see and touch. However the worldwide wellbeing movement, which grows daily, is beginning to change this. To end the discrimination in mental health, in 2005 the LSE's Centre for Economic Performance founded a Mental Health Policy Group to make the case for proper treatment for mentally ill people in England and to show how it could be provided. Much of the case described above was developed by that group (Centre for Economic Performance's Mental Health Policy Group, 2006). Fortunately, the government listened and in 2008 it launched the Improving Access to Psychological Therapies (IAPT) program, which basically followed the proposals of our group (Clark, 2011).

This 6-year plan aimed to ensure that by Year 6 the NICE Guidelines were being delivered throughout the country. The method was a new service for which most of the staff would have to receive a year's training on top of whatever mental health training they already had. The service would need roughly 8,000 therapists, of whom 6,000 would have to be trained. In addition, there should be employment support workers (1 for every 8 therapists) to help people stay in work or regain employment if they had lost it.[6] The program has gone remarkably well and has been continued by the present government. Recovery rates are now approaching 50% and are improving as more and more of the therapists become experienced and fewer are trainees.

In IAPT every patient's outcome is monitored session by session, so that more is known about outcomes than in most other parts of the NHS. We can also see from comparing the Wave 1 services that recovery rates are higher where NICE guidelines are followed and where the staff are more experienced (Gyani, Shafran, Layard, & Clark, 2011). So far the objective we have set is quite limited—an ability by 2015 to treat 15% of the diagnosable population each year at an annual cost of around £300 million. As we approach that goal, we become increasingly aware of the challenge coming from co-morbidity with physical illness. To deal with that another 5-year program will have to be proposed in the government's next Spending Review that would take coverage up to 25% by 2020.

This chapter has focused mainly on adults, where the labor market evidence is clear cut. But of course it would be best if we could prevent most adult mental illness in the first place. This brings us to the question of child mental illness and mental health promotion in schools and elsewhere.

Prevention

Half of all adults with mental illness have shown it by the age of 15. Table 7.9 shows the prevalence of mental disorders in childhood, again from a government survey of households.

Table 7.10 shows the other problems which mentally ill children have when they are children. Children with mental health problems are at least five times more likely than others to play truant or to be excluded, as well as being much more likely to smoke, take drugs, and, worst of all, to self-harm.

Table 7.11 shows how people's adult lives develop according to the scale of their behavioral difficulties in childhood. The left-hand column is essentially those children who have conduct disorder and the right-hand column is the best-behaved 50%. There is an extraordinary difference between the

Table 7.9. Prevalence of Mental Illness in Children

Children (5–16)	Percentage
Emotional disorders	4
Conduct disorder/ADHD	6
Total	10

Source: Green, McGinnity, Meltzer, Ford, and Goodman (2005).

Table 7.10. How Mental Health Problems Contribute to Other Childhood Problems (Children aged 5–16).

Percentage who:	Children with:		
	Emotional Disorders	Conduct Disorders	No Disorder
Play truant	16	22	3
Have ever been excluded from school	12	34	4
Smoke regularly (age 11–16)	19	30	5
Have ever used hard drugs (age 11–16)	6	12	1
Have ever self-harmed	19	18	2

Source: Green, McGinnity, Meltzer, Ford, and Goodman (2005).

Table 7.11. Subsequent Outcomes for Children with Behavioral Difficulties at Ages 7–9.

Percentage who subsequently	Children whose childhood conduct was in	
	Worst 5%	Best 50%
Committed violent offences (21–25)	35	3
Were drug-dependent (21–25)	20	5
Became a teenage parent	20	4
Were welfare-dependent (at age 25)	33	9
Attempted suicide (ever)	18	4

Source: Fergusson, Horwood, and Ridder (2005).

two groups in the extent to which they go on to commit violent crime, to become teenage parents, or to live off welfare. Even with controls, these differences remain huge. It is because we have not tackled mental illness that these problems are just as they were in Beveridge's day—or in some ways worse. The case for early intervention is based on the extent to which childhood disorder predicts for the individual a life of misery, and for society a load of costs.

Table 7.12 shows the subsequent taxpayer cost of children with conduct disorder, compared with other children.[7] The issue, of course, is whether anything can be done and whether it is cost-effective. There has been much

Table 7.12. Costs to the Taxpayer—From Criminal Justice, Social Care, and Remedial Help between Ages 10 and 28 (£).

Child with conduct disorder at age 10	70,000
Child with conduct problems at age 10	24,000
Child with none of the above at age 10	7,000

Source: Scott, Knapp, Henderson, and Maughan (2001). London sample.

less research on the treatment of children than of adults, but, as for adults, there are well-established treatments that are recommended by NICE.

Treatments for Children

For children with anxiety problems, CBT typically leads to 50% recovery rates, and for children with mild to moderate conduct disorder parent training produces improvement in two thirds of cases. These are quite cheap treatments. For serious conduct disorder much more intensive work is needed, such as multisystemic therapy costing around £6,000.

The shocking thing is that only a quarter of all the million or so children in England who need treatment are receiving it, and yet child mental health services are now being reduced due to cuts in English local authority funding. This is simply inhuman—most physical problems continue to be almost automatically treated, while the human spirit is treated as marginal.

So the case for treatment is above all humanitarian. But it is also cost-saving. Unfortunately the cost-saving is more difficult to compute for children than for adults, since many of the costs which are saved come many years later, and very few treatment trials of children follow them up for long enough to record all these savings.

Prevention: Schools

This brings up the issue of preventing mental illness in the first place. The first point is that good intentions are not enough—many well-intentioned programs carried out with the best will in the world have been found to make no difference. One recent example was the British government's pilots of social and emotional learning in secondary schools (Humphrey, Lendrum, & Wigelsworth, 2010). The evaluators correctly attributed this to insufficient structure and insufficient manualization.

170

The programs that produce the best results are those that are highly structured (which is also true of psychological therapy). In the United States the CASEL collaboration has done a meta-analysis of 180 programs typically lasting around 20 hours in half-sized classes. The average short-run effects are to raise those who take the program by around 10 percentile points on emotional state, behavior, and achievement (Payton et al., 2008). Some programs have, of course, much better results than average.

In the United Kingdom the LSE's Centre for Economic Performance (CEP) took the lead in organizing pilots of the University of Pennsylvania's Resilience Program for all the 11-year-olds in 22 secondary schools. This is an 18 hour program that teaches the children to observe and manage their own thoughts and feelings, and to understand and respond to the thoughts and feelings of others. The largest effects (compared with controls) were on the children who started off in the most depressed 40% of the class. For them their degree of depression was reduced by 0.2 standard deviations, but by 3 years later the effect had gone (Challen, Machin, Noden, & West, 2011).

This problem of fading effects arises in many programs; for most of them we have no idea of their long-term effects because they have simply not been followed up. One encouraging exception is the so-called Good Behavior Game (Ialongo et al., 1999; Kellam et al., 2008) piloted in Baltimore. Each beginning primary school class is divided into 3 teams and each team is scored according to the number of times a member of the team breaks one of the behavior rules. If there are fewer than five infringements all members of the team get a reward. Children in the treatment and control groups were followed up right up to age 19–21, and those in the treatment group had significantly lower use of drugs, alcohol, and tobacco and significantly lower frequency of anti-social personality disorder.

There is one obvious feature of this program: the amount of time when the game was played totaled around 200 hours. Aristotle was right—habit is central to the development of character and we shall only produce a more mentally healthy school population if we spend more time on it. First, we need a more values-based school ethos, but, second, we need a sustained evidence-based curriculum for personal, social, and health education lasting throughout school life. The CEP has now devised a balanced mix of evidence-based programs that would provide 140 hours of the curriculum in secondary schools, and the Centre will be piloting it over a 5 year period (Layard, Coleman, & Hale, 2011).

Workplace

Another place where mental health could be improved is, of course, at the workplace. Better mental health is very much in the employers' interests, given the problems of absence and turnover which I discussed earlier. In 17 out of 19 OECD countries work-related mental problems are up. Surveys of individuals show that the worst time in their day is when they are in the presence of their line manager (Kahneman, Krueger, Schkade, Schwarz, & Stone, 2004). We need better job design and a more pro-active way of handling absence. In many countries managers are not allowed to ring up their sick employees and ask how they are and what the problem is. We have got to become a lot more open about mental health problems, and to get treatment for those who need it.

Social Sciences

But basic to all this will be a better understanding of the role of mental health in all aspects of our national life. So let me end on this, and the way in which social science can contribute.

What we need now is a complete model of the life-course. Emotional wellbeing should be the central variable of interest—the ultimate criterion by which we judge the state of our society. But, to understand how this evolves, we have to know how it affects a person's conduct, educational performance, physical health, and (in adulthood) their employment, earnings, and performance as parents. And we also need to know how these other things then affect emotional wellbeing.

So in Figure 7.4 each dot is, in principle, affected by every dot that is prior to it in time, including of course the person's family background and the shocks and interventions they have experienced. The dotted lines indicate just one equation in the model.

Our current understanding of this picture is very patchy. It is a bit like our understanding of macroeconomics in the late 1940s. Bits and pieces were known about the parts of the economy, but to make real progress required an estimated model which showed how much each bit mattered. Scholars in Oxford and Philadelphia led the way in developing one.

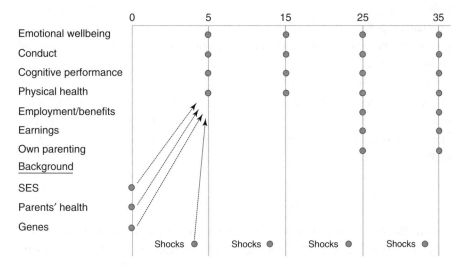

Figure 7.4. Model of Life Course.

Similarly, today we know lots of bits and pieces about subjective wellbeing but we still lack a model—a quantitative model in which the relative importance of all the factors is properly shown. The CEP is setting about estimating such a model using the mass of cohort data that now exists in Britain and abroad.

For this model to be of use for analyzing policy interventions, it must be fully causal—the estimated equations must tell you how any variable$_t$ would change if an earlier shock were introduced into the model. But there is always the danger that the observed relationships in the model are not truly causal but reflect the common influence of some unobserved variable which persists over time. The most obvious omitted variable is the genes, which are omitted in most of modern social science. We have to get these in, and that is why we plan that some of our work will use data on twins or adoptees to enable us to control properly for the genes.

Ultimately the aim is to lead to better policy through a more sensible kind of cost-effectiveness analysis than is currently used. If you think about the welfare state, most of the benefits cannot be measured in units of "willingness to pay." Think, for example, of health, social care, law and order, the environment, and of course the relief of poverty. The benefits can only meaningfully be measured in units of emotional wellbeing or life satisfaction. To measure them we should use the model in conjunction with experimental data, to estimate how life satisfaction changes in response to policy interventions. The model also gives us a better fix on the net costs of an intervention (after the gross costs have been adjusted for all the savings or extra costs incurred as a result).

We have already seen an example of that for CBT. So in 25 years' time there's a real chance that we will have much better methods of cost-effectiveness analysis—and governments which focus much more on what really matters for our people.

Action for Happiness

But, in the end, what happens will depend ultimately on individuals—what they do themselves and what they get their governments to do. That is why a year ago a social movement was launched called Action for Happiness whose members pledge to try to create the most happiness they can in the world around them and the least misery.[8] That is how we should lead our own lives. But we should also expect our policymakers to adopt policies that have the same effect. Foremost among them is much more attention to mental health.

Conclusion

This objective is unlikely to be achieved unless each country has a separate cabinet minister for "mental health and social care." This could include mental health promotion and treatment from the cradle to the grave. Within the healthcare system it would establish parity of treatment for mental illness and physical illness. It would also cover nontherapeutic services of care for children and old people. And it would pressurize other ministries, like the ministry of education, to make wellbeing a major objective of policy.

For social services the lesson is clear. One of its central purposes should be to uncover the determinants of human wellbeing. Likewise mental health should routinely be considered as an influence on any other important outcome, be it earnings, crime, or family stability. And every survey should include questions about mental health. If we want to improve the wellbeing of our society, we need a change of tack. Economic growth is not the magic bullet, and happiness depends more on the quality of our relationships and our own inner peace. Mental health is vital for both of these. Improving it could be the most important single step forwards in the twenty-first century.

Notes

1. A version of this chapter first appeared in the IZA Journal of Labor Policy. http://www.izajolp.com/content/2/1/2. It is based on a lecture delivered at the LSE in March 2012.

2. Source: British Cohort Study. Malaise score is based on the following 24 questions (1 = yes) divided by 24: Often have backache; Feel tired most of the time; Often feel miserable or depressed; Often have bad headaches; Often get worried about things; Usually have great difficulty in falling/staying asleep; Usually wake unnecessarily early in the morning; Wear yourself out worrying about your health; Often get into a violent rage; People often annoy and irritate you; At times had twitching of the face, head, or shoulders; Often suddenly become scared for no good reason; Scared to be alone when there are no friends near you; Easily upset or irritated; Frightened of going out alone or meeting people; Constantly keyed up and jittery; Suffer from indigestion; Suffer from an upset stomach; Poor appetite; Every little thing gets on your nerves and wears you out; Heart often races like mad; Often have bad pains in your eyes; Troubled with rheumatism or fibrositis; Ever had a nervous breakdown.

3. Naylor et al. (2012) estimate that since one third of LTC patients have mental illness and treating LTC costs roughly 5% of GDP, the cost of their mental illness is 0.8% of GDP ($1/2 \times 1/3 \times 5\%$).

4. This is consistent with the recovery rates and cross-sectional evidence quoted earlier. For the U.S. data see (Wells et al., 2000) and (Rollman et al., 2005). For patients in Wave 1 of IAPT (see later in chapter) 47.5% of the patients were in employment (and not receiving sick pay) when they began treatment. Immediately after treatment ended the proportion was 49.5%, but more will have returned to work in the following weeks and months. Analysis by Alex Gyani. The change in numbers on sick pay and benefits equaled the change in numbers employed (without sick pay). On other outcomes of IAPT, see Gyani et al. (2011).

5. Survey by the Royal College of General Practitioners carried out in 2010.

6. For evidence that CBT is more effective than pure social support, see the following. For long-term unemployed in Britain, group CBT compared with social support led 4 months later to employment rates of 49% for CBT and 28% for social support (Proudfoot, Gray, Carson, Guest, & Dunn, 1999). An Australian study of benefit claimants compared 8 hours of group CBT plus 8 hours of job search assistance to 16 hours of job search assistance only. After 4 weeks the employment rate was 53% for the CBT-plus group and 20% for the job search group (Della-Posta and Drummond, 2006).

7. These costs omit reduced earnings, mental illness and the costs of narcotic drugs, smoking and suicide. This has been estimated in present value terms at £225,000 (Friedli & Parsonage, 2007).
8. actionforhappiness.org. It now has over 30,000 members from over 140 countries.

References

Almlund, M., Duckworth, A. L., Heckman, J., & Kautz, T. (2011). Personality, psychology and economics. In E. A. Hanushek, S. Machin, & L. Woessmann (Eds.), *Handbook of the economics of education*, Volume 4 (pp. 1–182). Hilversum: Elsevier.

Beveridge, W. (1942). *Report on social insurance and allied services*. London: HMSO.

Centre for Economic Performance's Mental Health Policy Group (2006). *The depression report: A new deal for depression and anxiety disorders*. London: London School of Economics and Political Science.

Challen, A., Machin, S., Noden, P., and West, A. (2011). *Evaluation of the UK resilience programme, final report*. London: Department for Education.

Chiles, J. A., Lambert, M. J., & Hatch, A. L. (1999). The impact of psychological interventions on medical cost offset: A meta-analytic review. *Clinical Psychology Scientific Practice, 6*(2), 204–220.

Clark, D. M. (2011). Implementing NICE guidelines for the psychological treatment of depression and anxiety disorders: The IAPT experience. *International Review of Psychiatry, 23*(4), 318–327.

Davidson, R., Jackson, D., & Kalin, N. (2000). Emotion, plasticity, context and regulation: Perspectives from affective neuroscience. *Psychological Bulletin, 126*, 890–906.

Della-Posta, C., & Drummond, P. D. (2006). Cognitive behavioural therapy increases re-employment of job seeking worker's compensation clients. *Journal of Occupational Rehabilitation, 16*(2), 223–230.

Duckworth, A. L, & Seligman, M. E. P. (2005). Self-discipline outdoes IQ in predicting academic performance of adolescents. *Psychological Science, 16*(12), 939–944.

Fergusson, D. M., Horwood, L. J., & Ridder, E. M. (2005). Show me the child at seven: The consequences of conduct problems in childhood for psychosocial functioning in adulthood. *Journal of Child Psychology and Psychiatry, 46*(8), 837–849.

Friedli, L., & Parsonage, M. (2007). *Mental health promotion: Building an economic case*. Belfast: Northern Ireland Association for Mental Health.

Green, H., McGinnity, A., Meltzer, H., Ford, T., & Goodman, R. (2005). *Mental health of children and young people in Great Britain, 2004*. London: Office for National Statistics.

Gyani, A., Shafran, R., Layard, R., & Clark, D. (2011). *Enhancing recovery rates in IAPT services: Lessons from analysis of the year one data.* London: Department of Health. Retrieved from http://www.iapt.nhs.uk/silo/files/enhancing-recovery-rates--iapt-year-one-report.pdf

Humphrey, N., Lendrum, A., & Wigelsworth, M. (2010). *Social and emotional aspects of learning (SEAL) programme in secondary schools: National evaluation.* London: Department of Education.

Ialongo, N. S., Werthamer, L., Kellam, S. G., Brown, C. H., Wang, S., & Lin, Y. (1999). Proximal impact of two first-grade preventive interventions on the early risk behaviors for later substance abuse, depression, and antisocial behavior. *American Journal of Community Psychology, 27*(5), 599–641.

Kahneman, D., Krueger, A., Schkade, D., Schwarz, N., & Stone, A. (2004). A survey method for characterizing daily life experience: The day reconstruction method (DRM). *Science, 306,* 1776–1780.

Kellam, S. G., Brown, C. H., Poduska, J. M., Ialongo, N. S., Wang, W., Toyinbo, P., . . . Wilcox, H. C. (2008). Effects of a universal classroom behavior management program in first and second grades on young adult behavioral, psychiatric, and social outcomes. *Drug Alcohol Dependency. 95,* Suppl. 1, S5–S28.

Layard, R. (2010). Measuring subjective wellbeing. *Science, 327,* 534–535.

Layard, R., Clark, A. E., Cornaglia, F., Powdthavee, N., & Vernoit, J. (2013). *What predicts a successful life? A life-course model of wellbeing.* Mimeo. London: London School of Economics and Political Science, CEP.

Layard, R., Coleman, J., & Hale, D. (2011). *Using tested programmes for secondary PSHE.* Mimeo. London: London School of Economics and Political Science.

Lepine, J. P., Gastpar, M., Mendlewicz, J., & Tylee, A. (1997). Depression in the community: The first pan-European study DEPRES (Depression Research in European Society). *International Clinical Psychopharmacology, 12*(1), 19–29.

Lundborg, P., Nilsson, A., & Rooth, D.-O. (2011). *Early life health and adult earnings: Evidence from a large sample of siblings and twins* (IZA Discussion Paper no. 5804). Bonn: IZA.

McManus, S., Meltzer, H., Brugha, T., Bebbington, P., & Jenkins, R. (2009). *Adult psychiatric morbidity in England, 2007: Results of a household survey.* London: National Centre for Social Research.

MIND (2010). *We need to talk. Getting the right therapy at the right time.* London: MIND.

Naylor, C., Parsonage, M., McDaid, D., Knapp, M., Fossey, M., & Galea, A. (2012). *Long-term conditions and mental health: The cost of co-morbidities.* London: The King's Fund and Centre for Mental Health.

Nimnuan, C., Hotopf, M., & Wessely, S. (2001). Medically unexplained symptoms: An epidemiological study in seven specialities. *Journal of Psychosomatological Research, 51*(1), 361–367.

Organisation for Economic Co-operation and Development (OECD) (2011). *Mental health and work: Evidence, challenges and policy directions.* Paris: OECD.

Payton, J. W., Weissberg, R. P., Durlak, J. A., Dymnicki, A. B., Taylor, R. D., Schellinger, K. B., & Pachan, M. (2008). *The positive impact of social and emotional learning for kindergarten to eighth-grade students: Findings from three scientific reviews*. Chicago, IL: Collaborative for Academic, Social and Emotional Learning (CASEL).

Proudfoot, J., Gray, J., Carson, J., Guest, D., & Dunn, G. (1999). Psychological training improves mental health and job-finding among unemployed people. *International Archives of Occupational and Environmental Health, 72*(suppl.) S40–S42.

Rollman, B. L., Belnap, B. H., Mazumdar, S., Houck, P. R., Zhu, F., Gardner, W., . . . Shear, M. K. (2005). A randomized trial to improve the quality of treatment for panic and generalized anxiety disorders in primary care. *Archives of General Psychiatry, 62*(12) 1332–1341.

Roth, A., & Fonagy, P. (2005). *What works for whom?* New York: Guilford Press.

Sainsbury Centre for Mental Health (2007). *Mental health at work: Developing the business case* (Policy paper 8). London: Sainsbury Centre for Mental Health.

Scott, S., Knapp, M., Henderson, J., & Maughan, B. (2001). Financial cost of social exclusion: Follow-up study of antisocial children into adulthood. *British Medical Journal, 323*(7306) 1–5.

Singleton, N., Bumpstead, R., O'Brien, M., Lee, A., & Meltzer, A. (2001). *Psychiatric morbidity among adults living in private households, 2000.* London: Office for National Statistics.

Timmins, N. (2001). *The five giants: A biography of the welfare state.* London: Harper Collins.

Wells, K. B., Sherbourne, C., Schoenbaum, M., Duan, N., Meredith, L., Unutzer, J., . . . Rubenstein, L. V. (2000). Impact of disseminating quality improvement programs for depression in managed primary care: A randomized controlled trial. *Journal of the American Medical Association, 283*(2), 212–220.

World Health Organization. (2002). *The World Health Report 2002—Reducing risks, promoting healthy life.* Geneva: World Health Organization.

Further Reading

Layard, R. (2011). *Happiness: Lessons from a new science* (2nd ed.). London: Penguin.

Centre for Economic Performance's Mental Health Policy Group (2012). *How mental illness loses out in the NHS.* London: London School of Economics and Political Science.

Part 2

Promoting Wellbeing
The Economic Case for Action

8

Investing in the Wellbeing of Young People

Making the Economic Case

David McDaid and A-La Park

London School of Economics and Political Science, U.K.

Candace Currie

University of St Andrews, U.K.

Cara Zanotti

University of South Australia, Australia

Introduction

The importance of childhood in molding us as adults has long been recognized. The sixteenth-century missionary St Francis Xavier is supposed to have said "give me the child until he is seven and I will give you the man." Five hundred years later the film maker Michael Apted continues to work on a series for British television called *7 Up*. This has followed a group of children from a diverse range of backgrounds every 7 years from the age of 7, so far until the age of 56; the assumption at the time of making the first series was that each child's socioeconomic status and personal circumstances would influence their life chances. Today, policy makers around the world are looking for evidence-informed actions to give children the best start in life. As we shall illustrate, economic arguments have lent further weight to the importance of early intervention in childhood,

The Economics of Wellbeing: Wellbeing: A Complete Reference Guide, Volume V.
Edited by David McDaid and Cary L. Cooper.
© 2014 John Wiley & Sons, Ltd. Published 2014 by John Wiley & Sons, Inc.
DOI: 10.1002/9781118539415.wbwell08

including contributions by the Nobel laureate economist James Heckman (Heckman, 2013) and Richard Layard writing in an earlier chapter in this volume.

This chapter will look in detail at the economic case for investing in measures to promote and protect the wellbeing of young people. We look at what is known about the long-term benefits of good wellbeing, as well as the consequences of poor wellbeing. We consider the potential economic costs and benefits of investing in actions to promote wellbeing and improve health. We then provide an overview of the potential cost-effectiveness of different strategies to promote wellbeing and prevent the onset of poor health and adverse life events.

We draw on a range of sources to look at impact. These include the Health Behaviour of School-aged Children study (HBSC) that has surveyed young people across Europe and North America five times since 1983. It focuses on social context, health outcomes, health behaviors, and risk behaviors—key factors that influence young people's health and wellbeing, opportunities and life chances (Currie et al., 2012). We also draw on work reviewing the economic benefits of promoting the mental and physical wellbeing of children (McDaid & Park, 2011; McDaid, Park, Currie, & Zanotti, 2011), supplemented by a further rapid review of the literature. All monetary data in the chapter have been converted to US$ and inflated to 2010 prices using the IMF World Economic Outlook Database 2011.

Why Is Economics Relevant to Child and Adolescent Wellbeing?

Fostering good wellbeing in children and young people is of great importance. Such wellbeing is influenced by many factors, such as the level of material resources available, access to and quality of education, psychological and physical health status, housing and the environment (Bradshaw, Martorano, Natali, & de Neuborg, 2013). Adverse experience and poor wellbeing in childhood may have long-lasting and profound consequences, which not only last into adulthood but affect future generations. It is important not only to have a good sense of what contributes to good wellbeing in childhood but also what actions can work to help promote and protect wellbeing. This means having access to good epidemiological and sociological data. It also requires carefully conducted evaluations of different actions targeted at different populations in different contexts and settings.

Many different questions might be asked. What, for instance, are the short-, mid- and long-term outcomes of these actions? Can they have an impact on school performance or influence social status in adulthood? Can they help provide young people with the skills to cope with different and difficult situations in life when they arise?

So where does economics fit in? If resources were limitless, it would be relatively straightforward to argue for investment in wellbeing promotion actions of proven effectiveness. Resources are, however, scarce, and careful choices have to be made about how to utilize what is available. Decisions are even more important in the context of economic downturns where health, social care, and education budgets are under even greater pressure. Evidence on effectiveness alone is insufficient for decision making; in addition to knowing what works and in what context, information on the economic impact of potential interventions is required. Such economic evidence is increasingly a formal element of decision-making processes, and can, as we shall see, in some circumstances be compelling in putting forward a case for policy change.

There are at least four key economic questions that it can be helpful to address in order to help provide decision makers with rationally based information to assist them with the difficult task of allocating resources (Knapp & McDaid, 2009) (see Box 8.1). We will consider these questions throughout the chapter, first beginning with the question of the impacts

---

Box 8.1.   Economic Questions to Inform Policy Making and Practice.

The costs of inaction: What are the economic consequences of *not* taking action to promote and protect the wellbeing of children and young people?

The costs of action: What would it cost to intervene by providing a promotive or preventive measure?

The cost-effectiveness of action: What is the balance between what it costs to intervene and what would be achieved in terms of better outcomes, e.g., emotional wellbeing, physical health, improved quality of life, educational performance?

The levers for change: What economic incentives can encourage more use of those interventions that are thought to be cost-effective and less use of those interventions which are not?

---

of not taking action—looking at what is known about any benefits gained through better wellbeing, as well as the consequences of poor wellbeing.

What Do We Know about the Long-Term Impacts of Wellbeing on Young People?

First, it is important to set out what aspects of child wellbeing we are focusing on in this chapter. As we have seen in earlier chapters in this volume, wellbeing can be thought of in many different ways, and this applies as much to children and young people as it does to adults. In recent years, in high-income countries wellbeing has been benchmarked using objective measures such as health status, access to education, quality of housing, and risky behaviors (Adamson, 2013).

Subjective wellbeing can also be measured through surveys of how children think and feel about their own lives and circumstances (Bradshaw et al., 2013). This latter approach can, however, be problematic, and cautions have been raised about its use—with some arguing that children with material disadvantage may nonetheless consider themselves to be satisfied with their life circumstances because they are unaware of what they are missing or are accepting of their circumstances (Ridge, 2002).

In addition, there are challenges in determining whether subjective wellbeing in children can reflect a long-term perspective rather than that of the immediate here and now. For this reason, while recognizing the importance of self-reported wellbeing in children and young people, we focus more on objective measures that are considered important to wellbeing, and in particular on issues related to health and education.

Positive Wellbeing

Most research that we discuss in this section focuses on looking at the long-term impacts of poor wellbeing on young people, as that is where the research evidence is concentrated. But we should not dismiss the value of positive wellbeing. Happiness in childhood is associated with social competence and good coping skills that lead to more positive outcomes in adulthood (Morgan et al., 2008). The HBSC 2009/2010 survey asked young people to rate their life satisfaction on a scale from 0 to 10, where a score of 6 or more was considered to be a high level of life satisfaction (Currie et al., 2012). While 79% and 86% of 15-year-old girls and boys

Table 8.1. Levels of High Life Satisfaction in 11- and 15-Year-Olds in Selected Countries in 2009/2010 HBSC Survey.

	11-year-olds who report high life satisfaction (%)		15-year-olds who report high life satisfaction (%)	
	Girls	Boys	Girls	Boys
Armenia	95	96	81	88
Canada	81	86	80	87
England	86	88	79	89
Hungary	86	88	75	82
Iceland	92	92	85	89
Romania	79	79	68	81
Turkey	70	74	58	63
United States	86	86	81	85
HBSC average	88	88	79	86

Source: Currie et al. (2012).

in the survey respectively reported having a high level of life satisfaction (Table 8.1), there was nonetheless a difference in positive levels of life satisfaction of as much as 10% for girls between the ages of 11 and 15. Low-income countries tend to have lower levels of positive satisfaction, but there can be great differences between the genders, as in Romania. Family affluence was significantly positively associated with high life satisfaction in nearly all countries.

Few researchers have looked at whether there are any long-term benefits of having good wellbeing in childhood. Yet this is important, as it can help determine whether there are any additional benefits to be gained over and above the avoidance of *negative* wellbeing. Should we, for instance, be concerned with the decreases in life satisfaction, for girls in particular, reported in the HBSC survey?

We can learn a little from work done analyzing follow-up data from a 1946 birth cohort study in Great Britain, where positive childhood wellbeing was assumed to be present in children whose teachers had rated them in the survey at ages 13 and 15 as being "very popular with other children," "unusually happy and contented," and "mak[ing] friends extremely easily" (Richards & Huppert, 2011). As Table 8.2 indicates, positive wellbeing in childhood was associated with more positive wellbeing and reduced risk of emotional problems when followed up to age 53. Those young people who had been rated as most positive by teachers had a 38% chance of

Table 8.2. Adulthood Wellbeing Outcomes in Happy Children at Ages 13 and 15 Compared to Children with No Positive Wellbeing Indicators.

Adult marker of wellbeing	Odds ratios and 95% confidence intervals
Life-course emotional profile (% moderate or severe) (age 53)	0.40 (0.32–0.50)
Work satisfaction and ambition (age 43) (%)	1.34 (1.04–1.71)
Work satisfaction (age 53)	1.29 (1.00–1.66)

Source: Richards and Huppert (2011).

moderate to severe emotional problems by the age of 53 compared to 65% in children with no positive ratings ($p < .001$). As Table 8.2 indicates, compared to children with no positive wellbeing, not only did positive children have a much lower likelihood of emotional problems, but they also had significantly higher likelihoods of work satisfaction at 43 ($p = .02$) and 53 years of age ($p = .05$). This research is encouraging, as it controlled for the presence of mental health problems, indicating that there are specific benefits associated with positive wellbeing. However, it is an area where much more research is needed. We still have very little information on the economic benefits associated with these better levels of positive wellbeing.

Impacts of Adverse Wellbeing

In contrast to the literature on positive wellbeing, there is a great deal of literature available on the many socioeconomic impacts of poor wellbeing in young people. Many adverse impacts may last well into adulthood (Allen, 2011; Case, Fertig, & Paxson, 2005; Case & Paxson, 2006; Fergusson, Horwood, & Ridder, 2005; Scott, Knapp, Henderson, & Maughan, 2001). These may include higher rates of health service use, increased contact with the criminal justice system, reduced levels of employment and often lower salaries when employed, and personal relationship difficulties. It is may also contribute to poor educational performance, which, in turn, may limit career options and the level of income that may be earned (Case & Paxson, 2006). Poor wellbeing in children can also have additional adverse consequences for parents, siblings and for their own future children. We look here at two aspects of poor health: obesity and mental health, as well as risky behaviors, educational opportunities and socio economic deprivation in childhood.

Health status.

Mental health. Some of the most powerful evidence can be seen in the findings of longitudinal studies conducted around the world that have tracked, in some cases over several decades, the long-term life consequences of poor mental health.

For example, one English study mapped the additional costs associated with conduct disorder (behavioral problems that reach the diagnostic threshold) and conduct problems (disruptive behavior, but not enough for diagnosis) in school compared to children with no behavioral problems from age 10 in 1970 to age 28 in 1988. As Figure 8.1 indicates, between the ages of 10 and 28, people who had conduct problems or conduct disorder in childhood imposed dramatically higher costs (about ten times greater) on society, particularly through criminal behavior and greater need of social work services, special education, and specialist health care (Scott et al., 2001). The authors also suggested greater investment in parenting programs. One U.K. study, which documented the health effects of parenting in mid-childhood, identified suboptimal parenting in a large proportion of the population (Waylen, Stallard, & Stewart-Brown, 2008). A systematic review of poor parent–child relationships also found that abusive relationships significantly increase the risk of anxiety, depression, suicidal behavior

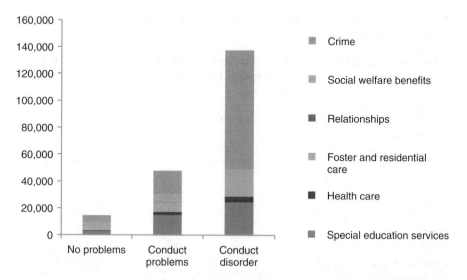

Figure 8.1. The Costs in Poor Mental Wellbeing by Age 28 for Young People with Behavioral Problems at Age 10 (US$ 2010). Adapted from Scott et al. (2001).

or post traumatic stress disorder in adulthood (Weich, Patterson, Shaw, & Stewart-Brown, 2009).

Analysis of the British 1946 birth cohort has reported significantly worse outcomes both for those children who had mild behavioral problems compared to no problems, as well as those with severe behavioral problems at age 13 compared to those with no problems (Colman et al., 2009). People who had mild or severe behavioral problems as children were more than twice or four times, respectively, as likely to have no educational qualifications compared to children with no problems. Both groups also had experienced significantly greater levels of life adversity than the general population and were working in manual jobs, while those with severe problems, unsurprisingly, were twice as likely to have reported multiple financial problems compared to the general population.

A study following up to age 25 children with behavioral problems between ages of 7 and 9, born in Christchurch, New Zealand, reported significantly worse outcomes in many areas of adult life that will have substantial economic impacts (Fergusson et al., 2005). Table 8.3 provides information on some of the outcomes showing results for the 5% of the cohort (46) children with the greatest level of behavioral problems at age 7–9 compared to the 50% (497) of the cohort with fewest behavioral problems at this age. There were striking differences in educational qualifications, with much higher rates of

Table 8.3. Socioeconomic Impacts by Age 25 of Behavioral Problems in Children Aged 7–9 in New Zealand.

Education / Employment outcome	50% of cohort of children with fewest behavioral problems	5% of children with most severe behavioral problems
No educational /vocational qualifications	6%	52%
University degree by age 25	36%	0%
Unemployed > 12 months between age 21 and 25	7%	17%
Welfare-dependent at 25	9%	33%
Became a parent before 20	6%	14%
Imprisoned ever	0%	8%
Drug-dependent	6%	15%
Mean gross income ($US 2010 prices)	$22,336	$16,063

All values between groups statistically significantly different (at least $p < .005$)

188

long-term unemployment. They were more likely to be welfare-dependent, to have been in prison, to be addicted to illegal drugs, and to become teenage parents. There was a mean difference of $6,273 in annual incomes (2010 prices).

This New Zealand study starkly shows the adverse impacts of poor wellbeing on educational achievements. Data in Great Britain from the 1958 National Child Development Study found persistent links between poor health in childhood and adult circumstances up to age 42 (Case et al., 2005; Palloni, Milesi, White, & Turner, 2009). In the United States, controlling for parental income, education, and social class, a direct link between poor child health and persistent significantly lower educational attainment, social economic status and poorer health than the general population can be observed (Case et al., 2005). Health problems that develop earlier in childhood at seven were also found to have a greater negative impact on educational attainment than those that developed at 16.

Using data from the U.S. Panel Study of Income Dynamics, the impacts of poor psychological health in childhood have been followed over 40 years. The reduction in earning power due to poor mental wellbeing in childhood was estimated to lead to an annual reduction in family income in adulthood of $10,866 or more than $313,000 over a working lifetime (Smith & Smith, 2010). The authors of this study suggested that their estimate would be "a significant understatement since it ignores the non-economic costs associated with these psychological disorders to individuals who experienced them. It also ignores the significant positive social costs with mental illness as treating children effectively will likely benefit their parents, siblings, classmates, and neighbors."

Obesity. The impacts of childhood obesity are perhaps overlooked in comparison to psychological health, but it is a significant issue. In the HBSC survey overall about 14% of 15-year-olds were overweight or obese, with average rates of 18% in boys and 10% in girls. The highest rates reported in the HBSC survey were to be found in the United States where 27% of girls and 34% of boys reported themselves to be obese or overweight (Currie et al., 2012). In most of these countries the risk of obesity was significantly lower in children from more affluent families.

Overweight children are more likely to become overweight adults (Deshmukh-Taskar et al., 2006; Krassas & Tzotzas, 2004). A systematic review of 11 studies that looked at the consequences in adulthood of childhood obesity reported risks of cardiometabolic morbidity to be as much as five times greater than in the nonobese child population (Reilly & Kelly, 2011). Overweight and obesity are strongly associated in adulthood with cardiovascular disease and diabetes, orthopaedic problems, and impaired psychological wellbeing (Gortmaker, Must, Perrin, Sobol, & Dietz, 1993).

Much of the data on the economic impact of obesity to date has focused on adults or the population as a whole, largely because there is a time lag between the onset of obesity and most major health impacts. Work undertaken by the OECD suggests that these costs are more than 1% of GDP per annum (Sassi, 2010). Where data are available on the costs of obesity for children, they tend to focus on the immediate direct costs of health care, as in Ireland, where inpatient hospital costs had risen in real terms from $9.34 million in 1997 to $20.66 million by 2004 (Vellinga, O'Donovan, & De La Harpe, 2008).

Lifetime medical costs of obesity have recently been modeled in the Netherlands from the age of 20 upwards and compared with the costs associated with smoking. Obesity had higher costs for individuals up to the age of 56 (van Baal et al., 2008). Obesity in young adults can be associated with an increased risk of premature withdrawal from the labor force, imposing additional costs on the public purse. Analysis of more than 1.1 million 18-year-old conscripts to the Swedish military over a 25-year period also reported significantly increased risks of between 30% and 300% for overweight to morbid obesity respectively for claiming disability pensions (Karnehed, Rasmussen, & Kark, 2007; Neovius, Kark, & Rasmussen, 2008).

Obesity can also have psychological impacts; children who are obese in some cultures may be at greater risk of social exclusion and bullying (Madowitz, Knatz, Maginot, Crow, & Boutelle, 2012; Mamun, O'Callaghan, Williams, & Najman, 2012). U.S. data on individuals aged 16 to 24 who were obese and were then followed up 7 years later, found that women had significantly lower levels of time in education, were less likely to be married, and had a lower socioeconomic status (Gortmaker et al., 1993). Men were less likely to be married but there was less impact on socioeconomic status, in line with other U.S. studies.

Risky behaviors.
Another aspect of wellbeing is engagement in risky behaviors. Here we consider three: tobacco and alcohol consumption and sexual behavior.

Alcohol consumption. The HBSC Survey 2009/2010 provided data on 15-year-olds who drank alcohol at least once a week (Currie et al., 2012).

Table 8.4. Percentage of 15-Year-Olds Who Drink at Least Once a Week. Highest 5 Countries/Regions HBSC Survey 2009/2010.

Girls (%)		Boys (%)	
Greece	34	Czech Republic	44
Czech Republic	33	Ukraine	44
Ukraine	30	Greece	43
Wales	29	Croatia	43
Austria	28	Italy	39
HBSC	17	HBSC	25

Table 8.4 shows the highest rates of consumption for boys and girls. On average 25% of boys and 17% of girls drank alcohol each week. Rates varied from a high of 34% of all 15-year-old girls in Greece to just 5% of girls in Iceland. Forty-four per cent of 15-year-old boys in the Czech Republic and the Ukraine consume alcohol every week compared to just 7% in Finland.

Risky drinking, including frequent and binge drinking, can have adverse psychological, social, and physical health consequences, including interpersonal violence, accidents, and unprotected sex. Adolescent binge drinking, identified through the 1970 British Birth Cohort Study, is a predictor of adversity and social exclusion in adult life, including increased risk of homelessness and lower socio economic status (Viner & Taylor, 2007). A systematic review of 54 studies looking at the long-term consequences of drinking behaviors for adolescents aged 15–19 found consistent evidence that higher alcohol consumption increases the risk of alcohol addiction and other related adverse events in adulthood (McCambridge, McAlaney, & Rowe, 2011). Evidence from Great Britain suggests that women who rarely or never drank at age 16 were significantly less likely to be binge drinkers in adulthood, while young men who drank heavily at age 16 were significantly more likely to be binge drinkers in adulthood than light drinkers (Jefferis, Power, & Manor, 2005).

The economic impacts on crime of the drunkenness in young people aged 10 to 17 in England have been estimated to be more than $9.54 million per annum: $7.25 million for violent crime and $2.29 million in property damage. It also estimated that the costs of attending acute emergency care units for 15–16 year olds due to drunkenness would be $7.64 million per annum (Jones, Stokes, & Bell, 2007). U.S. and South Korean studies also report substantial costs due to absence from the labor force and premature

Table 8.5. Percentage of 15-Year-Olds Who Smoke at Least Once a Week. Highest 5 Countries/Regions. HBSC Survey 2009/2010.

Girls (%)		Boys (%)	
Greenland	61	Greenland	53
Austria	29	Lithuania	34
Czech Republic	28	Latvia	32
Hungary	26	Ukraine	31
Croatia	25	Croatia	27
HBSC	17	HBSC	19

mortality (Miller, Levy, Spicer, & Taylor, 2006; Kim, Chung, Lee, & Park, 2010).

Smoking. Data from the 2009/2010 HBSC survey shows that rates of smoking at least once a week averaged 6% at age 13, increasing to 18% by age 15 (Currie et al., 2012). Table 8.5 shows the highest rates of smoking for 15-year-old boys and girls. In this survey rates of smoking for 15-year-olds tended to be higher in eastern Europe: 29% of Austrian girls and 28% of Czech girls were smoking every week at 15 compared with rates of just 7% in the United States and Iceland. Around a third of 15-year-old boys in Latvia and Lithuania were smoking every week compared with 8% of Canadians, and 9% of English, Icelandic, Norwegian, and U.S. boys. In the most deprived population in the survey, in Greenland, extraordinarily 61% of girls and 53% of boys were smoking every week.

The long-term economic impacts of smoking that starts specifically in childhood are not well documented, although much has been written about the economic impact of smoking in adults, in terms of health-care costs, premature mortality and time off work because of smoking-related illness (Parrott & Godfrey, 2004). Importantly, at least two thirds of adult smokers in very different country settings begin smoking in their teenage years (Freedman, Nelson, & Feldman, 2012; Giovino et al., 2012; Muttarak et al., 2013; Oh et al., 2010).

There is well-documented evidence on the harmful health effects of cigarette use, which can cause many chronic respiratory and cardiovascular diseases such as lung cancer, heart diseases, stroke, and hypertension (U.S. Department of Health and Human Services, 1994). The earlier an individual starts smoking, the more difficulty they will generally have in quitting smoking at a later age; the likelihood of dying of cancer due to smoking is three times higher if an individual begins smoking at 15 compared with someone who takes up smoking in their mid-20s (Department of Health, 1998).

Some useful evidence of economic impact in childhood can be taken from research looking at the impacts of passive smoking in children. Passive smoking in households is also an issue: a report from the Royal College of Physicians in England reported that children growing up with parents or siblings who smoke are also 90% more likely to become smokers themselves (Royal College of Physicians, 2010). The report also estimated that the future costs of treating smokers who take up the habit because of exposure to parental smoking as children, could be as much as $10.59 million annually, while almost the same level of costs, $10.41 million, would be incurred through lost productivity due to illness and smoking breaks every year. There will also be external costs, through passive smoking, to others from their own smoking as adults. It also found that passive smoking by parents leads to primary care visits by children costing $18 million and hospital admissions costing $25.26 million every year. Providing children with drugs to treat asthma developed as a result of passive smoking would cost a further €7.43 million every year (Royal College of Physicians, 2010).

Sexual behavior.   The promotion of safe and healthy sexual behavior is a key issue for young people. Unprotected sex carries with it the risk of unwanted teenage pregnancy, potential abortion, or single/early motherhood and sexually transmitted infections. As the 2009/2010 HBSC survey indicates (Table 8.6), about 23% of girls and 29% of boys had sexual intercourse by age 15 with rates as high as 48% for boys in Romania and 71% of girls in Greenland (Currie et al., 2012). Pregnancies also vary across the EU,

Table 8.6.   Percentage of 15-Year-Olds Who Have Had Sexual Intercourse. Highest 5 Countries/Regions HBSC Survey 2009/2010.

Girls (%)		Boys (%)	
Greenland	71	Romania	48
Wales	39	Greenland	46
Denmark	38	Armenia	45
Scotland	35	Ukraine	40
England	32	Denmark	38
HBSC	23	HBSC	29

ranging from about 12 per 1,000 women aged 15–19 in Italy to 59 in Bulgaria. Rates of over 50 per 1,000 are also found in Romania and the U.K. (Barnekow, Currie, Letsch, de Looze, & Morgan, 2009).

There is a wide body of literature on the long-term adverse consequences of poor sexual and reproductive health, particularly in respect of teenage pregnancy. Data from the United Kingdom also report that 43% of women who had their first child below the age of 20 are likely to be in low-income households, compared with 21% of households where the age of the mother at first birth was between 23 and 32 (Hobcraft & Kiernan, 2001). U.S. data also report that teenage mothers are much less likely to complete schooling than their peers who do not have a child until 30 (Hofferth, Reid, & Mott, 2001).

The children of teenage mothers are themselves more likely to be socially and economically disadvantaged (Boden, Fergusson, & Horwood, 2008). A study following a cohort of more than 1,000 children from birth to age 18 in New Zealand, found that children of teenage mothers were at between 1.5 and 9 times greater risk of having adverse outcomes compared to children whose mothers were over 30: 41% left school without any qualifications compared with just 1.1% for those with mothers over 30 ($p < .0001$); 16.7% were frequent offenders compared to 5.7% of the older group; ($p < .001$); 9% versus 1.4% attempted suicide ($p < 0.01$); 23% versus 9% were regular smokers ($p < .0001$). Children born into families with older mothers were more likely to be brought up in a more stable and nurturing environment (Fergusson & Woodward, 1999). Similar impacts on the children of teenage mothers have been reported in the United States (Hofferth & Reid, 2002).

All of these adverse outcomes have substantial economic consequences, but there appear to have been few attempts to actually quantify the economic costs of teenage pregnancy. In England the annual costs of teenage pregnancy to the health system have been estimated in one study to be $158 million per annum; social welfare payments to mothers who do not enter work in the 3 years following birth can range between $47,440 and €62,421 (Dennison, 2004). The study also noted that they are also much more likely to require targeted help and support in respect of issues such as housing, education, employment, and training. The education economist Rebecca Maynard in the United States estimated that the annual incremental costs to the public purse (through the need for social welfare payments and health care costs) of childbearing among teenagers is more than double the costs for women who give birth in their twenties (Maynard, 1997).

In 2004 she estimated that the costs in the United States attributable to adverse outcomes in the children of teenage mothers were $10.44 billion per annum (Hoffman, 2006). Of these costs 23% can be attributed to the increased time that these children were likely to spend in prison compared to the children of mothers over the age of 20.

Education and income.
Poor educational status, for instance, increases the risk of being a teenage mother, which, in turn, increases the risks to the health of a child who then may not achieve a good education (Fiscella & Kitzman, 2009). Equally, low-income households are at increased risk of poor childhood health, which, in turn, increases the risk of the next generation also being in a low-income household. Systematic reviews of long-running interventions to improve childhood development and educational opportunities for children have a positive and persistent impact on cognitive development and education attainment.

Even in societies with strong social protection systems, lower levels of income inequality, and good access to education, poverty in childhood still has adverse outcomes in adulthood. Work in Norway looking at data over 10 years on children in families receiving social welfare payments because of their low incomes indicates that most are likely to eventually claim such payments themselves as adults (Lorentzen, Dahl, & Harsløf, 2011). Low childhood socioeconomic status in Norway has also been associated with increased mortality for most causes of death, other than breast cancer, during young adulthood (ages 25–35) in a study looking at people born between 1955 and 1965 (Strand & Kunst, 2007).

What Do We Know about the Economic Benefits of Promoting and Protecting the Wellbeing of Young People?

We now turn to the three remaining economic questions in Box 8.1 and consider the merits of investing in actions to promote wellbeing. As we will show, this is encouraging; potentially there are a number of different actions that generate substantial economic returns because of the long-lasting adverse impacts to health and other aspects of life resulting from poor wellbeing in childhood. Indeed, the economist James Heckman has argued the greatest economic returns are to be made by focusing on early intervention in childhood such as supportive services for new mothers and their infants, preschool support and actions in schools (Heckman, 2006, 2013). He noted that such investment not only reduces inequalities between disadvantaged children and their peers, but broadly "promotes schooling, raises the quality of the workforce, enhances the productivity of schools and reduces crime, teenage pregnancy and welfare dependency. They raise earnings and promote social attachment" (Heckman, 2006). There are economic returns to be made from actions later in the life course, such as during the transition from adolescence to adulthood, but these are likely to be less pronounced, as children will already have been influenced by earlier life events and the emotional and cognitive skills that they have already acquired.

Here we describe interventions that are about much more than maintaining health. They include actions to strengthen emotional resilience, as well as good noncognitive skills including motivation, perseverance, assets, and capabilities. Non-health-sector interventions can include social welfare support for those on low incomes, as well as special educational support. In this section of the chapter we highlight examples of some of the potential economic payoffs from investment in actions to promote health, decrease risky behaviors, and address social-economic disadvantage.

Protecting and Promoting Health

Psychological wellbeing.
Robust reviews indicate that effective interventions to promote and protect the psychological wellbeing of children include antenatal and perinatal maternal mental health programs, parenting support programs in infancy and preschool years with a focus on maternal sensitivity and infant bonding, parenting programs targeted at the general or high-risk populations with a focus on child behavior, and specialist parent support programs for very high-risk groups, where parents may have severe mental health problems or may be neglecting their children (Stewart-Brown & Schrader-McMillan, 2011).

School also provides a good opportunity to engage with children. A range of interventions can be delivered in school for the benefit of mental health, social, emotional, and educational outcomes (Weare & Nind, 2011). The characteristics of more effective school interventions include teaching skills, focusing on positive mental health, starting early with the youngest children and continuing with older ones, operating for a lengthy period of time, embedding this work within the school curriculum, and better liaison with parents. These interventions can, however, be ineffective if not implemented with clarity, intensity, and fidelity. A recent systematic review (Corrieri et al., 2013) identified 24 trials in schools of interventions to prevent depression. Sixteen reported significant lower levels of depression, although the clinical size of these effect differences was very small but did persist over the long term for both universal and targeted interventions.

There is a literature on the cost-effectiveness of some of these interventions (McDaid & Park, 2011; Mihalopoulos, Vos, Pirkis, & Carter, 2011). Ensuring that new mothers and their children come into regular contact with health visitors can be highly cost-effective and help promote better maternal–infant bonding. The Nurse Family Partnership program developed in New York in the 1980s (Olds, Henderson, Phelps, Kitzman, & Hanks, 1993) followed up 400 women from different socioeconomic backgrounds over 15 years (Olds et al., 1997). The economic case for home visiting for all women, not just those at high risk, was strong (Karoly et al., 1998; Karoly, Kilburn, & Cannon, 2005). Benefits outweighed costs by a factor of 5.7 to 1 for high-risk women and 1.26 to 1 for low-risk women.

A randomized controlled trial of health visitors who delivered psychological therapies to women at high risk of post-natal depression also improved outcomes at lower costs than health visitor usual care. There was a 90% chance that this would be cost-effective in an English context (Morrell et al., 2009). Home visiting was also compared with participation in a mother–child attachment group intervention in Canada. While no difference in effects was reported, costs were significantly lower in the attachment group (Niccols, 2008). In the United Kingdom a controlled trial of an intensive home visiting and social support program for vulnerable families where children could be at risk of abuse or neglect reported a cost per unit improvement in maternal sensitivity and infant cooperativeness of $5,682 (Barlow et al., 2007; McIntosh, Barlow, Davis, & Stewart-Brown, 2009). With this study the challenge is to judge whether this improvement in wellbeing represents value for money, as it uses a clinical outcome measure that cannot be compared with other uses of resources within the health-care system.

Looking at parenting programs, the more robust evidence tends to focus on children already identified as being at risk of emotional health problems rather than the population as a whole. An evaluation of one parenting program in Wales, the Webster-Stratton Incredible Years (IY) program, found it to be cost-effective for all 3–5-year-old children at risk of conduct disorder, but even more cost-effective if targeted at children with the highest risk of developing conduct disorder (Edwards, Ceilleachair, Bywater, Hughes, & Hutchings, 2007). Analysis from a trial looking at 3–8-year-old children in the United States also suggests that combining the parenting component of IY with child-based training and teacher training, even though more expensive, can be more cost-effective (Foster, 2010). In an Australian context, another parenting program delivered to all children, with stepped care actions targeted at children with behavioral problems and their parents, known as Triple-P, has been modeled to be cost-effective in most circumstances (Mihalopoulos et al., 2011). The costs and benefits of parenting programs to prevent conduct disorders have also recently been modeled in England over a 25-year period. Overall benefits exceed the costs of the program by more than 8:1 because of the substantial costs of crime in adolescence and adulthood that can be avoided (Bonin, Stevens, Beecham, Byford, & Parsonage, 2011).

The cost-effectiveness of after-school screening and subsequent psychological intervention has been compared with usual health support in the curriculum for Australian teenagers (aged 11–17 years) with elevated depressive symptom levels (Mihalopoulos, Vos, Pirkis, & Carter, 2012). Looking just at impacts on the health system, the intervention was found to be cost-effective in 98% of all scenarios modeled, with a baseline cost of $3,500 per disability adjusted life year (DALY) avoided. In the United States a controlled trial targeted at-risk-group teenagers (13–18 years) who had parents with depressive disorder (Lynch et al., 2005). They were offered a 15-session cognitive behavioral intervention. From a societal perspective the incremental cost per QALY gained was $9,275. This remained robust under various sensitivity analyses, suggests that the intervention would be cost-effective in most high-income country settings.

There is also economic evidence supporting school-based wellbeing promotion programs. The Caring School Community scheme developed in the United States (Battistich, Schaps, Watson, & Solomon, 1996) aimed at strengthening students' connectedness to school—an important element for increasing academic motivation and achievement and for reducing drug use, violence, and delinquency. It can be delivered for just a handful of dollars per pupil and has been estimated to potentially generate a return on investment of 28:1, looking only at impacts on drug dependency and violence (Aos, Lieb, Mayfield, Miller, & Pennucci, 2004). Implementation of evidence-based promotion programs as part of another scheme, the Communities That Care program, also suggests net benefits of between 5:1 and 10:1, even when looking only at the benefits of reduced smoking and delinquency (Kuklinski, Briney, Hawkins, & Catalano, 2012).

The Seattle Social Development Project implemented a teacher and parent intervention, including child social and emotional development, for 6 years. The children involved in the project were then followed up from age 12 to 21 (Hawkins, Kosterman, Catalano, Hill, & Abbott, 2005). Costs of $5,412 per child for the project were outweighed by benefits from the avoidance of violence, smoking, and drug abuse that were three times as great. Again this analysis is conservative, as no monetary value was placed on significant improvements seen in mental and emotional health (Aos et al., 2004).

Another school-based intervention is the Good Behavior Game (GBG), an approach that seeks to instil positive behaviors in children through participation in a game, with prizes given to winning teams who behave better (Kellam et al., 2011). Focusing solely on the economic benefits from evidence on a reduction in tobacco use rather than on any of its other wellbeing benefits, an economic analysis reported a return on investment of 25:1 (Aos et al., 2004).

Thus, the economic evidence for interventions to promote better psychological wellbeing is promising. However, a major limitation remains a lack of evidence on the long-term impacts of use of these programs; we do not know, for instance, whether their effects decay over time or if additional follow-up "booster" programs can improve their long-term effectiveness. At the same time, acceptability issues, particularly to intervention providers, including schools and mental health professionals, need to be considered before any large-scale implementation, especially when transferring programs between very different socioeconomic contexts, both within and across countries.

Tackling obesity.
Despite the potential long-term impacts of overweight and obesity in childhood there have only been a handful of economic studies looking to tackle this issue. Work in Australia looking at the economic case for prevention in general identified a number of programs where savings to the health-care system over the life of the child outweighed the costs of intervention (Carter et al., 2009). These included education programs to reduce television viewing, reduction in TV advertising for high-fat and/or high-sugar foods and drinks directed at children (Magnus, Haby, Carter, & Swinburn, 2009), family-based general practitioner programs targeted

at families of overweight or moderately obese children (Moodie, Haby, Wake, Gold, & Carter, 2008) and school-based educational programs to encourage better nutritional intake, reduced consumption of sugary drinks, and participation in physical activity (Carter et al. 2009). Not all interventions have been found to be cost-effective—these include a "Walking School Bus" program for primary school children, drug therapy, and gastric banding (Carter et al., 2009), an active transport program for primary school children (Moodie, Haby, Galvin, Swinburn, & Carter, 2009) and an after-school physical activity program (Moodie, Carter, Swinburn, & Haby, 2010). In contrast, in Spain, a controlled trial of more than 1,000 nine- and ten-year-olds, where some schools implemented a structured program of after school physical activities, three times a week for 90 minutes per session, was reported to cost less than the usual after-school physical activity programs that were being offered and to lead to a reduction in overweight in girls but an increase in body fat in boys (Moya Martinez et al., 2011; Salcedo Aguilar et al., 2010).

Economic models have also been used to help estimate some of the potential long-term impacts of different interventions to prevent/tackle obesity. In the United States a controlled trial involving 10 secondary schools in Boston looked at short-term (2-year) changes in body mass index following the implementation of an interdisciplinary curriculum intended to decrease TV and fatty food consumption, as well as increase the intake of fruit, vegetables, and moderate exercise. Modeling was then used to predict the transition to obesity from age 14 to 40. The program only appeared to be effective in girls (perhaps emphasizing the need for more contextual research on the acceptability of interventions) and overall the program was estimated to cost just $5,076 per QALY gained (Wang, Yang, Lowry, & Wechsler, 2003).

A combination of actions including the use of food labeling, food advertising self-regulation, school-based intervention, mass media campaigns, and physician-dietician counselling in primary care had a cost per DALY gained of less than $10,000 in OECD countries (Sassi, 2010). Another economic model in the United Kingdom using data on the effectiveness of lifestyle interventions for children reported a cost per life year gained of $20,589 (Hollingworth et al., 2012). Both of these models also suggest that intervention is cost-effective, albeit acknowledging that it would take many years for all the benefits to be gained. However, one challenge with these economic payoffs is that it remains to be seen whether a reduction in body mass index in childhood can be maintained in adult life.

Addressing Risky Behaviors

Actions to prevent alcohol-related harm.

Much of the economic analysis to date tends to focus on actions targeted at adults. This includes interventions which will also have some impact on younger people. Advertising bans and increases in taxation can help reduce alcohol consumption in a cost-effective manner, as evidenced in Estonia (Chisholm, Rehm, Van Ommeren, & Monteiro, 2004; Lai, Habicht, Reinap, Chisholm, & Baltussen, 2007).

Modeling work for the National Institute of Health and Care Excellence (NICE) in England on school-based interventions to prevent and reduce alcohol-related harm among children and young people concluded that they are likely to be cost-effective because of substantial adverse costs avoided (Jones et al, 2007). A family-focused intervention in the United States, the Iowa Strengthening Families Program (ISFP), had the objective of delaying the start of drinking alcohol. It consisted of seven sessions with 11–12-year-old students from 33 rural schools and their parents. Benefits of the intervention exceeded costs by a ratio of 9:1 (Spoth, Guyll, & Day, 2002). Evaluation of various alcohol and drug prevention programs in the United States that were targeted at children and young people has also generated favorable benefit-to-cost ratios, ranging from 5:1 to 100:1 (Aos et al., 2004).

Actions to prevent the uptake of smoking in children and young people.

Given that it has been known for a considerable period of time that the harmful health consequences of smoking begin early in life, a number of economic evaluations have looked specifically at interventions to either prevent the uptake of smoking in young people, or, alternatively, to provide them with support to quit. Most of these studies have been conducted in the United States, showing very favorable cost-effectiveness ratios generating significant savings. One example from elsewhere concerns a potentially cost-effective intervention in Germany, where school classes for children aged 11–14 were given incentives to be smoke-free for 6 months. Prizes, including trips abroad, were on offer to the best-performing class. Students and their teachers monitored performance. Smoking increased by 16% in the intervention group compared with 21% in the control group ($p < .001$). Taking a lifetime perspective and looking at impacts on the health system and participation in the workforce the program was found to be cost-effective. For every $1 spent there would be a return of $3.6.

In the Netherlands a generic school-based program was estimated to have a cost per QALY gained of $25,174 (Vijgen, van Baal, Hoogenveen, de Wit, & Feenstra, 2008). In the United States an enhanced nationwide school-based anti-tobacco education program was compared with the status quo (Tengs, Osgood, & Chen, 2001). Modeling outcomes and costs over 50 years, depending on assumptions about the decaying effects of the intervention, cost per QALY gained ranged from $5,860 to $405,277. If only 30% of program effects were assumed to end after 4 years, it had a favorable cost per QALY gained of $23,839, with similar results reported from a Canadian study (Wang & Crosset, 2001).

In Florida, a cost-effectiveness analysis looking at a two-year statewide school-based smoking cessation program, the American Lung Association's Not On Tobacco (N-O-T) for young people aged 17 to 25 years, was also highly cost-effective compared to a brief intervention (Dino, Horn, Abdulkadri, Kalsekar, & Branstetter, 2008). A review for NICE of a generic school-based smoking prevention program also involved economic modeling (Jit, Barton, Chen, & Uthman, 2009). This looked at the long-term economic costs and benefits as a result of prevention of smoking in adulthood, based on different assumptions about the delay/decrease in the initiation of smoking. Under most scenarios the intervention was very cost-effective with a cost per QALY gained ranging from $5,733 to $24,271. The case for investing in a mass media campaign to prevent smoking uptake in young people aged between 11 and 18 was also estimated as part of this NICE review. This appears to be even more cost-effective at a cost of $4,127 per QALY gained. U.S. studies combining mass media campaigns with school tobacco prevention programs (Secker-Walker, Worden, Holland, Flynn, & Detsky, 1997) and with increased taxation have also been reported as cost-effective or even cost-saving (Fishman & Ebel, 2005).

Cost-effective actions to improve sexual health.
Few economic evaluations have been conducted of education and behavioral interventions to prevent teenage pregnancy. One exception is the evaluation of a neighborhood program targeted at disadvantaged adolescents of both sexes between the ages of 11 and 18 in New Britain, Connecticut (Rosenthal et al., 2009). This intervention involved education about life, family, sex, academic support and tutoring, career and vocational guidance, artistic expression, and access to mental health services. It looked at the impacts on the income of fathers, foster care, and long-term costs linked to poor outcomes for children of teenage mothers. The long-term economic

impacts on participants in the program to age 30 (due to benefits of increased educational opportunities) were estimated. Taking this long-term perspective, the net benefits of the program were $11,262 per participant.

In an earlier study, in the absence of previous cost-effectiveness studies, work was undertaken in England for NICE to assess the case for investing in counselling, emergency contraception, and abortions to avoid unwanted conceptions in women under the age of 18. Emergency contraception at a cost of $7,850 per conception avoided was by far the least costly option; the costs per conception averted for one-to-one counselling by a primary care nurse would be in excess of $86,375 (Lewis & Barham, 2006). This analysis did not model any longer term health and non-health benefits and the costs of an unwanted conception. However, there are also likely to be benefits from counselling due to a reduction in sexually transmitted disease which were not factored into this analysis. The study, which also looked at the cost-effectiveness of screening and subsequent treatment for sexually transmitted infections, largely in US populations, generally reported screening to be cost-effective in reducing further infections (Barham, Lewis, & Latimer 2007).

Preschool Interventions

There are many broad social welfare actions that may help improve the wellbeing of children, which we cannot go into in detail here. For instance, as discussed by McDaid and Wahlbeck in a later chapter in this volume, family income support programs at times of economic crisis can be protective of psychological wellbeing. We have also already noted the benefits of good access to support services such as health visitors.

Here we highlight briefly the economic case for investing in extra measures to support the preschool education of very young children and give additional support to children in the first years of school. Systematic reviews of long-running interventions to improve childhood development and educational opportunities for children demonstrate they can have a positive and persistent impact on cognitive development and education attainment (Camilli, Vargas, Ryan, & Barnett, 2010; Nores & Barnett, 2010). They can also be associated with a range of improved outcomes to adulthood, although it may be difficult to replicate all of the benefits of these studies when scaled up to national level programs (Barnett, 2011).

There is also some information on their long-term economic impacts. The most well-known study concerns the Perry Pre-School Study where, between 1962 and 1967, disadvantaged three- and four-year-old children living in an urban setting were randomized between one group who received high-quality preschool education for 2.5 hours per day, plus home visits and tutoring, and another who did not. The study found that adults at age 40 who had received the preschool program had higher earnings, were more likely to hold a job, had committed fewer crimes, and were more likely to have graduated from high school than adults who did not have preschool education. By age 40 substantial economic benefits of 13:1 had been generated, with 87% of benefits being due to crime avoided, with other benefits from reduced costs to the education system, increased taxes on earnings, and avoidance of welfare payments. This is conservative as benefits in terms of improved health were not considered (Schweinhart et al., 2005).

The long-term costs and benefits of another pre-school education program, Abecedarian, have also been evaluated (Barnett & Masse, 2007). The program, delivered in rural North Carolina, provided up to 10 hours a day of educational experiences, plus good nutrition and health support, to children from their first year of life until they entered kindergarten (up to 5 years). Participants were followed up to the age of 21. Benefits were reported to outweigh costs by almost 4:1, including benefits for future earnings, better health through avoidance of smoking, primary and secondary school education savings, and reduced welfare use. Costs of the program included public funding towards additional participation in higher education.

Another program in Chicago, Child Parent Centers, delivered in 24 different locations from the age of three, along with nutritional support and outreach to parents and continued to age nine, has also been assessed. Participants were followed to age 21 and benefit–cost ratios between 6:1 and 10:1 were observed (Temple & Reynolds, 2007). Models have also been used to estimate the potential benefits and costs of preschool programs: with better future adult earnings alone estimated to generate benefit–cost ratios of between 3:1 and 4:1 (Bartika, Gormley, & Adelstein, 2012).

Conclusion

This chapter has highlighted the many long-term consequences of poor wellbeing that emerges in childhood. While St Francis Xavier may have been wrong to assume that our adult characters are fully determined by life experiences before the age of seven, it is clear that many cost-effective actions to promote and protect wellbeing can be delivered in the first years of life, or even before birth, by addressing the wellbeing needs of families. There are also many actions targeted at young people aged well above seven, particularly to address risky behaviors and behavioral problems and to promote healthy lifestyles.

Challenges remain. In particular, while longitudinal studies have given us powerful information on the consequences of poor wellbeing, less has been said about the economic benefits of positive wellbeing as opposed to the absence of impairments to wellbeing. Furthermore, when it comes to looking at the effectiveness of interventions, with the exception of some early education interventions and health visitor visiting schemes, we still know little about the actual long-term benefits of interventions. Models have been used to project benefits, but these have made many assumptions about the extent to which the positive benefits of interventions are maintained. There now needs to be long-term follow-up of participants to adulthood of more interventions, including parenting programs.

We also need to understand more about the reasons why young people do or do not engage in wellbeing-promoting programs, so as to better understand how they can be improved and also aid in their potential implementation in many different countries with very different cultural and socioeconomic contexts. Addressing these issues will help facilitate ever more judicious investment so as to maximize opportunities to give our children the best start in life.

References

Adamson, P. (2013). *Child wellbeing in rich countries: A comparative overview.* Florence: UNICEF Office of Research—Innocenti.

Allen, G. (2011). *Early intervention: The next steps.* London: Department of Work and Pensions. http://www.dwp.gov.uk/docs/early-intervention-next-steps.pdf.

Aos, S., Lieb, R., Mayfield, J., Miller, M., & Pennucci, A. (2004). *Benefits and costs of prevention and early intervention programs for youth.* Olympia, WA: Institute for Public Policy.

Barham, L., Lewis, D., & Latimer, N. (2007). One to one interventions to reduce sexually transmitted infections and under the age of 18 conceptions: A systematic review of the economic evaluations. *Sexually Transmitted Infections, 83*(6), 441–446.

Barlow, J., Davis, H., McIntosh, E., Jarrett, P., Mockford, C., & Stewart-Brown, S. (2007). Role of home visiting in improving parenting and health in families at risk of abuse and neglect: Results of a multicentre randomised controlled trial and economic evaluation. *Archives of Disease in Childhood, 92*(3), 229–233.

Barnekow, V., Currie, C., Letsch, C., de Looze, M., & Morgan, A. (2009). *A snapshot of the health of young people in Europe.* Copenhagen: World Health Organization, Regional Office for Europe.

Barnett, W. S. (2011). Effectiveness of early education intervention. *Science, 333*(6045), 975–978.

Barnett, W. S., & Masse, L. N. (2007). Comparative benefit–cost analysis of the Abecedarian program and its policy implications. *Economics of Education Review, 26*(1), 113–125.

Bartika, T. J., Gormley, W., & Adelstein, S. (2012). Earnings benefits of Tulsa's pre-K program for different income groups. *Economics of Education Review, 31,* 1143–1161.

Battistich, V., Schaps, E., Watson, M., & Solomon, D. (1996). Prevention effect of the child development project: Early findings from an ongoing multisite demonstration trial. *Journal of Adolescent Research, 11,* 12–35.

Boden, J. M., Fergusson, D. M., & Horwood, L. J. (2008). Early motherhood and subsequent life outcomes. *Journal of Child Psychology and Psychiatry, 49*(2), 151–160.

Bonin, E., Stevens, M., Beecham, J., Byford, S., & Parsonage, M. (2011). Parenting interventions for the prevention of persistent conduct disorders. In M. Knapp, D. McDaid & M. Parsonage (Eds.), *Mental health promotion and prevention: The economic case* (pp. 6–8). London: Department of Health.

Bradshaw, J., Martorano, B., Natali, L., & de Neuborg, C. (2013). *Children's subjective wellbeing in rich countries.* Working Paper 2013–03. Florence: UNICEF Office of Research.

Camilli, G., Vargas, S., Ryan, S., & Barnett, W. S. (2010). Meta-analysis of the effects of early education interventions on cognitive and social development. *Teachers College Record, 112*(3), 579–620.

Carter, R., Moodie, M., Markwick, A., Magnus, A. Vos, T. Swinburn, B., & Haby, M. M. (2009). Assessing cost-effectiveness in obesity (ACE-obesity): An overview of the ACE approach, economic methods and cost results. *BMC Public Health, 9,* 419.

Case, A., Fertig, A., & Paxson, C. (2005). The lasting impact of childhood health and circumstance. *Journal of Health Economy, 24*(2), 365–389.

Case, A., & Paxson, C. (2006). Children's health and social mobility. *Future Child, 16*(2), 151–173.

Chisholm, D., Rehm, J., Van Ommeren, M., & Monteiro, M. (2004). Reducing the global burden of hazardous alcohol use: A comparative cost-effectiveness analysis. *Journal of Studies on Alcohol and Drugs, 65*(6), 782–793.

Colman, I., Murray, J., Abbott, R. A., Maughan, B., Kuh, D., Croudace, T. J., & Jones, P. B. (2009). Outcomes of conduct problems in adolescence: 40 year follow-up of national cohort. *British Medical Journal, 338,* a2981.

Corrieri, S., Heider, D., Conrad, I., Blume, B., Konig, H. H., & Riedel-Heller, S. G. (2013). School-based prevention programs for depression and anxiety in adolescence: A systematic review. *Health Promotion International.* doi: 10.1093/heapro/dat001.

Currie, C., Zanotti, C., Morgan, A., Currie, D., de Looze, M., Roberts, C., . . . Barnekow, V. (2012). *Social determinants of health and well-being among young people. Health Behaviour in School-aged Children (HBSC) study: International report from the 2009/2010 survey.* Copenhagen: WHO Regional Office for Europe.

Dennison, C. (2004). *Teenage pregnancy: An overview of the research evidence.* London: Health Development Agency.

Department of Health (1998). *Smoking kills: A white paper on tobacco (Cm 4177).* Norwich: The Stationery Office.

Deshmukh-Taskar, P., Nicklas, T. A., Morales, M., Yang, S. J., Zakeri, I., & Berenson, G. S. (2006). Tracking of overweight status from childhood to young adulthood: The Bogalusa heart study. *European Journal of Clinical Nutrition, 60*(1), 48–57.

Dino, G., Horn, K., Abdulkadri, A., Kalsekar, I., & Branstetter, S. (2008). Cost-effectiveness analysis of the Not On Tobacco program for adolescent smoking cessation. *Prevention Science, 9*(1), 38–46.

Edwards, R. T., Ceilleachair, A., Bywater, T., Hughes, D. A., & Hutchings, J. (2007). Parenting programme for parents of children at risk of developing conduct disorder: Cost effectiveness analysis. *British Medical Journal, 334*(7595), 682.

Fergusson, D. M., Horwood, L. J., & Ridder, E. M. (2005). Show me the child at seven: The consequences of conduct problems in childhood for psychosocial functioning in adulthood. *Journal of Child Psychology and Psychiatry, 46* 837–849.

Fergusson, D. M., & Woodward, L. J. (1999). Maternal age and educational and psychosocial outcomes in early adulthood. *Journal of Child Psychology and Psychiatry, 40*(3), 479–489.

Fiscella, K., & Kitzman, H. (2009). Disparities in academic achievement and health: The intersection of child education and health policy. *Pediatrics, 123*(3), 1073–1080.

Fishman, P. A., & Ebel, B. E. (2005). Cigarette tax increase and media campaign: Cost of reducing smoking-related deaths. *American Journal of Preventive Medicine, 29*(1), 19–26.

Foster, E. M. (2010). Costs and effectiveness of the fast track intervention for antisocial behavior. *Journal of Mental Health Policy and Economics, 13*(3), 101–119.

Freedman, K. S., Nelson, N. M., & Feldman, L. L. (2012). Smoking initiation among young adults in the United States and Canada, 1998–2010: A systematic review. *Prevention of Chronic Disease, 9*, E05.

Giovino, G. A., Mirza, S. A., Samet, J. M., Gupta, P. C., Jarvis, M. J. Bhala, N. . . . Asma, S. (2012). Tobacco use in 3 billion individuals from 16 countries: An analysis of nationally representative cross-sectional household surveys. *The Lancet, 380*(9842), 668–679.

Gortmaker, S. L., Must, A., Perrin, V, Sobol, A. M., & Dietz, W. H. (1993). Social and economic consequences of overweight in adolescence and young adulthood. *New England Journal of Medicine, 329*(14), 1008–1012.

Hawkins, J. D., Kosterman, R., Catalano, R. F., Hill, K. G., & Abbott, R. D. (2005). Promoting positive adult functioning through social development intervention in childhood: Long-term effects from the Seattle Social Development Project. *Archives of Pediatrics and Adolescent Medicine, 159*(1), 25–31.

Heckman, J. (2006). *The economics of investing in children. Policy Briefing No 1.* Dublin: UCD Geary Institute. http://www.ucd.ie/geary/static/publications/policybriefings/geary_report1.pdf.

Heckman, J. (2013). *Giving kids a fair chance.* Boston, MA: MIT Press.

Hobcraft, J., & Kiernan, K.. (2001). Childhood poverty, early motherhood and adult social exclusion. *British Journal of Sociology, 52*(3), 495–517.

Hofferth, S. L., & Reid, L. (2002). Early childbearing and children's achievement and behavior over time. *Perspectives on Sexual and Reproductive Health, 34*(1), 41–49.

Hofferth, S. L., Reid, L., & Mott, F. L. (2001). The effects of early childbearing on schooling over time. *Family Planning Perspectives, 33*(6), 259–267.

Hoffman, S. (2006). *By the numbers: The public costs of teen childbearing.* Washington, DC: National Campaign to Prevent Teen Pregnancy.

Hollingworth, W., Hawkins, J., Lawlor, D. A., Brown, M., Marsh, T., & Kipping, R. R. (2012). Economic evaluation of lifestyle interventions to treat overweight or obesity in children. *International Journal of Obesity (London), 36*(4), 559–566.

Jefferis, B. J., Power, C., & Manor, O. (2005). Adolescent drinking level and adult binge drinking in a national birth cohort. *Addiction, 100*(4), 543–549.

Jit, M., Barton, P., Chen, Y. F., & Uthman, O. (2009). *School-based interventions to prevent the uptake of smoking among children and young people: Cost-effectiveness model.* Birmingham: University of Birmingham.

Jones, L., Stokes, E., & Bell, M. (2007). *A review of the effectiveness and cost-effectiveness of interventions delivered in primary and secondary schools to prevent and/or reduce alcohol use by young people under 18 years old: Addendum. Additional economic evidence prepared for the Public Health Interventions Advisory Committee (PHIAC).* Liverpool: Liverpool John Moores University.

Karnehed, N., Rasmussen, F., & Kark, M. (2007). Obesity in young adulthood and later disability pension: A population-based cohort study of 366,929 Swedish men. *Scandinavian Journal of Public Health, 35*(1), 48–54.

Karoly, L. A, Greenwood, P. W., Everingham, S. S., Houbé, J., Kilburn, M. R., Rydell, C. P., . . . Chiesa, J. (1998). *Investing in our children: What we know and don't know about the costs and benefits of early childhood interventions.* Santa Monica: RAND Corporation.

Karoly, L. A., Kilburn, M. R., & Cannon, J. S. (2005). *Early childhood interventions. Proven results, future promise.* Santa Monica: RAND Corporation.

Kellam, S. G., Mackenzie, A. C., Brown, C. H., Poduska, J. M., Wang, W., Petras, H., & Wilcox, H. C. (2011). The good behavior game and the future of prevention and treatment. *Addiction Science and Clinical Practice*, 6(1), 73–84.

Kim, J., Chung, W., Lee, S., & Park. C., (2010). [Estimating the socioeconomic costs of alcohol drinking among adolescents in Korea] [in Korean]. *Journal of Preventive Medicine and Public Health*, 43(4), 341–351.

Knapp, M., & McDaid, D. (2009). Making an economic case for prevention and promotion. *International Journal of Mental Health Promotion*, 11(3), 49–56.

Krassas, G. E., & Tzotzas, T. (2004). Do obese children become obese adults?: Childhood predictors of adult disease. *Pediatric Endocrinology Reviews*, 1(suppl. 3), 455–449.

Kuklinski, M. R., Briney, J. S., Hawkins, J. D., & Catalano, R. F. (2012). Cost-benefit analysis of communities that care outcomes at eighth grade. *Preventive Science*, 13(2), 150–161.

Lai, T., Habicht, J., Reinap, M., Chisholm, D., & Baltussen, R. (2007). Costs, health effects and cost-effectiveness of alcohol and tobacco control strategies in Estonia. *Health Policy*, 84(1), 75–88.

Lewis, D., & Barham, L. (2006). *Economic modeling of interventions to reduce the transmission of chlamydia and other sexually transmitted infections and to reduce the rate of under eighteen conceptions*. London: NERA Economic Consulting.

Lorentzen, T., Dahl, E., & Harsløf, I. (2011). Welfare risks in early adulthood: A longitudinal analysis of social assistance transitions in Norway. *International Journal of Social Welfare*, 21, 408–421.

Lynch, F. L., Hornbrook, M., Clarke, G. N., Perrin, N., Polen, M. R., O'Connor, E., & Dickerson, J. (2005). Cost-effectiveness of an intervention to prevent depression in at-risk teens. *Archives of General Psychiatry*, 62(11), 1241–1248.

Madowitz, J., Knatz, S., Maginot, T., Crow, S. J., & Boutelle, K. N. (2012). Teasing, depression and unhealthy weight control behaviour in obese children. *Pediatric Obesity*, 7(6), 446–452.

Magnus, A., Haby, M. M., Carter, R., & Swinburn, B. (2009). The cost-effectiveness of removing television advertising of high-fat and/or high-sugar food and beverages to Australian children. *International Journal of Obesity (London)*, 33(10), 1094–1102.

Mamun, A. A., O'Callaghan, M. J., Williams, G. M., & Najman, J. M. (2012). Adolescents bullying and young adults body mass index and obesity: A longitudinal study. *International Journal of Obesity (London)*. doi: 10.1038/ijo.2012.182.

Maynard, R. (1997). *Kids having kids: Economic costs and social consequences of teen pregnancy*. Washington DC: Urban Institute Press.

McCambridge, J., McAlaney, J., & Rowe, R. (2011). Adult consequences of late adolescent alcohol consumption: A systematic review of cohort studies. *PLoS Medicine*, 8(2), e1000413.

McDaid, D., & Park, A.-L. (2011). Investing in mental health and well-being: Findings from the DataPrev project. *Health Promotion International*, 26(suppl. 1), i108–i139.

McDaid, D, Park, A.-L., Currie, C., & Zanotti, C. (2011). *Making the case for investing in the health of young people: Assessing the economic impact of poor* health and actions to promote and protect better health of children in Europe. Edinburgh: University of Edinburgh.

McIntosh, E., Barlow, J., Davis, H., & Stewart-Brown, S. (2009). Economic evaluation of an intensive home visiting programme for vulnerable families: A cost-effectiveness analysis of a public health intervention. *Journal of Public Health (Oxford)*, *31*(3), 423–433.

Mihalopoulos, C., Vos, T., Pirkis, J., & Carter, R. (2011). The economic analysis of prevention in mental health programs. *Annual Review of Clinical Psychology*, *7*, 169–201.

Mihalopoulos, C., Vos, T., Pirkis, J., & Carter, R. (2012). The population cost-effectiveness of interventions designed to prevent childhood depression. *Pediatrics*, *129*(3), e723–c730.

Miller, T. R., Levy, D. T., Spicer, R. S., & Taylor, D. M. (2006). Societal costs of underage drinking. *Journal of Studies on Alcohol*, *67*(4), 519–528.

Moodie, M., Carter, R. C., Swinburn, B. A., & Haby, M. (2010). The cost-effectiveness of Australia's Active After-School Communities program. *Obesity (Silver Spring)*, *18*(8), 1585–1592.

Moodie, M., Haby, M., Galvin, L., Swinburn, B., & Carter, R. (2009). Cost-effectiveness of active transport for primary school children—Walking School Bus program. *International Journal of Behavioral Nutrition and Physical Activity*, *6*, 63.

Moodie, M., Haby, M., Wake, M., Gold, L., & Carter, R. (2008). Cost-effectiveness of a family-based GP-mediated intervention targeting overweight and moderately obese children. *Economics and Human Biology*, *6*(3), 363–376.

Morgan, A., Currie, C., Due, P., Nic Gabhainn, S., Rasmussen, M., Samdal, O., & Smith, R. (2008). *Mental well-being in school-aged children in Europe: Associations with social cohesion and socioeconomic circumstances.* Copenhagen: World Health Organization Regional Office for Europe. http://www.euro.who.int/__data/assets/pdf_file/0010/76483/Hbsc_Forum_2007_mental_well-being.pdf.

Morrell, C. J., Warner, R., Slade, P., Dixon, S., Walters, S., Paley, G., & Brugha, T. (2009). *Psychological interventions for postnatal depression: Cluster randomised trial and economic evaluation. The PoNDER trial* (Health technology assessment 13). http://www.hta.ac.uk/fullmono/mon1330.pdf.

Moya Martinez, P., Sanchez Lopez, M., Lopez Bastida, J., Escribano Sotos, F., Notario Pacheco, B., Salcedo Aguilar, F., & Martinez Vizcaino, V. (2011). [Cost-effectiveness of an intervention to reduce overweight and obesity in 9-10-year-olds. The Cuenca study] [in Spanish]. *Gaceta Sanitaria*, *25*(3), 198–204.

Muttarak, R., Gallus, S., Franchi, M., Faggiano, F., Pacifici, R., Colombo, P., & La Vecchia, C. 2013). Why do smokers start? *European Journal of Cancer Prevention*, *22*(2), 181–186.

Neovius, M., Kark, M., & Rasmussen, F. (2008). Association between obesity status in young adulthood and disability pension. *International Journal of Obesity (London)*, *32*(8), 1319–1326.

Niccols, A. (2008). "Right from the start": Randomized trial comparing an attachment group intervention to supportive home visiting. *Journal of Child Psychology and Psychiatry, 49*(7), 754–764.

Nores, M., & Barnett, W. S. (2010). Benefits of early childhood interventions across the world: (Under) investing in the very young. *Economics of Education Review, 29*(2), 271–282.

Oh, D. L., Heck, J. E., Dresler, C., Allwright, S., Haglund, M., Del Mazo, S. S., . . . Hashibe, M. (2010). Determinants of smoking initiation among women in five European countries: A cross-sectional survey. *BMC Public Health, 10*, 74.

Olds, D. L., Eckenrode, J., Henderson, C. R., Jr., Kitzman, H., Powers, J., Cole, R.,. . . Luckey, D. (1997). Long-term effects of home visitation on maternal life course and child abuse and neglect. Fifteen-year follow-up of a randomized trial. *Journal of the American Medical Association, 278*(8), 637–643.

Olds, D. L., Henderson, C. R., Jr., Phelps, C., Kitzman, H., & Hanks, C. (1993). Effect of prenatal and infancy nurse home visitation on government spending. *Medical Care, 31*(2), 155–174.

Palloni, A., Milesi, C., White, R. G., & Turner, A. (2009). Early childhood health, reproduction of economic inequalities and the persistence of health and mortality differentials. *Social Science Medicine, 68*(9), 1574–1582.

Parrott, S., & Godfrey, C. (2004). Economics of smoking cessation. *British Medical Journal, 328*(7445), 947–949.

Reilly, J. J., & Kelly, J. (2011). Long-term impact of overweight and obesity in childhood and adolescence on morbidity and premature mortality in adulthood: Systematic review. *International Journal of Obesity (London), 35*(7), 891–898.

Richards, M., & Huppert, F. A. (2011). Do positive children become positive adults? Evidence from a longitudinal birth cohort study. *Journal of Positive Psychology, 6*(1), 75–87.

Ridge, T. (2002). *Child poverty and social exclusion*. Bristol: Policy Press.

Rosenthal, M. S., Ross, J. S., Bilodeau, R., Richter, R. S., Palley, J. E., & Bradley, E. H. (2009). Economic evaluation of a comprehensive teenage pregnancy prevention program: Pilot program. *American Journal of Preventive Medicine, 37*(6 suppl. 1), S280–S287.

Royal College of Physicians (2010). *Passive smoking and children*. London: Royal College of Physicians.

Salcedo Aguilar, F., Martinez-Vizcaino, V., Sanchez Lopez, M., Solera Martinez, M., Franquelo Gutierrez, R., Serrano Martinez, S., . . . Rodriguez-Artalejo, F. (2010). Impact of an after-school physical activity program on obesity in children. *The Journal of Pediatrics, 157*(1), 36–42 e3.

Sassi, F. (2010). *Fit not fat*. Paris: OECD.

Schweinhart, L. J., Montie, J., Xiang, Z., Barnett, W. S., Belfield, C. R., & Nores, M. (2005). *Lifetime effects: The High/Scope Perry Preschool study through age 40*. (Monographs of the High/Scope Educational Research Foundation, 14). Ypsilanti, MN: High/Scope Educational Research Foundation.

Scott, S., Knapp, M., Henderson, J., & Maughan, B. (2001). Financial cost of social exclusion: Follow up study of antisocial children into adulthood. *British Medical Journal, 323*(7306), 191.

Secker-Walker, R. H., Worden, J. K., Holland, R., Flynn, B., & Detsky, A. (1997). A mass media programme to prevent smoking among adolescents: Costs and cost effectiveness. *Tobacco Control, 6,* 207–212.

Smith, J. P., & Smith, G. C. (2010). Long-term economic costs of psychological problems during childhood. *Social Science Medicine, 71*(1), 110–115.

Spoth, R. L., Guyll, M., & Day, S. X. (2002). Universal family-focused interventions in alcohol-use disorder prevention: Cost-effectiveness and cost-benefit analyses of two interventions. *Journal of Studies of Alcohol, 63*(2), 219–228.

Stewart-Brown, S. L., & Schrader-McMillan, A. (2011). Parenting for mental health: What does the evidence say we need to do? Report of Workpackage 2 of the DataPrev project. *Health Promotion International, 26*(suppl. 1), i10–i28.

Strand, B. H., & Kunst, K. (2007). Childhood socioeconomic position and cause specific mortality in early adulthood. *American Journal of Epidemiology, 165,* 85–93.

Temple, J. A., & Reynolds, A. J. (2007). Benefits and costs of investments in preschool education: Evidence from the Child–Parent Centers and related programs. *Economics of Education Review, 26*(1), 126–144.

Tengs, T. O., Osgood, N. D., & Chen, L. L. (2001). The cost-effectiveness of intensive national school-based anti-tobacco education: Results from the tobacco policy model. *Preventive Medicine, 33*(6), 558–570.

U.S. Department of Health and Human Services (1994). *Youth and tobacco: Preventing tobacco use among young people: A report of the Surgeon General.* Atlanta, GA: Department of Health and Human Services.

van Baal, P. H., Polder, J. J., de Wit, G. A., Hoogenveen, R. T., Feenstra, T. L., Boshuizen, H. C., . . . Brouwer, W. B. (2008). Lifetime medical costs of obesity: Prevention no cure for increasing health expenditure. *PLoS Medicine, 5*(2), e29.

Vellinga, A., O'Donovan, D., & De La Harpe, D. (2008). Length of stay and associated costs of obesity related hospital admissions in Ireland. *BMC Health Service Research, 8,* 88.

Vijgen, S. M., van Baal, P., Hoogenveen, R. T., de Wit, G. A., & Feenstra, T. L. (2008). Cost-effectiveness analyses of health promotion programs: A case study of smoking prevention and cessation among Dutch students. *Health Education Research, 23*(2), 310–318.

Viner, R. M., & Taylor, B. (2007). Adult outcomes of binge drinking in adolescence: Findings from a UK national birth cohort. *Journal of Epidemiology and Community Health, 61*(10), 902–907.

Wang, L. Y., & Crosset, L. S. (2001). Cost-effectiveness of a school-based tobacco-use prevention program. *Archives of Pediatric and Adolescent Medicine, 155*(9), 1043–1050.

Wang, L. Y., Yang, Q., Lowry, R., & Wechsler, H. (2003). Economic analysis of a school-based obesity prevention program. *Obesity Research, 11*(11), 1313–1324.

Waylen, A., Stallard, N., & Stewart-Brown, S. (2008). Parenting and health in midchildhood: A longitudinal study. *European Journal of Public Health, 18*(3), 300–305.

Weare, K., & Nind, M. (2011). Mental health promotion and problem prevention in schools: What does the evidence say? *Health Promotion International 26*(suppl. 1), i29–i69.

Weich, S., Patterson, J., Shaw, R., & Stewart-Brown, S. (2009). Family relationships in childhood and common psychiatric disorders in later life: Systematic review of prospective studies. *British Journal of Psychiatry, 194*(5), 392–398.

Further Readings

Adamson, P. (2013). *Child wellbeing in rich countries: A comparative overview.* Florence: UNICEF Office of Research—Innocenti.

Currie, C., Zanotti, C., Morgan, A., Currie, D., de Looze, M., Roberts, C., . . . Barnekow, V. (2012). *Social determinants of health and well-being among young people. Health Behaviour in School-aged Children (HBSC) study: International report from the 2009/2010 survey.* Copenhagen: WHO Regional Office for Europe.

Heckman J. (2013). *Giving kids a fair chance.* Boston, MA: MIT Press.

Karoly, L. A., Kilburn, M. R., & Cannon, J. S. (2005). *Early childhood interventions. Proven results, future promise.* Santa Monica: RAND Corporation.

Knapp, M., McDaid, D., & Parsonage, M. (Eds.) (2011). *Mental health promotion and mental illness prevention: The economic case.* London: Department of Health.

Nores, M., & Barnett, W. S. (2010). Benefits of early childhood interventions across the world: (Under) investing in the very young. *Economics of Education Review, 29*(2), 271–282.

9

Investing in Wellbeing in the Workplace

More Than Just a Business Case

David McDaid and A-La Park

London School of Economics and Political Science, U.K.

Why Should We Be Interested in Mental Health and Wellbeing at Work?

Wellbeing can be thought of as "a dynamic state in which the individual is able to develop their potential, work productively and creatively, build strong and positive relationships with others and contribute to their community. It is enhanced when an individual is able to fulfil their personal and social goals and achieve a sense of purpose in society" (BIS, 2008, p. 10). Work makes a contribution to our wellbeing. We simply cannot leave our mental health and wellbeing at the door of the workplace. Employment in a good working environment is beneficial to physical and mental wellbeing. Moreover, for people who have experienced poor mental health, maintaining or returning to employment can also be a vital element in the recovery process, helping to build self-esteem, confidence, and social inclusion (Perkins, Farmer, & Litchfield, 2009). This chapter provides an overview of some of the economic arguments for investing in actions to protect mental health and wellbeing at work, before going on to review what is known about the cost-effectiveness of different interventions and considering how this evidence base may be further strengthened. Where any monetary values are reported in this chapter these have been converted to 2010 US dollars using the IMF World Economic Outlook Database.

The Economics of Wellbeing: Wellbeing: A Complete Reference Guide, Volume V.
Edited by David McDaid and Cary L. Cooper.
© 2014 John Wiley & Sons, Ltd. Published 2014 by John Wiley & Sons, Inc.
DOI: 10.1002/9781118539415.wbwell09

Box 9.1. highlights some of the different arguments that can be made for investing in mental health and wellbeing within workplaces, and we will look at each in turn. Is there a public health argument for actions in the workplace, given that we spend so much time there? Do we need supports to meet challenges arising from the changing nature of workplaces and work pressures? Should we invest to promote social inclusion? Are there economic incentives for both business and the wider economy?

> **Box 9.1.** The Case for Investing in Mental Health and Wellbeing at Work.
>
> Contributing to population health goals
> Addressing the psychosocial impact of the changing nature of work
> Promoting social inclusion
> Economic impacts on business
> Economic impacts for governments and society

Contributing to Population Health Goals

Mental-health-promoting actions that take place within the workplace can contribute to general population health goals. For instance, in the European Union (EU) as a whole 64% of the population aged 15–64 were in employment in 2011 (Eurostat, 2012). From a public health perspective the workplace is therefore an important setting where potentially health-promoting activities can be delivered in a more cost-effective fashion. Actions at work also provide an opportunity for the early identification of risk factors for poor health. This public-health approach means that action in the workplace is about much more than simply focusing on the prevention of mental health problems and poor wellbeing that may be linked to a poor work environment; it is also about those non-work-related problems that may become visible and sometimes exacerbated within some working environments.

The Psychosocial Impact of the Changing Nature of Work and Organizational Restructuring

While some levels of stress and high demands at work can be good for health, a poor workplace environment can have an adverse impact on health and lead to excess levels of what psychologists call psychological distress, which, in turn, can lead to the development of poor mental and physical health. Many models and theories have been put forward to explain the reasons for psychological distress (Levi et al., 2000). One key theory suggests that the level of stress at work experienced by an individual depends on the interaction between three different elements of the psychosocial work environment: demand, control and support (Karasek & Theorell, 1990). Jobs characterized by a combination of high workload demands and insufficient control of the situation by the employee are most likely to lead to psychological distress. The level of support that an individual receives from their line manager can, however, act as a buffer: individuals who feel valued may be at lower risk of experiencing psychological distress.

Another potential explanation for psychological distress may be an imbalance between efforts and rewards in the workplace (Siegrist, 1996). High efforts and low rewards increase the risk of psychological distress and poor mental health. Individuals may not feel that they are receiving a high enough salary for work, but equally they may feel that they are being taken for granted or not held in high esteem by colleagues and managers (de Jonge, Bosma, Peter, & Siegrist, 2000; Lau, 2008). This may have economic consequences for companies if staff morale is poor and/or if there is an impact on productivity and absenteeism.

A major challenge that we all must now face is the changing nature of the way in which we all work in the twenty-first century. This may further increase the risk of psychological distress. Jobs increasingly involve working to tight deadlines. Vulnerabilities to psychosocial stress, burnout, and mental health problems are becoming more challenging as the nature of work continues to change, moving away from traditional occupations towards service-sector jobs with high levels of demand and work intensity. The boundaries between home life and work are also becoming blurred, especially in the service sector.

A poor working environment can increase the risk of psychosocial stress, which is itself a predictor of future depression and anxiety (Chandola, 2010). In Belgium a survey of 1,500 employees found that in 2008 more than 40% experienced undue stress at work. It also found that 60% of employees who receive little or no support from their superiors are frequently stressed within the workplace, whereas this rate reaches only 32% for employees who receive much assistance and support from their superiors. It noted that 18% of the employees suffering from considerable stress were likely to perform less well within their organizations compared to 7% of those without undue stress (Zebra Zone, 2008).

There is evidence that the workplace environment is deteriorating. Overall satisfaction with working conditions has declined over time among respondents to the five European Working Conditions Surveys since 1991 (European Foundation for the Improvement of Living and Working Conditions [EFILWC], 2010). Less than 20% were "very satisfied" with their working conditions in 2010, a steady decrease since 1991 when this rate was closer to 30%. The latest European Working Conditions Survey in 2010 also indicated that at least 20%, and in some countries (Sweden and Finland) more than 50%, of those surveyed had experienced substantial restructuring or reorganization in their workplaces over the previous 3 years (EFILWC, 2010).

There is a continuing shift away from heavy industry and agriculture towards the service sectors and the knowledge economy (where there is a need for high levels of potentially stressful consumer interaction) or high-technology sectors (where it may be difficult to keep up with the pace of change). Mental health problems are much more common in service sector occupations such as banking, education, and public administration than they are in heavy industry or construction (Black, 2008; Eurostat, 2010), although this may also, in part, be due to higher prevalence rates of depression and anxiety in women who make up a larger share of the service-sector workforce. In some countries there is also a demographic change in the workforce, not only accommodating more women but also older workers, new migrants, and those who shift between employment sectors when skill requirements change. All of these groups may be at greater risk of poor wellbeing.

The situation may be compounded by new working practices, such as increased use of temporary/short-term employment contracts. While this may be intended to help adapt economies to the challenges of competing in a global marketplace, one consequence may be a feeling of increased job insecurity, for instance, where there is a possibility of outsourcing tasks to external locations. Restructuring can also increase job demands and workload, which increases the chances of burnout and poor mental health (Kieselbach, Nielsen, & Triomphe, 2010).

Protecting the psychological wellbeing of employees may be particularly important during such a time of economic transition and restructuring. As McDaid and Wahlbeck indicate in Chapter 11 in this volume, historically, economic downturns that lead to increases in unemployment can increase risks to mental health and wellbeing (Laszlo et al., 2010; Stuckler, Meissner, Fishback, Basu, & McKee, 2012; Wahlbeck & McDaid, 2012). Fears over jobs and downsizing in both the public and private sectors are important risk factors for psychosocial stress and mental health problems (Campbell, Worral, & Cooper, 2000; Cheng, Chen, Chen, & Chiang, 2005). They compound the challenges that are always faced by continuous change and restructuring. Data from the European Working Conditions Survey 2010 indicate that feelings of job insecurity have been increasing for all types of employment (EFILWC, 2010), but are most pronounced for those in low-skilled manual jobs. Twenty-three percent of these workers felt their jobs to be insecure compared to 11% of highly skilled clerical workers. These fears are not restricted to the private sector. Even though the full effects of the economic downturn had not been felt in the United Kingdom by 2010, a survey of public-sector employees found that 20% of them thought they were "likely" to lose their jobs, a rise of 11% since spring 2009 when the downturn was first on the radar (Chandola, 2010).

Promoting Social Inclusion

Another important reason for investing in support at work is that it is critical to promoting social inclusion. We have indicated that around two thirds of the adult population in high-income countries are in employment; however, rates of employment for people with all types of mental health problem are much lower, despite an expressed preference by many people with mental health problems to be in work (Perkins et al., 2009). A better working environment can help improve employment rates of people who develop mental health problems. Failure to improve puts additional costs on governments who have to provide social welfare support for people who would prefer to be in employment.

Employers may be reluctant to retain individuals with known mental health problems believing that they are likely to be less productive or more disruptive in the workplace (Kaszynski & Cechnicki, 2011; Perkins et al., 2009). Firms may also lack the technical knowledge and awareness of what is required to accommodate people with mental health problems on their return to the workplace. Surveys in Ireland and Scotland reported that more than 70% of employers did not know enough about the law regarding mental health in the workplace (National Economic and Social Forum, 2007; See Me Scotland, 2006).

Economic Impacts for Business

Investing in improving the overall level of wellbeing within the workplace can have multiple benefits to employers. The workplace can provide a healthy culture and environment that is psychologically supportive to the workforce, helping to foster and maintain wellbeing. Not only are improved levels of psychological and physical wellbeing associated with better workplace performance, but they can also help improve the level of staff retention, improve employee–employer dialogue, and encourage the greater levels of creativity and innovation that are vital to dynamic business and enhance the reputation of the workplace (Michaels & Greene, 2013; Robertson & Cooper, 2011; Wang & Samson, 2009).

One example of this can be seen in a survey of nearly 29,000 employees across 10 industries in 15 countries around the world. The survey looked at the relationship between wellness and business effectiveness (Dornan & Jane-Llopis, 2010; Wang & Samson, 2009). Ninety-one percent of employees in the survey were working in the private sector. Participants were asked to self-report on attitudes, performance, and conditions directly related to the effectiveness of their organization. The survey found that, in organizations where health and wellbeing were perceived by employees to be well managed, organizational performance was more than 2.5 times greater than in those where they were perceived to be poorly managed.

Seventy-two percent of those who rated their organization highly for actively promoting health and wellbeing (including work/life balance) also rated it highly for encouraging creativity and innovation. This was equivalent to an almost fourfold increase in creativity and innovation, compared with a sevenfold decrease in companies where health and wellbeing were perceived to be poorly managed. Companies where health and wellbeing were poorly managed were also four times less likely to retain staff talent within a 12-month period compared to companies with a good approach to health and wellbeing (Wang & Samson, 2009).

In contrast, a mentally unhealthy workforce has adverse economic consequences for business. In many countries employers will be directly responsible for paying at least some of the costs of sickness benefits to their employees for a specified period of time. There can be substantial immediate productivity losses due to sickness absenteeism. Even very minor levels of depression are associated with productivity losses (Beck et al., 2011). Where there is a loss of highly skilled workers due to poor health, additional recruitment and training costs may be incurred by employers (McDaid, 2007).

In addition to absenteeism, businesses have to contend with presenteeism—poor performance while at work due to excess stress and mental health problems (Aronsson, Gustafsson, & Dallner, 2000; McDaid, 2007). It remains difficult to measure and few estimates of its costs have been made, although some studies suggest that its impact may be as much as five times greater than the costs of absenteeism alone (Sanderson & Andrews, 2006). Presenteeism is also itself a strong predictor of future poor mental and physical health (Janssens, Clays, Clercq, Bacquer, & Braeckman, 2013; Leineweber, Westerlund, Hagberg, Svedberg, & Alexanderson, 2012; Taloyan et al., 2012), which itself may imply additional costs where employers are responsible for paying the health-care costs of their employees. Another reason for investing in measures to protect and promote wellbeing is because of the spillover impacts of poor mental wellbeing to other workers: there can be a detrimental impact on those working in teams. Sickness absence may also lead to an increased workload and potential risk of work-related stress in remaining team members.

There can also be reputational and legal consequences of having an unhealthy workplace. If a business is perceived to have high levels of absenteeism, it may potentially have an adverse impact on its reputation. This might be seen, rightly or wrongly, by both the general public and potential future recruits as a signal of the low priority that a company places on having a healthy workforce. Potentially, it might lose customers and procurement contracts. Within the workforce there can be a detrimental impact on morale and staff loyalty. Poor mental health and excess work-related stress can also increase the risk of accidents due to human error; this in turn could lead to litigation and compensation claims in some circumstances. There are also increased risks of people developing physical health problems, including cardiovascular disease and diabetes, if they experience depression and anxiety disorders. This can also increase the risks of further work absenteeism (De Hert et al., 2011).

Achieving Economic Goals for Government and Society

Better wellbeing at work can also have major benefits for governments and wider society (Beddington et al., 2008) as it implies reduced rates of absenteeism, presenteeism, and consequently less poor health. Typically at

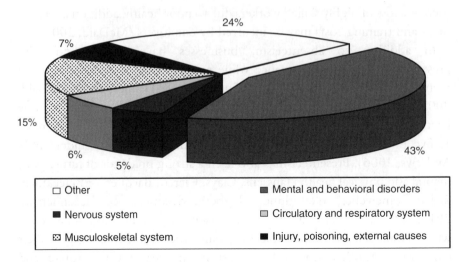

Figure 9.1. Reason for Disability Benefit Claims in Great Britain 2008–2012. Adapted from Department of Work and Pensions (2013).

least two thirds of the costs of common mental health problems are for lost productivity. The costs are substantial; for instance, the costs of major depression in 30 European countries were estimated to be US$109 billion in 2010 while costs for all anxiety disorders accounted for a further €88 billion (Olesen, Gustavsson, Svensson, Wittchen, & Jonsson, 2012). This may be due either to poor performance while at work, sick leave, or early retirement on the grounds of poor mental health, as well as exclusion from the workplace due to discrimination linked to an individual's mental health status.

In high-income countries governments usually are responsible for paying the majority of long-term sickness and disability benefits for people absent from work because of poor mental health. These can be substantial as illustrated in the case of Great Britain in Figure 9.1 where it can be seen that 43% of all disability benefits for the period 2008 to 2012 were due to mental and behavioral disorders (Department of Work and Pensions, 2013). As Figure 9.2 shows, not only are there many more disability claims related to mental health problems compared with other health problems, there are also greater numbers of people who have been claiming benefits for between 2 and 5 years.

Levels of absenteeism, unemployment and long-term disability claims due to psychosocial stress and mental health problems have been increasing

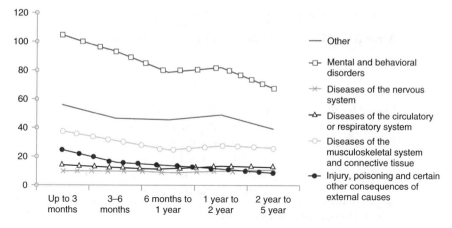

Figure 9.2. Duration of Employment and Support Allowance Claims in Great Britain 2008–2012. Adapted from Department of Work and Pensions (2013).

in high income countries; in many countries they have now overtaken musculoskeletal problems as the leading cause of days of absence from work and withdrawal from the labor market (Organisation for Economic Cooperation and Development, 2012).

Better wellbeing at work can thus reduce the need for publicly funded health-care systems to deal with the consequences of some adverse health events that might have been better identified and avoided through early intervention at work. Moreover, an improvement in productivity in the workplace contributes to the economic performance of nations. Improvements in workplace productivity may increase the level of profit achieved by the private sector, and thus additional tax revenues may be raised for the public purse. In the public sector, improved efficiency through improved workplace productivity may be achieved—something that is very important given the pressure on public expenditure in many countries.

What Do We Know about Actions to Promote Mental Health and Wellbeing in the Workplace?

Having looked at the economic case for promoting and protecting mental health and wellbeing at work, we now consider what is known about the cost-effectiveness of different actions that might be taken.

Table 9.1. Multiple Risk Factors to Wellbeing.

Areas for action	Examples of issues to be addressed
Lifestyle	Physical activity, nutrition, weight management, alcohol use, tobacco use, sleep, risky behaviors
Mental health	Stress, abusive behavior, harassment, anxiety, depression, resilience
Physical health	Musculoskeletal, cardiovascular, medical history, general health
Engagement	Commitment, satisfaction, advocacy, pride, workplace factors

Source: Dornan and Jane-Llopis (2010).

Before looking at this evidence base, it is important to remember that measures to promote better mental wellbeing and address factors that contribute to undue work-related stress and poor mental health should, ideally, be embedded within an overarching framework for wellness and health promotion in the workplace. As Table 9.1 highlights, a sustainable approach to wellness at work that can have benefits for both employers and employees will need to address multiple risk factors to wellbeing. Measures are needed to promote a healthy workplace environment and good level of engagement between employers and employees, as well as foster general healthy lifestyle promotion and monitor physical health (Dornan & Jane-Llopis, 2010). Although we do not focus on these issues in this chapter, but instead concentrate on psychosocial issues, it should be noted that there is a literature on the economics of many of these interventions that the reader may wish to look at (see, e.g., Allen, Lewis, & Tagliaferro, 2012; Baicker, Cutler, & Song, 2010; Milani & Lavie, 2009; Pelletier, 2005).

Turning to mental health and wellbeing, many different effective interventions have been identified (Corbiere, Shen, Rouleau, & Dewa, 2009; Kuoppala, Lamminpaa, & Husman, 2008; Martin, Sanderson, & Cocker, 2009). Actions can be implemented at both an organizational level within the workplace and/or targeted at specific individuals. The former category includes measures to promote awareness of the importance of mental health and wellbeing at work for managers and risk management for stress and poor mental health, for instance, looking at job content, working conditions, terms of employment, social relations at work, modifications to physical working environment, flexible working hours, improved employer–employee communication, and opportunities for career progression. Actions targeted

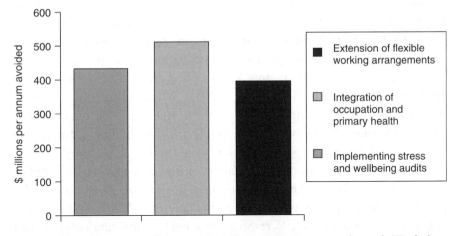

Figure 9.3. Estimation of Annual Benefits to UK Economy through Workplace Mental Health and Wellbeing Promotion (2010 US$). Adapted from BIS (2008).

at individuals can include modifying workloads, providing cognitive behavioral therapy, relaxation and meditation training, time management training, exercise programs, journaling, biofeedback, and goal setting.

Most of existing economic literature has focused on the case for interventions targeted at individuals rather than organizational level interventions (Bhui, Dinos, Stansfeld, & White, 2012; Cancelliere, Cassidy, Ammendolia, & Cote, 2011; Corbiere et al., 2009; Hamberg-van Reenen, Proper, & van den Berg, 2012; McDaid & Park, 2011; Richardson & Rothstein, 2008). This is perhaps not surprising, as there have been few controlled trials of organizational workplace-health-promoting interventions, let alone interventions where mental health components can be identified, and even fewer where information on the costs and consequences of the intervention are provided (Corbiere et al., 2009). In part, this may reflect challenges in evaluating organizational-level actions, but it will also be due to commercial sensitivities and the reluctance of employees and trade unions to participate in evaluations that assess workplace performance.

One controlled study looked at a combination of organizational and individual stress management measures for customer sales representatives at a telecommunications company in the United States. While it did report improvements in emotional wellbeing following the introduction of the program, as well as a marked improvement in productivity and absenteeism, the program's value for money could not be considered as its costs were not provided (Munz, Kohler, & Greenberg 2001). Figure 9.3 shows the results of modeling work undertaken as part of the U.K. Foresight Study on Mental Capital and Wellbeing. This suggests that substantial economic costs could be avoided every year through investment in stress and wellbeing audits ($434 million), better integration of occupational and primary health-care systems ($513 million) and an extension in flexible-working-hours arrangements ($394 million) (BIS, 2008). Where other organizational interventions are concerned, however, there appears to be no economic analysis looking at the benefits of better training of line managers to recognize risk factors for poor wellbeing, even though this is one of the key recommendations made on effective interventions at work (NICE, 2009b).

There have been a number of economic assessments of general health promotion and wellness programs, particularly in a U.S. context, where employers are usually directly responsible for the health-care costs of their employees. In general, this literature points to a positive return on investment in these corporate wellness programs, because of the avoidance of health-care costs. A review of general wellness programs (the focus is usually more on weight and smoking than mental wellbeing) reported a reduction in health care costs of $3.27 and $2.73 in absenteeism costs for every $1 spent on these programs (Baicker et al., 2010) .

Some of the evaluations of wellness programs report both stress- and/or mental-health-related outcomes in addition to looking at impacts on business in terms of productivity, absenteeism, and staff turnover. In the United States the Johnson and Johnson wellness program, which includes stress management, has been associated with a reduction in health-care costs of $225 per employee per annum (Ozminkowski et al., 2002), while a 4-year analysis of the Highmark company wellness program, including stress management classes and online stress management advice, reported a return on every $1 invested of $1.65 when looking at the impact on health-care costs (Naydeck, Pearson, Ozminkowski, Day, & Goetzel, 2008).

One study that did report mental health outcomes looked at the economic case for investing in a multi-component, workplace-based health-promotion program in the United Kingdom. Participants were provided with a personalized health and wellbeing report on personal health areas in need of improvement, and practical suggestions as to how to achieve the recommended changes were given. Participants also gained access to a personalized lifestyle web portal that included articles, assessments, and interactive online behavior-change programs. They also received tailored emails every 2 weeks on relevant personal wellness topics, as well as packs of information and seminars on key health topics. Using a pre-post test study design, participants were found to have significantly reduced health risks, including work-related stress and depression, reduced absenteeism, and improved workplace performance. The cost of the intervention to the company was $135 per employee; there was a 6-fold return on investment due to a reduction in absenteeism and improvements in workplace productivity (Mills, Kessler, Cooper, & Sullivan, 2007). A similar intervention delivered to employees in the computing industry reported improvements in stress levels while decreasing the costs of health care service use by more than one third. This, it was noted, would more than cover the costs of the intervention (Rahe et al., 2002).

Also in the United States, participants in a health risk assessment and disease management scheme were compared to matched controls in other companies that did not have health promotion programs. Overall levels of risk to health were significantly reduced, while there was also a significant reduction in the prevalence of depression, although rates of anxiety significantly increased. There were net cost savings from a health-care-payer perspective, although the costs of participation in the health promotion program were not reported (Loeppke et al., 2008).

In Canada, an uncontrolled evaluation of a comprehensive workplace-health-promotion program, including information for stress management, reported a significant reduction in stress levels, signs of stress, and feelings of depression at the end of a 3-year study period. While costs of the program were not reported, staff turnover and absenteeism decreased substantially (Renaud et al., 2008).

A small controlled study explored the use of biofeedback to prevent stress and poor health in correctional officers working in a youth detention facility in the United States. This led to an improvement in psychological wellbeing and physical health, but also to improvements in productivity levels and incremental cost savings of more than $1,000 over 3 months, although the sample size was too small to be significant. However, the study did not monetize the value of reported productivity gains (McCraty, Atkinson, Lipsenthal, & Arguelles, 2009).

Some studies have also modeled the potential economic benefits of investing in mental wellbeing at work. Modeling analysis of a comprehensive approach to promote mental wellbeing at work, quantifying some of the business case benefits of improved productivity and reduced absenteeism was produced as part of guidance developed by the National Institute for Health and Care Excellence (NICE) in the United Kingdom. It suggested that productivity losses to employers as a result of undue stress and poor mental health could fall by 30%; for a 1,000-employee company there would be a net reduction in costs in excess of $473,000 (NICE, 2009a).

The economic benefits of participation in general wellbeing programs were also recently modeled in a U.K. context. Implementing a multi-component wellness program similar to one shown to be effective in the United States (Mills et al., 2007) could, from a business perspective alone, bring a return on the investment in such a program of $9 for every $1 invested. In addition, there would be further economic benefits to the health and social security systems from a reduction in the health problems (mental and physical) developing in the workplace (McDaid, King, Park, & Parsonage, 2011).

Avoiding absenteeism in the workplace can also mean that business and public sector organizations avoid the costs associated with having to hire temporary staff to provide cover or avoid unnecessary delays in providing services. Another analysis looking at the English National Health Service (NHS) workforce reported potential economic gains from reducing absence levels to the levels seen in the private sector that would be the equivalent of having more than 15,000 additional staff available every day to treat patients. This would amount to an annual cost saving to the English NHS of £500 million per annum (Boorman, 2009).

What Do We Know about Cost-Effective Actions to Help People with Mental Health Problems Remain in Employment?

Among interventions to help people with mental health problems remain in, or return to, work, specialist occupational health physicians and psychologists can play a key role in providing services. Counseling can be effective for employees identified as having job-related stress and mental health problems. Cognitive behavior therapy (CBT) can also be effective in treating people with stress and/or mental health problems (Bhui et al., 2012; Pomaki, Franche, Murray, Khushrushahi, & Lampinen., 2012). For example, in a study of health-care workers in the United Kingdom who had recently experienced stress-related absenteeism from work, it was found that those employees who made use of a computerized version of CBT had significantly better short-term improvements in symptoms of depression and anxiety compared to a comparator group of employees receiving standard care (Grime, 2004).

Much of the economic analysis undertaken to date on actions to help people with mental health problems remain in work has been done in the United States. Cost-effectiveness studies that have looked at the use of improved care management, including psychotherapy and medication, suggest that the costs of running such programs are more than outweighed by the savings made in terms of lower levels of absenteeism, better performance at work, and higher rates of job retention (Lo Sasso, Rost, & Beck, 2006; Wang et al., 2006; Wang, Simon, & Kessler, 2008).

For example, in the United States individuals who were identified through a workplace screening program and then subsequently received CBT and medical support had significantly better mental health outcomes, higher rates of job retention, and more hours worked (an additional two weeks) at 12 months compared to those individuals receiving usual care alone (Wang et al., 2007). The business case again was strong: there was a positive return on investment to the company because of the avoidance of hiring and training new staff. A randomized controlled trial has also been conducted with civil servants in Maine, USA where employees identified as having depression were provided with telephone-based counseling involving CBT, work coaching or modification, and better care coordination with primary care physicians. Significant improvements in mental health were achieved with productivity cost savings due to reduced absenteeism of $6,041 per participant per year (Lerner et al., 2012) .

Economic analysis modeling the costs and benefits of investment in screening for depression followed by enhanced care including CBT in a U.K. context also suggests that intervention is highly cost-effective. Over a 2-year period the rate of return to a 500-employee company paying for the program would be in the region of $5 for every $1 spent. In the second year, costs to the health service equivalent to half the cost of the intervention program would also be saved (McDaid, King, & Parsonage, 2011).

How Can We Facilitate Greater Investment in Workplace Mental Health and Wellbeing Promotion?

We have demonstrated that there are economic benefits to be gained from having more mentally healthy workforces. Most of this evidence comes from the United States where employers have a direct incentive to protect the health of their employees, as they pay for health-care coverage (Dewa, McDaid, & Ettner, 2007). In countries where health care is funded through taxation or social health insurance, there is perhaps less of an economic incentive for smaller businesses to provide their own workplace-health-promotion services.

There may be economic benefits to be gained through better integration of primary care, in particular, with occupational health services. State support for occupational health services varies considerably. Greater support for occupational health services from tax- or social-insurance-funded health-care systems could help in the provision of a range of appropriate services in workplaces. As this chapter notes, many of the approaches needed to promote and protect mental health at work should be implemented at an organizational level. Governments might also consider incentivizing companies, perhaps through tax breaks, to invest in actions to address workplace mental health at an organizational level.

Long-term sickness benefits remain the responsibility of social welfare systems. Adjusting these systems so as potentially to place more responsibility on employers for some of these costs might also increase the priority given to mental health in the workplace. Such a development would require careful consideration of the potential impacts on business and also any adverse impacts on the willingness of employers to recruit individuals with a history of health problems

Many good practices in workplace health promotion may be found in large private companies or in large public-sector organizations. Another particular area for action therefore may be to provide financial incentives for small business to invest in mental-health-promotion activities. Without such incentives it may not be feasible for them to implement effective programs. In England NICE recommended that organizations such as the NHS and local author-ities collaborate with small and medium-sized enterprises, so as to allow them access to public sector occupational health services (NICE, 2009c).

Regardless of differences in formal system structures, there is a need for employees, trade unions, existing occupational health services, public health services, and workplaces to work in partnership with government to help facilitate greater implementation and uptake of workplace mental health and wellbeing actions. Given the sensitivity of the issue, employees and employers should work together towards the implementation of procedures to address psychosocial health risks in organizations, making use of existing guidelines where available.

In practice, this could mean providing more support for greater involve-ment of workers in workplace risk assessment, given the experience that workers have of their own workplaces. National and international stakeholders, including governments, can also work more together to help foster an exchange of best practices as regards psychosocial risk assessment and the transferability of approaches between national contexts; to raise awareness of workplace risk assessment to include psychosocial hazards; and to foster cooperation with other relevant stakeholders on this issue and organize training courses.

The exchange of good practices, among enterprises and nations, should, naturally, also include international organizations such as the World Health Organization, the International Labour Organization and the Organisation for Economic Cooperation and Development, or initiatives such as the Workplace Wellness Alliance of the World Economic Forum, as well as nongovernmental organizations and service user or self-help associations.

Conclusions

Employment in a good working environment is beneficial to physical and mental health. From a public health perspective, the workplace is an important setting where health-promoting activities can take place. Actions at work also provide an opportunity for the early identification of risk factors for poor health. Poor work environments can increase the risk of excess levels of stress, potentially leading to poor wellbeing.

A holistic approach to action to promote and protect mental health and wellbeing is required. It requires actions to improve the structure and organization of workplaces, as well as investing in measures to strengthen the ability of individuals to cope with daily stressors. Much of this action is about organizational issues: it is about a better workplace culture, improved communication, better line management, flexible working opportunities to protect the work–life balance and opportunities for career development and rewards. But we also need to recognize that individuals ought also to take responsibility for their own health, given that much of their time remains outside the working environment.

What is clear is that the economic arguments for investment in workplace mental health are strong. There are economic returns to business, but there is also much more. If workplace-mental-health programs are well implemented, additional benefits can be harnessed, such as a reduced burden on health and social welfare systems. But strengthening awareness that these benefits can be achieved is critical for increased implementation.

This is particularly the case for business outside the United States, as well as for governments who may not perceive it as their place to provide any support for workplace-health-promotion schemes.

No one approach will fit all circumstances. Approaches that have proved effective in some contexts may need adaptation to be effective in other settings, such as in different countries or in different sectors of employment. Critically, responsibility for the implementation of cost-effective actions does not rest with the employer alone. It is also important to get the buy-in of other stakeholders such as the health system, occupational health departments, social welfare organizations, trade unions, and people with lived experience of poor mental health at work. Economics can help do this, by demonstrating that these stakeholders also benefit from better wellbeing at work.

Nearly all of the economic evidence cited in this chapter is from the United States, where employers have a strong incentive to take action, as they often are responsible for funding health care for their employees. Financial and regulatory incentives may be needed to stimulate investment in workplace health promotion, especially in small and medium-sized businesses, in contexts where health systems are funded by taxation or social health insurance. Governments should be prepared to do this, as they will share in the benefits of better wellbeing at work. They could, for example, include tax breaks for the provision of workplace-health-promotion programs, as well as schemes to make workplace-health-promotion resources in public sector organizations available to smaller businesses in their local communities. After all, work is a fundamental and positive aspect of life. We simply cannot leave our mental health and wellbeing at the door of the workplace.

References

Allen, J. C., Lewis, J. B., & Tagliaferro, A. R. (2012). Cost-effectiveness of health risk reduction after lifestyle education in the small workplace. *Preventing Chronic Disease, 9.* http://www.cdc.gov/pcd/issues/2012/11_0169.htm.

Aronsson, G., Gustafsson, K., & Dallner, M. (2000). Sick but yet at work. An empirical study of sickness presenteeism. *Journal of Epidemiological Community Health, 54*(7), 502–509.

Baicker, K., Cutler, D., & Song, Z. (2010). Workplace wellness programs can generate savings. *Health Affairs (Millwood), 29*(2), 304–311.

Beck, A., Crain, A. L., Solberg, L. I., Unutzer, J., Glasgow, R. E., Maciosek, M. V. & Whitebird, R. (2011). Severity of depression and magnitude of productivity loss. *Annals of Family Medicine, 9*(4), 305–311.

Beddington, J., Cooper, C. L., Field, J., Goswami, U., Huppert, F. A., Jenkins, R., . . . Thomas, S. M. (2008). The mental wealth of nations. *Nature*, *455*(7216), 1057–1060.

Bhui, K. S., Dinos, S., Stansfeld, S. A., & White, P. D. (2012). A synthesis of the evidence for managing stress at work: A review of the reviews reporting on anxiety, depression, and absenteeism. *Journal of Environmental Public Health*, *2012*, 515874.

BIS (Department for Business, Innovation and Skills) (2008). *Foresight mental capital and wellbeing project. Final project report*. London: The Government Office for Science.

Black, C. (2008). *Working for a healthier tomorrow*. London: Department of Work and Pensions.

Boorman, S. (2009). *NHS Health and Wellbeing. Final report*. London: Department of Health.

Campbell, F., Worral, L., & Cooper, C. (2000). *The psychological effects of downsizing and privatisation*. Wolverhampton Business School Working Paper Series (WP001/00), 1–20.

Cancelliere, C., Cassidy, J. D., Ammendolia, C., & Cote, P. (2011). Are workplace health promotion programs effective at improving presenteeism in workers? A systematic review and best evidence synthesis of the literature. *BMC Public Health*, *11*, 395.

Chandola, T. (2010). *Stress at work*. London: The British Academy.

Cheng, Y., Chen, C. W., Chen, C. J., & Chiang, T. L. (2005). Job insecurity and its association with health among employees in the Taiwanese general population. *Social Science and Medicine*, *61*(1), 41–52.

Corbiere, M., Shen, J., Rouleau, M., & Dewa, C. S. (2009). A systematic review of preventive interventions regarding mental health issues in organizations. *Work*, *33*(1), 81–116.

De Hert, M., Correll, C. U., Bobes, J., Cetkovich-Bakmas, M., Cohen, D., Asai, I., . . . Leucht, S. (2011). Physical illness in patients with severe mental disorders. I. Prevalence, impact of medications and disparities in health care. *World Psychiatry*, *10*(1), 52–77.

de Jonge, J., Bosma, H., Peter, R., & Siegrist, J. (2000). Job strain, effort–reward imbalance and employee well-being: A large-scale cross-sectional study. *Social Science and Medicine*, *50*(9), 1317–1327.

Department of Work and Pensions (2013). *DWP Statistics*. http://statistics.dwp.gov.uk/asd/.

Dewa, C. S., McDaid, D., & Ettner, S. L. (2007). An international perspective on worker mental health problems: Who bears the burden and how are costs addressed? *Canadian Journal of Psychiatry*, *52*(6), 346–356.

Dornan, A., & Jane-Llopis, E. (2010). *The wellness imperative: Creating more effective organisations*. Geneva: World Economic Forum.

EFILWC (European Foundation for the Improvement of Living and Working Conditions) (2010). *Changes over time—First findings from the fifth European*

Working Conditions Survey. Dublin: European Foundation for the Improvement of Living and Working Conditions.

Eurostat (2010). *Health and safety at work in Europe. 1999–2007*. Luxembourg: Publications Office of the European Union.

Eurostat (2012). *Employment statistics*. http://epp.eurostat.ec.europa.eu/statistics _explained/index.php/Employment_statistics.

Grime, P. R. (2004). Computerized cognitive behavioural therapy at work: A randomized controlled trial in employees with recent stress-related absenteeism. *Occupational Medicine (London)*, *54*(5), 353–359.

Hamberg-van Reenen, H. H., Proper, K. I. , & van den Berg, M. (2012). Worksite mental health interventions: A systematic review of economic evaluations. *Occupational and Environmental Medicine*, *69*(11), 837–845.

Janssens, H., Clays, E., Clercq, B. D., Bacquer, D. D., & Braeckman, L. (2013). The relation between presenteeism and different types of future sickness absence. *Journal of Occupational Health*. http://www.ncbi.nlm .nih.gov/pubmed/23485571.

Karasek, R., & Theorell, T. (1990). *Healthy work: Stress, productivity, and the reconstruction of working life*. New York: Basic Books.

Kaszynski, H., & Cechnicki, A. (2011). Polscy pracodawcy wobec zatrudniania osób chorujących psychicznie [Attitudes of Polish employers toward hiring mentally ill people]. *Psychiatria Polska*, *45*(1), 45–60.

Kieselbach, T., Nielsen, K., & Triomphe, C. E. (2010). *Psychosocial risks and health effects of restructuring*. Brussels: Commission of the European Communities.

Kuoppala, J., Lamminpaa, A., & Husman, P. (2008). Work health promotion, job well-being, and sickness absences-a systematic review and meta-analysis. *Journal of Occupational and Environmental Medicine*, *50*(11), 1216–1227.

Laszlo, K. D., Pikhart, H., Kopp, M. S., Bobak, M., Pajak, A., Malyutina, S., . . . Marmot, M. (2010). Job insecurity and health: A study of 16 European countries. *Social Science and Medicine*, *70*(6), 867–874.

Lau, B. (2008). Effort–reward imbalance and overcommitment in employees in a Norwegian municipality: A cross sectional study. *Journal of Occupational Medicine and Toxicology*, *3*, *9*. http://link.springer.com/article/ 10.1186%2F1745-6673-3-9.

Leineweber, C., Westerlund, H., Hagberg, J., Svedberg, P., & Alexanderson, K. (2012). Sickness presenteeism is more than an alternative to sickness absence: Results from the population-based SLOSH study. *International Archives of Occupational and Environmental Health*, *85*(8), 905–914.

Lerner, D., Adler, D., Hermann, R. C., Chang, H., Ludman, E. J., Greenhill, A., . . . Rogers, W. H. (2012). Impact of a work-focused intervention on the productivity and symptoms of employees with depression. *Journal of Occupational and Environmental Medicine*, *54*(2), 128–135.

Levi, L., Bartley, M., Marmot, M., Karasek, R., Theorell, T., Siegrist, J., . . . Landsbergis, P. (2000). Stressors at the workplace: Theoretical models. *Occupational Medicine*, *15*(1), 69–106.

Lo Sasso, A. T., Rost, K., & Beck, A. (2006). Modeling the impact of enhanced depression treatment on workplace functioning and costs: A cost-benefit approach. *Medical Care, 44*(4), 352–358.

Loeppke, R., Nicholson, S., Taitel, M., Sweeney, M., Haufle, V., & Kessler, R. C. (2008). The impact of an integrated population health enhancement and disease management program on employee health risk, health conditions, and productivity. *Population Health Managment, 11*(6), 287–296.

Martin, A., Sanderson, K., & Cocker, F. (2009). Meta-analysis of the effects of health promotion intervention in the workplace on depression and anxiety symptoms. *Scandinavian Journal of Work and Environmental Health, 35*(1), 7–18.

McCraty, R., Atkinson, M., Lipsenthal, L., & Arguelles, L. (2009). New hope for correctional officers: An innovative program for reducing stress and health risks. *Applied Psychophysiological Biofeedback, 34*(4), 251–272.

McDaid, D. (2007). The economics of mental health in the workplace: What do we know and where do we go? *Epidemiologia e Psichiatria Sociale, 16*(4), 294–298.

McDaid, D., King, D., Park, A., & Parsonage, M. (2011). Promoting wellbeing in the workplace. In M. Knapp, D. McDaid, & M. Parsonage (Eds.), *Mental health promotion and mental illness prevention: The economic case* (pp. 22–23). London: Department of Health.

McDaid, D., King, D., & Parsonage, M. (2011). Workplace screening for depression and anxiety disorders. In M. Knapp, D. McDaid & M. Parsonage (Eds.), *Mental health promotion and mental illness prevention: The economic case* (pp. 20–21). London Department of Health.

McDaid, D., & Park, A. L. (2011). Investing in mental health and well-being: Findings from the DataPrev project. *Health Promotion International 26*, Suppl. 1, i108–i139.

Michaels, C. N., & Greene, A. M. (2013). Worksite wellness: Increasing adoption of workplace health promotion programs. *Health Promotion Practice, 14*(4), 473–479.

Milani, R. V., & Lavie, C. J. (2009). Impact of worksite wellness intervention on cardiac risk factors and one-year health care costs. *American Journal of Cardiology, 104*(10), 1389–1392.

Mills, P. R., Kessler, R. C., Cooper, J., & Sullivan, S. (2007). Impact of a health promotion program on employee health risks and work productivity. *American Journal of Health Promotion, 22*(1), 45–53.

Munz, D. C., Kohler J. M., and Greenberg C. I. (2001). Effectiveness of a comprehensive worksite stress management program: Combining organizational and individual interventions. *International Journal of Stress Management, 8*, 49–62.

National Economic and Social Forum (2007). *Mental health and social inclusion.* Dublin: NESF.

Naydeck, B. L., Pearson, J. A., Ozminkowski, R. J., Day, B. T., & Goetzel, R. Z. (2008). The impact of the Highmark Employee Wellness programs on 4-year healthcare costs. *Journal of Occupational and Environmental Medicine*, 50(2), 146–156.

NICE (National Institute for Health and Care Excellence) (2009a). *Promoting mental wellbeing at work: Business case*. London: NICE.

NICE (2009b). *Promoting mental wellbeing through productive and healthy working conditions: Guidance for employers*. London: NICE.

NICE (2009c). *Workplace interventions that are effective for promoting mental wellbeing. Synopsis of the evidence of effectiveness and cost-effectiveness*. London: NICE.

Olesen, J., Gustavsson, A., Svensson, M., Wittchen, H. U., & Jonsson, B. (2012). The economic cost of brain disorders in Europe. *European Journal of Neurology*, 19(1), 155–162.

Organisation for Economic Cooperation and Development (2012). *Sick on the job? Myths and realities about mental health and work*. Paris: OECD Publishing.

Ozminkowski, R. J., Ling, D., Goetzel, R. Z., Bruno, J. A., Rutter, K. R., Isaac, F. & Wang, S. (2002) Long-term impact of Johnson & Johnson's health & wellness program on health care utilization and expenditures. *Journal of Occupational and Environmental Medicine*, 44(1), 21–29.

Pelletier, K. R. (2005). A review and analysis of the clinical and cost-effectiveness studies of comprehensive health promotion and disease management programs at the worksite: Update VI 2000–2004. *Journal of Occupational and Environmental Medicine*, 47(10), 1051–1058.

Perkins, R., Farmer, P., & Litchfield, P. (2009). *Realising ambitions: Better employment support for people with a mental health condition*. London: Department of Work and Pensions.

Pomaki, G., Franche, R. L., Murray, E., Khushrushahi, N., & Lampinen, T. M. (2012). Workplace-based work disability prevention interventions for workers with common mental health conditions: A review of the literature. *Journal of Occupational Rehabilitation*, 22(2), 182–195.

Rahe, R. H., Taylor, C. B., Tolles, R. L., Newhall, L. M., Veach, T. L., & Bryson, S. (2002). A novel stress and coping workplace program reduces illness and healthcare utilization. *Psychosomatic Medicine*, 64(2), 278–286.

Renaud, L., Kishchuk, N., Juneau, M., Nigam, A., Tereault, K., & Leblanc, M. C. (2008). Implementation and outcomes of a comprehensive worksite health promotion program. *Canadian Journal of Public Health*, 99(1), 73–77.

Richardson, K. M., & Rothstein, H. R. (2008). Effects of occupational stress management intervention programs: A meta-analysis. *Journal of Occupational Health Psychology*, 13(1), 69–93.

Robertson, I., & Cooper, C. (2011). *Wellbeing: Productivity and happiness at work*. Basingstoke: Palgrave Macmillan.

Sanderson, K., & Andrews, G. (2006). Common mental disorders in the workforce: Recent findings from descriptive and social epidemiology. *Canadian Journal of Psychiatry*, 51(2), 63–75.

See Me Scotland (2006). *See me so far: A review of the first four years of the Scottish anti-stigma campaign*. Edinburgh: See Me Scotland.

Siegrist, J. (1996). Adverse health effects of high-effort/low-reward conditions. *Journal of Occupational Health Psychology*, *1*(1), 27–41.

Stuckler, D., Meissner, C., Fishback, P., Basu, S., & McKee, M. (2012). Banking crises and mortality during the Great Depression: Evidence from US urban populations, 1929–1937. *Journal of Epidemiological Community Health*, *66*(5), 410–419.

Taloyan, M., Aronsson, G., Leineweber, C., Magnusson Hanson, L., Alexanderson, K., & Westerlund, H. (2012). Sickness presenteeism predicts suboptimal self-rated health and sickness absence: A nationally representative study of the Swedish working population. *PLoS One*, *7*(9), e44721.

Wahlbeck, K., & McDaid, D. (2012). Actions to alleviate the mental health impact of the economic crisis. *World Psychiatry*, *11*(3), 139–145.

Wang, H., & Samson, K. (2009). *Wellness and productivity management: A new approach to increasing performance*. Philadelphia: Right Management Inc.

Wang, P. S., Patrick, A., Avorn, J., Azocar, F., Ludman, E. J., McCulloch, J., . . . Kessler, R. C. (2006). The costs and benefits of enhanced depression care to employers. *Archives of General Psychiatry*, *63*(12), 1345–1353.

Wang, P. S., Simon, G. E., Avorn, J., Azocar, F., Ludman, E. J., McCulloch, J., . . . Kessler, R. C. (2007). Telephone screening, outreach, and care management for depressed workers and impact on clinical and work productivity outcomes: A randomized controlled trial. *Journal of the American Medical Association*, *298*(12), 1401–1411.

Wang, P. S., Simon, G. E., & Kessler, R. C. (2008). Making the business case for enhanced depression care: The National Institute of Mental Health–Harvard Work Outcomes Research and Cost-effectiveness Study. *Journal of Occupational and Environmental Medicine*, *50*(4), 468–475.

Zebra Zone (2008). *Stress au travail. Belgique 2008* [Stess at work. Belgium 2008]. Brussels: Securex.

Further Readings

More on the wellbeing and economic benefits of work can be found in various reports on wellbeing and work prepared as part of the Foresight Mental Capital and Wellbeing Project. London: Government Office for Science, 2008. These are available at http://www.bis.gov.uk/foresight/our-work/projects/published-projects/mental-capital-and-wellbeing/reports-and-publications.

See also various reports on workplace health promotion produced by the National Institute for Health and Care Excellence in England. These are available at http://guidance.nice.org.uk/PHG/Published.

Knapp, M., McDaid, D., & Parsonage, M. (Eds.). (2011). *Mental health promotion and mental illness prevention: The economic case*. London: Department of Health.

Robertson, I., & Cooper, C. (2011) *Wellbeing: Productivity and happiness at work*. Basingstoke: Palgrave Macmillan.

10

Promoting the Health and Wellbeing of Older People

Making an Economic Case

A-La Park and David McDaid

London School of Economics and Political Science, U.K.

Anna K. Forsman

National Institute for Health and Welfare (THL), Finland
and Nordic School of Public Health NHV, Sweden

Kristian Wahlbeck

Finnish Association for Mental Health, Finland

Introduction

This chapter focuses on the wellbeing of older people. It looks at what is known about some of the economic impacts of poor wellbeing in older age, as well as the potential economic benefits of better wellbeing. It then identifies effective actions that may be taken to promote and protect the wellbeing of people over the age of 55 and reflects on what is known about their cost-effectiveness.

The chapter draws on a range of sources including previous systematic reviews of the effectiveness of different health-promoting interventions (Forsman, Nordmyr, & Wahlbeck, 2011; Forsman, Schierenbeck, & Wahlbeck, 2011; Lee et al., 2012), guidelines on health promotion for older people, as well reviews of economic studies (McDaid & Park, 2011; Windle

The Economics of Wellbeing: Wellbeing: A Complete Reference Guide, Volume V.
Edited by David McDaid and Cary L. Cooper.
© 2014 John Wiley & Sons, Ltd. Published 2014 by John Wiley & Sons, Inc.
DOI: 10.1002/9781118539415.wbwell10

et al., 2008). Where any monetary values are reported in the chapter, these have been converted to 2010 U.S. dollars using the IMF World Economic Outlook Database.

Why Is Economics Relevant to the Wellbeing of Older People?

As we shall indicate, there are economic benefits that come from focusing on protecting the wellbeing of older people, given the substantial contributions that they make to the economy. It is important, therefore, to understand what contributes to, or detracts from, good wellbeing. It is equally important to know what actions can work to help promote and protect wellbeing. This requires carefully conducted evaluations of different actions targeted at different populations in different contexts and settings, to determine not only their effectiveness but also their acceptability to target population groups such as older people.

So, where does economics fit in? Well, if resources were limitless it would be relatively straightforward to argue for investment in any wellbeing promotion action that worked. We don't, however, live in Utopia; resources are scarce and careful choices have to be made about how to utilize what is available. Decisions are even more important in the context of economic downturns where health and social care and other budgets come under great pressure. Quite simply, evidence of effectiveness alone is insufficient for decision making; in addition to knowing what works and in what context, information on the economic impact of potential interventions is required. Such economic evidence is increasingly a formal element of decision-making processes, and, as we shall see, can, in some circumstances, be compelling in putting forward a case for policy change.

There are at least four key economic questions that can be helpful to decision makers (Knapp & McDaid, 2009). First we are interested in the *costs of inaction*: what are the economic consequences of *not* taking action to promote and protect the wellbeing of older people? After all, if there are few consequences from not protecting wellbeing, then should it in fact be a priority? Policy makers will also want to know what are the *costs of action*? In other words, what are the resource requirements and economic costs of providing any intervention, and what would this mean for the scaling-up of an effective service nationwide?

240

Given that resources are limited, there are opportunity costs associated with any investment we make. If we invest in a Tai Chi program to promote the wellbeing of community-dwelling older people, those resources are no longer available to be used for another activity, such as befriending programs. That is where economic evaluation comes in, as it allows the *cost-effectiveness* of any action to be determined. For instance, we can estimate how much it costs to implement a Tai Chi program and look at the impact it has on psychological wellbeing, and compare these with the cost and impacts of one or more alternative interventions. A final area where economics may have a role to play is in the *use of economic incentives* to influence behavior, perhaps providing funding for transport so that older people without their own transport can attend Tai Chi classes, or providing subsidies or tax breaks to not-for-profit groups to develop community health promotion programs.

We will consider all of these questions throughout the chapter, beginning by looking at whether there are economic benefits that may be gained through better wellbeing, before then looking at what the economic consequences of not taking action may be.

What Are the Potential Economic Payoffs of Focusing on Wellbeing?

Many of the benefits of better wellbeing, such as higher levels of satisfaction with our lives and the world in which we live, are difficult to quantify in monetary terms, but are intrinsically of importance in their own right. They also have been explicitly acknowledged to be important by governments and other bodies formulating new measurements of national wellbeing (Beaumont, 2012; Stiglitz, Sen, & Fitoussi, 2010). But there are some more easily identified economic payoffs that can be identified and we focus on two here—healthy aging and the positive contributions of older people to economic outputs.

Healthy Aging

Investing in measures to promote wellbeing can help promote healthy aging. Healthy aging is a key policy objective in many countries to try to counter the effects of demographic change. We know that the global population is aging at an unprecedented rate, with the number of people over the age of

241

60 expected to exceed the number of people under the age of 15 for the first time by 2045 (United Nations, 2009). In Ireland, for example, about one quarter of the population will be over the age of 65 by 2046 putting pressure on the sustainability of the pension system and risking greater health and social care costs (Baker & Ring, 2013).

The number of oldest old is also growing, or "exploding" to use the words of Roger Thatcher, former director of the Office of Population Censuses and Surveys and Registrar General for England and Wales (Thatcher, 2001). The increased likelihood of survival into later life, including to very old ages, has been a trend in developed countries throughout the second part of the last century (Serra, Watson, Sinclair, & Kneale 2011). If these trends continue, then in the United Kingdom alone, over a quarter of children born in 2011 and about 20% of younger people now under 20 can expect to celebrate their 100th birthday (Evans, 2011).

Increased life expectancy is, of course, something to be celebrated, especially if this means that we will extend the number of years where we can live in good health, rather than extending time spent in poor heath. If wellbeing does indeed protect health and reduce the risk of some future health events, then investing in wellbeing now will continue to have economic payoffs in future. This is because we can avoid some future health and social welfare costs.

Harnessing the Economic Power of Older People

A second important economic argument for investing in the wellbeing of older people is that this can help harness even more of the economic power of what we have established is a growing demographic. Far from being a burden to the economy, older people make a substantial positive contribution to any economy. For example, work in the United Kingdom suggests that in 2010, after accounting for extra pension, health, and social care costs, people over the age of 65 still made a net contribution of more than $65 billion to the economy (WRVS, 2011). This, it is predicted, will rise to more than $125 billion by 2030.

These economic benefits not only include the spending power of older people, but also their increasing role in paid work beyond traditional retirement ages, as well as through volunteering and caring responsibilities, perhaps for spouses but also for grandchildren. In 2010 the economic benefits from volunteering and looking after grandchildren in the United Kingdom by people aged over 65 were estimated to be $17.2 billion and

$4.4 billion per annum respectively. This says nothing about the staggering $57 billion in informal care provided by older people to adult family members. The Women's Royal Voluntary Service (WRVS) report also identifies other benefits which are more difficult to value monetarily but of great importance: for example, older people may act as "social glue" in their local communities, contributing to community cohesion and social capital, providing leadership in local clubs and faith groups or providing advice and support to young people.

A survey of more than 2,000 people over the age of 55 in the United Kingdom in 2012 found that, on average, that they are involved in charitable activities for 75 hours per year, with a further 73 hours on voluntary activities in their communities (MGM Advantage, 2012). The survey also found that they provide 326 hours of informal care per annum. All of this implies that if the older population can remain healthier for longer then there is scope for further increasing these economic benefits. If better wellbeing can help us achieve this goal then the case for investment will become even more persuasive.

What Are the Economic Consequences of Poor Wellbeing in Older People?

In addition to the positive economic benefits to be gained from better wellbeing, we can document some of the adverse consequences of poor wellbeing. Wellbeing is influenced by much more than health status. There are ten different domains considered in measures of national wellbeing now being used in the United Kingdom (Beaumont, 2012). As well as looking at our income, wealth, and health status, other domains include the environment in which we live, our education and skills, the quality of the relationships we have with other people, and our roles in society. In this section we highlight some of the impacts of just a few of these influences on wellbeing: the risk of social isolation, our mental and physical health status, and income.

Social Isolation

We begin by looking at social isolation. This is a key risk factor for poor wellbeing. It may become even more important in future years given the increasing number of people in many high-income countries who are living alone. In the United States, figures from the Census Bureau indicate that

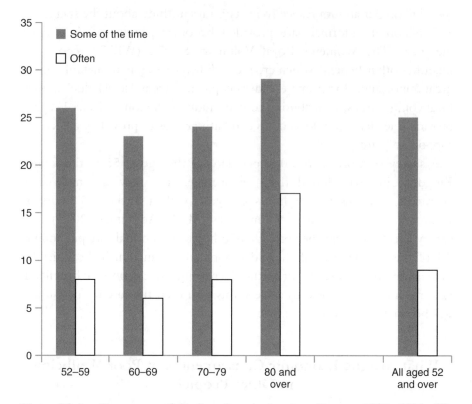

Figure 10.1. Frequency of Feeling Lonely by Age Group, 2009–2010 (%). English Longitudinal Survey on Ageing 2009–2010. Respondents were asked "How often do you feel lonely?" and responded "Hardly ever," "Some of the time," or "Often." Adapted from Beaumont (2013).

the number of people living alone had increased from 17% in 1970 to 27% in 2010 (Lofquist, Lugaila, O'Connell, & Feliz, 2012). Similar changes in living arrangements can be seen around the globe. In 2005 about one out of every seven older people lived alone; more than one third of all older women lived alone (United Nations, 2005).

It is not surprising then that many people have to deal with loneliness. Figure 10.1 illustrates how common feeling lonely can be in older people, using data from the 2009–2010 Wave of the English Longitudinal Study on Ageing (ELSA) (Beaumont, 2013). Forty-six percent of those aged 80 and over reported being lonely often or some of the time compared to 34% of all those aged 52 and over. Those aged 80 and over were also considerably more likely to report being lonely often than other age groups: 17% of the over 80s reported being lonely often compared to an average of 9% of

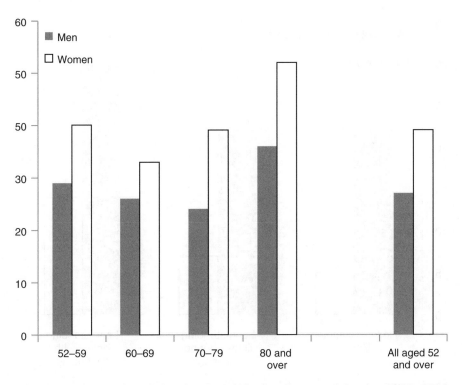

Figure 10.2. Frequency of Feeling Lonely by Age Group and Gender, 2009–2010 (%). English Longitudinal Survey on Ageing 2009–2010. Respondents were asked "How often do you feel lonely?" and responded "Hardly ever," "Some of the time," or "Often." Adapted from Beaumont (2013).

all respondents. A higher percentage of women than men reported feeling lonely either some of the time or often in each age group: 39% of all women aged 52 and over reported this frequency of feeling lonely compared to 27% of men (Figure 10.2).

Rates of loneliness were also markedly higher in people with long-standing health problems that place limits on their daily activities. Twenty-seven percent of those who did not report any long-standing illness said that they had been lonely some of the time or often compared with 45% of those with a long-standing illness that limited their activities (Figure 10.3).

Limited social networks and geographical isolation are risk factors to the wellbeing of older people. Using data from ELSA, social isolation rather than loneliness has also been associated with a 25% increased risk of mortality compared to those who were not socially isolated; loneliness was not found to increase risk of mortality (Steptoe, Shankar, Demakakos, & Wardle,

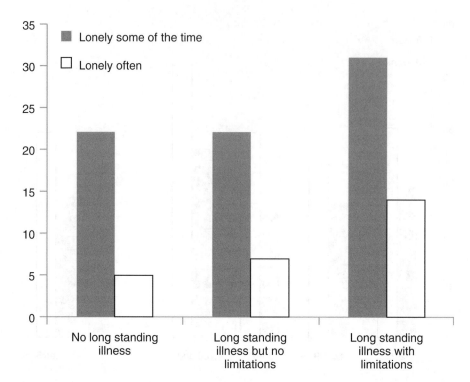

Figure 10.3. Frequency of Loneliness by Long-Standing Illness Status, 2009–2010 (%). English Longitudinal Survey on Ageing 2009–2010. Respondents were asked "How often do you feel lonely?" and responded "Hardly ever," "Some of the time," or "Often." They were also asked whether they had a long-standing illness and whether it limited their daily activities such as pushing a vacuum cleaner. Adapted from Beaumont (2013).

2013). In the Netherlands, however, a 10-year follow-up of men over the age of 65, found that those who had previously reported themselves to be lonely had a 30% increased risk of mortality compared to the rest of the study sample (Holwerda et al., 2012).

Elsewhere lower levels of contact with friends and neighbors were associated with significantly greater rates of depression in a survey of more than 6,800 older people living in two areas of Sweden and Finland (Forsman, Nyqvist, Schierenbeck, Gustafson, & Wahlbeck, 2012). The authors also looked at what they called "cognitive social capital," which they defined as trust in friends and neighbors. Low levels of trust were associated with higher rates of depression. Data from the European Study of Adult Wellbeing also reports a positive association between the number of close contacts and mental wellbeing (Burholt &Windle, 2006).

Inevitably, older people will experience bereavements. This is another determinant of social isolation and loneliness. The death of a spouse is a major life event; one recent European longitudinal analysis indicates that married older people who lose a spouse are at significantly increased risk of having depressive symptoms compared to married couples who do not experience such a bereavement (Schaan, 2013). In this study the impact of bereavement did not differ by gender, but appeared more pronounced where the married couple had a good quality of relationship. The ELSA survey in England also found that "people who perceived that their spouse was able to give them high levels of social support reported much higher levels of wellbeing than either married people who did not perceive their spouse gave them high levels of social support or people without a spouse or partner" (Demakakos, McMunn, & Steptoe, 2010, p. 10).

Widowed people in Nordic countries in the study by Schaan had lower levels of depressive symptoms compared to those in southern Europe; similar studies have also reported that older people tend to be less lonely in northern European countries (Dykstra, 2009). This might conceivably be due to the better levels of social support and social protection to be found in these countries. Scandinavian older adults may be satisfied with their lives when they have more privacy and independent living arrangements, relative, for instance, to their Italian or Greek counterparts, who will have been more used to frequent social contacts at an earlier age (Reher, 1998).

In China findings of higher levels of depression in widowed people have been attributed to the lower levels of support from family and friends (Zhang & Li, 2011). The situation is however complex and may be very different in different contexts and cultures: analysis in South Korea of more than 9,000 older people in a cross-sectional survey found significantly higher rates of depression in widowed or divorced men but not in women (Jang et al., 2009).

Poor Mental and Physical Health

Health status is, of course, one key element of wellbeing, and we would do well to remember the words of the Roman poet Juvenal who spoke of the need for "a sound mind in a sound body," recognizing the links between physical and mental wellbeing and the importance of protecting both as we age.

Individuals have different levels of coping ability and resilience to life events. Personal resilience is a multidimensional product of perceived self-esteem and self-efficacy by individuals throughout their life course. It is protective against the risk of poor psychological wellbeing and depression. Resilience needs to be strengthened as much as possible because depression is expected to become the largest contributor to the worldwide burden of disease by 2030 and already is the most common mental health problem in older people (de Beurs et al., 2005). The economic costs of depression in later life are substantial; for instance, analysis in the United States of almost 9,000 people over the age of 60 found that their health care costs were about 50% higher than their non-depressed counterparts over a 6-month period (Katon, Lin, Russo, & Unutzer, 2003); substantial higher costs have been reported elsewhere, e.g., in Germany (Luppa et al., 2013) or Quebec (Vasiliadis et al., 2013). The majority of suicides are linked to depression; and older people in most countries have the highest rates of completed suicide (O'Connell, Chin, Cunningham, & Lawlor, 2004).

In high-income countries studies suggest that around 12% of older people are affected by clinically significant levels of depression at any one time (Copeland et al., 2004); rates as high as 16% have been reported in some studies (Forlani et al., 2013; Regan, Kearney, Savva, Cronin, & Kenny, 2013). Rates of depression increase with age; for instance, one Norwegian cohort study of more than 16,000 people found significant increases in incidence at all ages above 76, with the highest annual incidence rates of more than 10% seen in those aged between 86 and 90 (Solhaug, Romuld, Romild, & Stordal, 2012).

Older men, in particular those who have been bereaved, may be more likely to neglect self-care and become vulnerable to various illnesses leading to higher mortality due to lack of cooking skills and information on proper nutrition and self-care tasks. Unhealthy lifestyles in turn have an impact on wellbeing. The Australian Wellbeing, Eating and Exercise for a Long Life (WELL) study included 2,644 people aged 55 to 64. It found that older people were more likely to report low levels of self-rated health if they also had low levels of fruit and vegetable intake and physical activity. One more serving unit of fruit or vegetables or an hour of physical activity during leisure time was linked with a 10% higher chance of reporting their health as good or better (Sodergren, McNaughton, Salmon, Ball, & Crawford, 2012).

Functional limitations at older age can also have a detrimental effect on wellbeing. Data from the ELSA survey in England shows that more than 45%

of older people with two or more limitations in their activities of daily living (ADL) have high levels of depressive symptoms compared to just 11% of those without any limitations (Demakakos et al., 2010). With advancing age, older people tend to have multiple morbid conditions; this also can increase demands on informal family carers, which in turn can affect their wellbeing.

Poverty

Relative poverty is also a risk factor for poor wellbeing. Financially better-off people tend to have a smaller number of depressive symptoms, higher levels of life satisfaction and quality of life, and lower levels of loneliness (Burholt & Windle, 2006). Data from the ELSA survey in England indicates that 27.5% of people in the poorest quintile in 2008–2009 had clinical levels of depression compared with only 7.2% of the wealthiest group (Demakakos et al., 2010).

A lack of future financial security can also cause undue stress and increase the risk of falling into debt; we have seen that unmanageable debt in the general adult population is linked to an increased risk of developing depressive disorders (Meltzer, Bebbington, Brugha, Farrell, & Jenkins, 2013). Future generations around the globe may receive considerably less in pensions compared to current day pensioners due to the strain on the economic system. This again increases the potential risk of poverty in old age.

One consequence of a lack of income may be insufficient funds to adequately heat a home. This can be of critical importance as many older people may spend a great majority of their time at home. Evidence indicates that this "fuel poverty" has a detrimental impact on health, including more respiratory health problems and declining psychological wellbeing (de Vries & Blane, 2012). A lack of funds also potentially leads to social exclusion and isolation, which, as we have already highlighted, can have substantial adverse consequences for wellbeing.

Are Measures to Protect and Promote Wellbeing in Older People Cost-Effective?

In this section we look at what is known about the cost-effectiveness of a number of different actions that may potentially help promote and protect wellbeing in older people. These include psychological therapies and health education, social supports, and other measures to tackle social and geographical isolation such as befriending, new media, or group activities.

The evidence base on what works still remains comparatively limited for this age group. A recent meta-analyses of studies with psychological or social interventions to prevent depression in older people reported a small but statistical effect; this being most pronounced for the use of social activities (Forsman, Nordmyr, et al., 2011; Forsman, Schierenbeck, et al., 2011; Lee et al., 2012). There is also evidence that actions targeted at high-risk groups of older people, such as those with chronic physical illness or the bereaved, can be effective (Cuijpers, Smit, Lebowitz, & Beekman, 2011). We then go on to briefly look at the economic case for investing in some actions outside the health system, such as measures to tackle poverty and improve access to lifelong learning. The benefits of volunteering or continued participation in work are also considered.

Group Activities

Various group activities can help promote the wellbeing of older people. They can help counter loneliness and social isolation. For instance regular participation in exercise classes by older people in a northern city in England was associated with better mental health at a cost per Quality Adjusted Life Year (QALY) gained of $21,453 (Munro, Nicholl, Brazier, Davey, & Cochrane, 2004). This would be considered to be cost-effective in most high-income-country contexts. The benefits achieved were thought to have been due to social engagement rather than the exercise per se.

Similarly, several studies have reported beneficial effects to psychological wellbeing of group-based Tai Chi for older people, but little is known about cost-effectiveness (Taylor-Piliae, Haskell, Waters, & Froelicher, 2006; Wang et al., 2010). However, if other health benefits are considered, then the economic case may become more attractive. In fact, the economic benefits of home exercise, group-based physical activity, and Tai Chi in reducing the risks of falls in older people have been modeled in Australia (Church, Goodall, Norman, & Haas, 2012). In this analysis Tai Chi was found to be most cost-effective at a cost of $28,648 per QALY, gained. Thus, any additional benefits to psychological wellbeing from Tai Chi could only make this intervention even more cost-effective.

In Finland, a trial of psychosocial group therapy for lonely older people was also reported to lead to significant improvements in psychological wellbeing, with a net mean reduction in health-care costs per participant of $1,030 (Pitkala, Routasalo, Kautiainen, & Tilvis, 2009). Another economic evaluation examined group-based occupational therapy sessions to promote healthy lifestyle change in the

United States. It was found to be cost-effective, improving quality of life over 9 months, without significantly increasing costs (Hay et al., 2002).

Addressing Social Isolation through New Media

The Internet is an important part of life today, and the medium is being used by an increasing number of older people for everyday transactions, such as banking and shopping, as well as for keeping in touch with friends and relatives. In a recent U.K. survey a quarter of all 65–74-year-olds were using social media and 44% were banking online; but in contrast to young adults few people over the age of 55 were using mobile phones to access the Internet (OFCOM, 2012). As of April 2012, 53% of Americans over the age of 65 were also using the Internet or email (Zickuhr & Madden, 2012).

The Internet is seen as a credible source of health-related information for older people (even through quality controls are limited), particularly in rapidly growing economies (McDaid & Park, 2010). These surveys indicate that in both the United Kingdom and the United States email is used much more than social media platforms; similar findings have been reported in Australia (Sum, Mathews, & Hughes, 2009). People aged between 55 and 75 have shown very positive attitudes towards use of the Internet or e-mail correspondence with families and friends, finding it easy to use (Adams, Stubbs, & Woods, 2005).

However, little is known about the cost-effectiveness of these technologies for older people. Nonetheless, they do represent a low cost means of communication, which has been associated with improvement in psychological wellbeing (Sum, Mathews, Pourghasem, & Hughes, 2009). Psychological therapies and self-help materials, such as those discussed in the next section, can also be delivered online, helping to reduce some costs and reaching people who may not otherwise be able to participate in group-based activities.

Stepped Care Including Use of Psychological Therapies

Some economic analysis supports the use of stepped care as a cost-effective means of preventing depression and anxiety among older people. A study in the Netherlands tested the effect of a stepped-care program for older people with sub-clinical-threshold depressive symptoms identified in primary care (van't Veer-Tazelaar et al., 2009). Stepped care encompassed (1) watchful waiting, (2) guided self-help using bibliotherapy, (3) problem solving and (4) referral to a primary care physician for further evaluation and treatment when required. The intervention was successful in reducing the incidence of anxiety or depressive disorders by 50%, with effects maintained over 12 months (van't Veer-Tazelaar et al., 2011). Modelling analysis based on trial data reported an incremental cost of $5,204 for a depression-free year (van't Veer-Tazelaar et al., 2010). The intervention had a 57% likelihood of being more cost-effective than routine primary care at a willingness to pay ceiling of $6,000 for a depression-free year. The authors concluded that this would be cost-effective in most high-income-country contexts.

Home Visiting Programs

In many high-income countries home visiting programs form part of the package of services to support older people. In a systematic review on economic evidence for the promotion of mental health and wellbeing (McDaid & Park, 2011), several studies looked at different types of home visiting interventions to promote wellbeing and reduce the risk of depression. The results were equivocal. Neither a home visit program by nurses in the Netherlands (Bouman et al., 2008), nor a program to promote the befriending of older people at home in England, were found to be effective or cost-effective (Charlesworth et al., 2008; Wilson et al., 2009).

A more promising economic study from the Netherlands compared a home visiting service provided by trained volunteers with a brochure providing information on depression. This program was targeted at older people who had been widowed for between 6 and 9 months and who were experiencing some degree of loneliness (Onrust, Smit, Willemse, van den Bout, & Cuijpers, 2008). Although improvements in quality of life were marginal the intervention still had a 70% chance of being cost-effective, with a baseline cost per QALY gained of $10,366.

In Canada a trial of an enhanced home nursing program for the over 75s, including education about healthy lifestyles, better coordination of community services, use of empowerment strategies to bolster the personal emotional resources and provision of support for family carers, was also associated with a significant improvement in mental wellbeing. There were no additional costs compared to usual home nursing care (Markle-Reid et al., 2006). Further analysis of similar multi-component home nursing programs in Canada also reported significantly improved quality of life at no extra cost to the health or long term care services (Markle-Reid, Browne, & Gafni, 2013).

Volunteering and Employment

Everybody wants to feel valued, respected, and understood. Older people are no exception, but some may struggle to make the transition from work to retirement. This loss of role can increase the risk of poor wellbeing and depression. Volunteering can provide meaningful ways to remain active in their communities. It is generally believed that volunteering can provide opportunities for social interaction and building social networks. In turn this can alleviate the feelings of loneliness, foster an altruistic spirit and a sense of purpose, and boost self-esteem.

In the United Kingdom, for example, a growing interest in volunteering throughout the life course peaks in the years right after retirement. Volunteering can help older people to experience a smooth transition from paid working stage to other post-retirement contributions to society. Almost one in four people aged 50 and over are involved in some type of voluntary activity in the UK (Lee, 2006).

Voluntary activities in late life can have physical and mental health benefits. One review reported that formal voluntary work for older people was associated with better self-reported health outcomes, physical health, social functioning, and greater satisfaction with life. While not having an impact on nursing home admission rates or a reduction in the likelihood of chronic physical health problems, volunteering was nonetheless linked with reduced depressive moods and improved survival (von Bonsdorff & Rantanen, 2011).

It should be noted that the benefits of volunteering can equally apply to paid work, perhaps on a part-time basis. An example of this comes from analysis of the Singapore Longitudinal Ageing Study. This showed positive health benefits from volunteering or continued participation in work (Schwingel, Niti, Tang, & Ng, 2009). Of 4,470 people aged 55 and over, the 10% who were engaged in volunteering, as well as the 12% who were in paid employment, had better cognitive function, less depressive symptoms and reported higher levels of mental/psychological wellbeing and life satisfaction, compared with their contemporaries who did not participate in work or volunteering activities after retirement.

Older volunteers can also help improve or maintain the quality of life of their peers. The Senior Companions Program in the United States consisted of volunteers aged 60 and above who received a small stipend to help housebound people living alone. They helped with activities such as purchasing groceries, preparing meals, providing transport when needed,

253

and, most importantly, providing regular human contact for at least 4 hours per week. The volunteers' life satisfaction scores were shown to improve significantly over 3 months compared with a waiting list control group of other future volunteers (Rabiner et al., 2003).

While volunteering sounds attractive, we should caution the reader that there is little robust information on its cost-effectiveness. However, volunteering, just like informal caring, is in itself a substantial contribution to economic output. We noted earlier in the chapter that, in the United Kingdom alone, volunteering is estimated to be worth $17 billion per annum (WRVS, 2011). The documented benefits to psychological wellbeing, if realized, potentially could also mean the avoidance of significant costs for treating and managing depression and related disorders. There are, of course, additional benefits to those that volunteers help; the American Association of Retired Persons has a successful Experience Corps program that operates in 20 cities in the United States helping children who are struggling with their reading and literacy (AARP, 2013). It may also help maintain the cognitive brain health of the volunteers (Carlson, 2011).

Lifelong Learning

Lifelong learning can also help older people maintain their mental wellbeing. Learning may help mitigate degenerative cognitive functional decline, as well promoting wellbeing via social networking in the class setting (BIS, 2008). Facilitating access to lifelong learning may imply investment in measures to help people who left education at a very early age prepare to take up learning opportunities as an adult in later life. However, in the United Kingdom, while more than half of all those who completed education at age 21 are willing to participate in learning later, only a quarter of people who left school at 16 would like to do this (Aldridge & Tuckett, 2009). Uptake may well be an issue, and little is known about the actual cost-effectiveness of investing in adult learning to promote wellbeing.

Tackling Poverty

While no formal cost-effectiveness studies on measures to tackle poverty could be identified, the merits of a number of measures might be assessed. These could include the benefits of financial literacy programs to help people plan early for pensions and the use of behavioral psychological techniques to encourage more people to pay into pensions (for instance by forcing people to opt out of rather than opt in to schemes). Other examples of schemes that could be evaluated include targeted social welfare benefits to those in most need, including informal carers, and financial incentives to encourage householders to install energy-efficiency measures in their homes.

Conclusion

This chapter has sought to show that there are powerful economic benefits that may be realized through better wellbeing in older age. Wellbeing can help support healthy aging, which in turn implies that the major positive contribution to the economy of older people may be further enhanced. Much is known about the risk factors to wellbeing. In many respects these are similar to those of the whole adult population, but issues of social isolation and loneliness, risks of psychological wellbeing linked to chronic health problems and changes in role and status following retirement may require tailored actions.

Happily, a range of cost-effective actions are available, although much more can be done to strengthen this evidence base as it has been assessed only in a handful of countries. In particular, economic modeling techniques might be used to synthesize existing information on the effectiveness of interventions to promote wellbeing with local cost and infrastructure data, so as to estimate the potential cost-effectiveness of interventions if implemented in different countries or settings where the capacity to do evaluation of this type remains limited.

References

AARP. (2013). *Volunteering can make a difference in a child's life*. http://www.aarp.org/experience-corps/experience-corps-volunteer/.

Adams, N., Stubbs, D., & Woods, V. (2005). Psychological barriers to Internet usage among older adults in the UK. *Medical Informatics and the Internet in Medicine, 30*(1), 3–17.

Aldridge, F., & Tuckett, A. (2009). *Narrowing participation. The NIACE survey on adult participation in learning*. Leicester: National Institute of Adult Continuing Education.

Baker, N., & Ring, E. (2013). Rapidly ageing population a financial time bomb. *Irish Examiner*, May 1.

Beaumont, J. (2012). *Measuring national wellbeing: A discussion paper on domains and measures*. London: Office for National Statistics.

Beaumont, J. (2013). *Measuring national wellbeing—Older people and loneliness, 2013*. London: Office for National Statistics.

BIS (Department for Business, Innovation and Skills) (2008). *Foresight mental capital and wellbeing project. Final project report*. London: The Government Office for Science.

Bouman, A., van Rossum, E., Evers, S., Ambergen, T., Kempen, G., & Knipschild, P. (2008). Effects on health care use and associated cost of a home visiting program for older people with poor health status: A randomized clinical trial in the Netherlands. *Journal of Gerontology A, Biological Sciences Medical Sciences, 63*(3), 291–297.

Burholt, V., & Windle, G. (2006). *The material resources and well-being of older people*. York: Joseph Rowntree Foundation.

Carlson, M. C. (2011). Promoting healthy, meaningful aging through social involvement: Building an Experience Corps. *Cerebrum, 10.* http://www.dana.org/news/cerebrum/detail.aspx?id=33556.

Charlesworth, G., Shepstone, L., Wilson, E., Thalanany, M., Mugford, M., & Poland, F. (2008). Does befriending by trained lay workers improve psychological well-being and quality of life for carers of people with dementia, and at what cost? A randomised controlled trial. *Health Technology Assessment, 12*(4), iii, v–ix, 1–78.

Church, J., Goodall, S., Norman, R., & Haas, M. (2012). The cost-effectiveness of falls prevention interventions for older community-dwelling Australians. *Australia and New Zealand Journal of Public Health, 36*(3), 241–248.

Copeland, J. R., Beekman, A. T., Braam, A. W., Dewey, M. E., Delespaul, P., Fuhrer, R., . . . Wilson, K. C. (2004). Depression among older people in Europe: The EURODEP studies. *World Psychiatry, 3*(1), 45–49.

Cuijpers, P., Smit, F., Lebowitz, B., & Beekman, A. (2011). Prevention of mental disorders in late life. In M. Abou-Saleh, C. Katona & A. Kumar (Eds.), *Principles and Practice of Geriatric Psychiatry* (pp. 844–849). Chichester: Wiley.

de Beurs, E., Comijs, H., Twisk, J. W., Sonnenberg, C., Beekman, A. T., & Deeg, D. (2005). Stability and change of emotional functioning in late life: Modelling of vulnerability profiles. *Journal of Affective Disorders, 84*(1), 53–62.

de Vries, R., & Blane, D. (2012). Fuel poverty and the health of older people: The role of local climate. *Journal of Public Health (Oxford).* doi: 10.1093/pubmed/fds094.

Demakakos, P., McMunn, A., & Steptoe, A. (2010). Well-being in older age: A multidimensional perspective. In J. Banks, C. Lessof, J. Nazroo, N. Rogers, M. Stafford, & A. Steptoe (Eds.), *Financial circumstances, health and well-being of the older population in England. The 2008 English Longitudinal Study Of Ageing (Wave 4)* (pp. 115–177). London: Institute of Fiscal Studies.

Dykstra, P. A. (2009). Older adult loneliness: Myths and realities. *European Journal of Ageing, 6*(2), 91–100.

Evans, J. (2011). *Number of future centenarians by age group—April 2011.* London: Department for Work and Pensions.

Forlani, C., Morri, M., Ferrari, B., Dalmonte, E., Menchetti, M., De Ronchi, D., & Atti, A. R. (2013). Prevalence and gender differences in late-life depression: A population-based study. *American Journal of Geriatric Psychiatry.* doi: 10.1016/j.jagp.2012.08.015.

Forsman, A. K., Nordmyr, J., & Wahlbeck, K. (2011). Psychosocial interventions for the promotion of mental health and the prevention of depression among older adults. *Health Promotion International, 26*(suppl. 1), i85–i107.

Forsman, A. K., Nyqvist, F., Schierenbeck, I., Gustafson, Y., & Wahlbeck, K. (2012). Structural and cognitive social capital and depression among older adults in two Nordic regions. *Aging and Mental Health, 16*(6), 771–779.

Forsman, A. K., Schierenbeck, I., & Wahlbeck, K. (2011). Psychosocial interventions for the prevention of depression in older adults: Systematic review and meta-analysis. *Journal of Aging and Health, 23*(3), 387–416.

Hay, J., LaBree, L., Luo, R., Clark, F., Carlson, M., Mandel, D., . . . Azen, S. P., (2002). Cost-effectiveness of preventive occupational therapy for independent-living older adults. *Journal of the American Geriatrics Society, 50*(8), 1381–1388.

Holwerda, T. J., Beekman, A. T., Deeg, D. J., Stek, M. L., van Tilburg, T. G., Visser, P. J., . . . Schoevers, R. A. (2012). Increased risk of mortality associated with social isolation in older men: Only when feeling lonely? Results from the Amsterdam Study of the Elderly (AMSTEL). *Psychological Medicine, 42*(4), 843–853.

Jang, S. N., Kawachi, I., Chang, J., Boo, K., Shin, H. G., Lee, H., & Cho, S. I. (2009). Marital status, gender, and depression: Analysis of the baseline survey of the Korean Longitudinal Study of Ageing (KLoSA). *Social Science and Medicine, 69*(11), 1608–1615.

Katon, W. J., Lin, E., Russo, J., & Unutzer, J. (2003). Increased medical costs of a population-based sample of depressed elderly patients. *Archives of General Psychiatry, 60*(9), 897–903.

Knapp, M., & McDaid, D. (2009). Making an economic case for prevention and promotion. *International Journal of Mental Health Promotion, 11*(3), 49–56.

Lee, M. (2006). *Promoting mental health and wellbeing in later life: A first report from the UK Inquiry into mental health and wellbeing in later life.* London: Age Concern and the Mental Health Foundation.

Lee, S. Y., Franchetti, M. K., Imanbayev, A., Gallo, J. J., Spira, A. P., & Lee, H. B. (2012). Non-pharmacological prevention of major depression among community-dwelling older adults: A systematic review of the efficacy of psychotherapy interventions. *Archives of Gerontology and Geriatrics, 55*(3), 522–529.

Lofquist, D., Lugaila, T., O'Connell, M., & Feliz, S. (2012). *Households and families: 2010. 2010 Census Briefs.* Washington, DC: U.S. Census Bureau.

Luppa, M., Konig, H. H., Heider, D., Leicht, H., Motzek, T., Schomerus, G., & Riedel-Heller, S. G. (2013). Direct costs associated with depressive symptoms in late life: A 4.5-year prospective study. *International Psychogeriatrics*, *25*(2), 292–302.

Markle-Reid, M., Browne, G., & Gafni, A. (2013). Nurse-led health promotion interventions improve quality of life in frail older home care clients: Lessons learned from three randomized trials in Ontario, Canada. *Journal of Evaluation in Clinical Practice*, *19*(1), 118–131.

Markle-Reid, M., Weir, R., Browne, G., Roberts, J., Gafni, A., & Henderson, S. (2006). Health promotion for frail older home care clients. *Journal of Advanced Nursing*, *54*(3), 381–395.

McDaid, D., & Park, A.-L. (2010). *Online health: Untangling the web*. London: BUPA.

McDaid, D., & Park, A.-L. (2011). Investing in mental health and well-being: Findings from the DataPrev project. *Health Promotion International*, *26*(suppl. 1), i108–i139.

Meltzer, H., Bebbington, P., Brugha, T., Farrell, M., & Jenkins, R. (2013). The relationship between personal debt and specific common mental disorders. *European Journal of Public Health*, *23*(1), 108–113.

MGM Advantage. (2012). *Rethinking retirement. Retirement Nation 2012.* Worthing, West Sussex: Marine and General Mutual Life Assurance Society.

Munro, J. F., Nicholl, J. P., Brazier, J. E., Davey, R., & Cochrane, T. (2004). Cost effectiveness of a community based exercise programme in over 65 year olds: Cluster randomised trial. *Journal of Epidemiology and Community Health*, *58*(12), 1004–1010.

O'Connell, H., Chin, A. V., Cunningham, C., & Lawlor, B. A. (2004). Recent developments: Suicide in older people. *British Medical Journal*, *329*(7471), 895–899.

OFCOM. (2012). *Adults media use and attitudes report*. London: OFCOM.

Onrust, S., Smit, F., Willemse, G., van den Bout, J., & Cuijpers, P. (2008). Cost-utility of a visiting service for older widowed individuals: Randomised trial. *BMC Health Services Research*, *8*, 128.

Pitkala, K. H., Routasalo, P., Kautiainen, H., & Tilvis, R. S. (2009). Effects of psychosocial group rehabilitation on health, use of health care services, and mortality of older persons suffering from loneliness: A randomized, controlled trial. *Journals of Gerontology Series A: Biological Sciences and Medical Sciences*, *64*(7), 792–800.

Rabiner, D. J., Scheffler, S., Koetse, E., Palermo, J., Ponzi, E., Burt, S., & Hampton, L. (2003). The impact of the senior companion program on quality of life outcomes for frail older adults and their families. *Home Health Care Services Quarterly*, *22*(4), 1–26.

Regan, C. O., Kearney, P. M., Savva, G. M., Cronin, H., & Kenny, R. A. (2013). Age and sex differences in prevalence and clinical correlates of depression: First results from the Irish Longitudinal Study on Ageing. *International Journal of Geriatric Psychiatry*. doi: 10.1002/gps.3955.

Reher, D. S. (1998). Family ties in Western Europe: Persistent contrasts. *Population and Development Review*, *24*, 203–234.

Schaan, B. (2013). Widowhood and depression among older europeans—The role of gender, caregiving, marital quality, and regional context. *Journal of Gerontology Series B, Psychological and Social Sciences, 68*(3), 431–442.

Schwingel, A., Niti, M. M., Tang, C., & Ng, T. P. (2009). Continued work employment and volunteerism and mental well-being of older adults: Singapore longitudinal ageing studies. *Age and Ageing, 38*(5), 531–537.

Serra, V., Watson, J., Sinclair, D., & Kneale, D. (2011). *Living beyond 100.* A report on centenarians. London: International Longevity Centre.

Sodergren, M., McNaughton, S. A., Salmon, J., Ball, K., & Crawford, D. A. (2012). Associations between fruit and vegetable intake, leisure-time physical activity, sitting time and self-rated health among older adults: Cross-sectional data from the WELL study. *BMC Public Health, 12,* 551.

Solhaug, H. I., Romuld, E. B., Romild, U., & Stordal, E. (2012). Increased prevalence of depression in cohorts of the elderly: An 11-year follow-up in the general population—the HUNT study. *International Psychogeriatrics, 24*(1), 151–158.

Steptoe, A., Shankar, A., Demakakos, P., & Wardle, J. (2013). Social isolation, loneliness, and all-cause mortality in older men and women. *Proceedings of the National Academy of Sciences of the United States of America, 110*(15), 5797–5801.

Stiglitz, J., Sen, A., & Fitoussi, J.-P. (2010). *Mismeasuring our lives: Why GDP doesn't add up. The Report by the Commission on the Measurement of Economic Performance and Social Progress.* New York: The New Press.

Sum, S., Mathews R. M., & Hughes I. (2009). Participation of older adults in cyberspace: How Australian older adults use the Internet. *Australasian Journal of Ageing, 28*(4), 189–193.

Sum, S., Mathews, R. M., Pourghasem, M., & Hughes, I. (2009). Internet use as a predictor of sense of community in older people. *Cyberpsychological Behavior, 12*(2), 235–239.

Taylor-Piliae, R. E., Haskell, W. L., Waters, C. M. & Froelicher, E. S. (2006). Change in perceived psychosocial status following a 12-week Tai Chi exercise programme. *Journal of Advanced Nursing, 54*(3), 313–329.

Thatcher, R. (2001). The demography of centenarians in England and Wales. *Population and Development Review, 13*(1), 139–156.

United Nations. (2005). *Living arrangements of older persons around the world.* New York: Department of Economic and Social Affairs, United Nations.

United Nations. (2009). *World population ageing* New York: Department of Economic and Social Affairs, United Nations.

van't Veer-Tazelaar, P. J., van Marwijk, H. W., van Oppen, P., van der Horst, H. E., Smit, F., Cuijpers, P., & Beekman, A. T. (2011). Prevention of late-life anxiety and depression has sustained effects over 24 months: A pragmatic randomized trial. *American Journal of Geriatric Psychiatry, 19*(3), 230–239.

van't Veer-Tazelaar, P. J., van Marwijk, H. W., van Oppen, P., van Hout, H. P., van der Horst, H. E., Cuijpers, P., . . . Beekman, A. T. (2009). Stepped-care prevention of anxiety and depression in late life: A randomized controlled trial. *Archives of General Psychiatry, 66*(3), 297–304.

van't Veer-Tazelaar, P. J., Smit, F., van Hout, H., van Oppen, P., van der Horst, H., Beekman, A., & van Marwijk, H. (2010). Cost-effectiveness of a stepped care intervention to prevent depression and anxiety in late life: Randomised trial. *British Journal of Psychiatry, 196*(4), 319–325.

Vasiliadis, H. M., Dionne, P. A., Preville, M., Gentil, L., Berbiche, D., & Latimer, E. (2013). The excess healthcare costs associated with depression and anxiety in elderly living in the community. *American Journal of Geriatric Psychiatry.* doi: 10.1016/j.jagp.2012.12.016.

von Bonsdorff, M. B., & Rantanen, T. (2011). Benefits of formal voluntary work among older people. *A review. Aging Clinicial and Experimental Research, 23*(3), 162–169.

Wang, C., Bannuru, R., Ramel, J., Kupelnick, B., Scott, T., & Schmid, C. H. (2010). Tai Chi on psychological well-being: Systematic review and meta-analysis. *BMC Complementary and Alternative Medicine, 10*, 23.

Wilson, E., Thalanany, M., Shepstone, L., Charlesworth, G., Poland, F., Harvey, I., . . . Mugford, M. (2009). Befriending carers of people with dementia: A cost utility analysis. *International Journal of Geriatric Psychiatry, 24*(6), 610–623.

Windle, G., Hughes, D., Linck, P., Russell, I., Morgan, R., Woods, B., . . . Yeo, S. T. (2008). *Public health interventions to promote mental well-being in people aged 65 and over: Systematic review of effectiveness and cost-effectiveness* London: NICE.

WRVS. (2011). *Gold age pensioners. Valuing the socio-economic contribution of older people in the UK*. Cardiff: WRVS.

Zhang, B., & Li, J. (2011). Gender and marital status differences in depressive symptoms among elderly adults: The roles of family support and friend support. *Aging and Mental Health, 15*(7), 844–854.

Zickuhr, K., & Madden, M. (2012). *Older adults and internet use.* Washington, DC: Pew Research Center.

Further Readings

More on the promoting the wellbeing of older people can be found in various reports on wellbeing and work prepared as part of the Foresight Mental Capital and Wellbeing Project. London: Government Office for Science, 2008. These are available at http://www.bis.gov.uk/foresight/our-work/projects/published-projects/mental-capital-and-wellbeing/reports-and-publications.

A variety of reports on the English Longitudinal Study of Ageing are available from the Institute for Fiscal Studies, http://www.ifs.org.uk/ELSA.

Forsman, A. K., Schierenbeck, I., & Wahlbeck, K. (2011). Psychosocial interventions for the prevention of depression in older adults: Systematic review and meta-analysis. *Journal of Aging and Health, 23*(3), 387–416.

11

Promoting and Protecting Mental Wellbeing during Times of Economic Change

David McDaid

London School of Economics and Political Science, U.K.

Kristian Wahlbeck

Finnish Association for Mental Health, Finland

Sporadic economic shocks and periods of economic transition are inevitable and not new. Even before the dawn of the Industrial Revolution, economies rose and declined, often linked to the strength of military power on land and at sea, or major changes in environmental conditions. During the eleventh and twelfth centuries Europe enjoyed an economic and agricultural boom. A slight warming of the climate and improved agricultural techniques allowed lands that had previously been marginal or even infertile to become fully productive. In the late twelfth and early thirteenth centuries, however, the climate once again began to cool. Decreased agricultural output could no longer support the same level of economic activity, and economies began to weaken. Private international banking and commercial ventures eventually succumbed to the recession that began in the fourteenth century. The consequences for health and wellbeing were stark: decades of famine and war, not to mention the small matter of the Black Death and its devastating effect on the European population (Dyer, 1989).

While detailed evidence on the links between this medieval recession and mental health and wellbeing may be missing, we can point to the wealth of

The Economics of Wellbeing: Wellbeing: A Complete Reference Guide, Volume V.
Edited by David McDaid and Cary L. Cooper.
© 2014 John Wiley & Sons, Ltd. Published 2014 by John Wiley & Sons, Inc.
DOI: 10.1002/9781118539415.wbwell11

knowledge gained in more recent years. The twentieth century witnessed an unprecedented number of economic shocks and transitions, coupled with major scientific innovation and social revolution. While economic growth has been associated with general improvements in population health, during periods of economic transition and structural change there may be adverse impacts on health and wellbeing, in part due to the population having to adjust to new types of employment, perhaps with different levels of social standing (Brenner, 2005). The Great Depression following the Wall Street Crash, as with a number of subsequent economic downturns, was associated with a mixed bag of positive and negative impacts on mortality. The rate of suicide increased in those directly affected by bankruptcy and the collapse of savings banks, while road-traffic accidents decreased thanks to the decline in car use over this period (Stuckler, Meissner, Fishback, Basu, & McKee, 2012). Long-term economic transition away from heavy industry, and a consequent rise in unemployment, have been associated with increases in all-cause mortality, and with death from heart disease in particular, as, for instance, in Scotland even after controlling for high levels of tobacco and alcohol consumption (Brenner, 1987). A meta-analysis of more than 42 studies covering 20 million people suggests that the risks of premature mortality are greatest in the first 10 years of unemployment, in men and in younger people (Roelfs, Shor, Davidson, & Schwartz, 2011). In the Swedish recession of the 1990s premature mortality from suicide increased with the duration of unemployment, unlike the situation for cancer, circulatory, and alcohol-related problems, which initially increased but then fell again in people with longer periods of unemployment (Garcy & Vagero, 2012). Interestingly, in Sweden there was no excess suicide mortality during the recession, but in the postrecession period unemployed men had an elevated mortality from suicide, which indicates a causal and contextual relationship between long-term unemployment and suicide (Garcy & Vagero, 2013). Cultural norms can also have an impact, perhaps compounding the magnitude of major social upheaval, as seen, for instance, in Russia after the collapse of the Soviet Union. But it is not all about downturns. Perceived inequality in society and its impact on psychological health are also important (Pickett & Wilkinson, 2010). In times of economic progress, such as occurred in Ireland during the late 1990s and early 2000s, suicide rates persistently increased, particularly among the young.

The impacts on health and wellbeing of the global economic crisis that began in late 2007 are now the subject of much debate. It is perhaps still too early to fully understand them all; the picture is far from clear. But what is clear is that austerity can destabilize public service budgets, and this has many consequences, including some affecting education, social welfare, and health-care systems. For instance in Greece, hospital budgets fell by about 40% (Kentikelenis et al., 2011), which, in turn, may have consequences for health and wellbeing.

Different societies can be more or less resistant to stressors, which can include economic upturns as well as crises. This is because health and wellbeing depend upon a variety of socioeconomic and environmental factors (Herrman, Saxena, & Moodie 2005). Policy choices can also influence the impact of any economic shock on wellbeing and health status. Unwise austerity measures in public services for children, families, and young people may run the risk of long-lasting and costly damage to mental and physical health and create an obstacle to economic recovery. Conversely, can measures to ensure that social safety nets and supports are in place increase the resilience of communities to economic shocks and mitigate the mental health impacts of fear of job loss, unemployment, loss of social status, and the stress-related consequences of economic downturns? This chapter looks first at some of the specific risks to wellbeing that are apparent during times of economic shock and then goes on to look at some of the actions that can be taken promote and protect mental health and wellbeing.

What Are the Potential Impacts on Mental Health and Wellbeing Arising from Economic Shocks?

While there may be longer-term impacts, in terms of communicable disease and chronic conditions such as cardiovascular disease, the most immediate impacts of economic shocks are on psychological wellbeing, including potentially increased risks of suicidal behavior and interpersonal violence. Both recessions and booms can widen social and income inequalities in societies, as, for instance, seen in Japan (Kondo, Subramanian, Kawachi, Takeda, & Yamagata, 2008). This, in turn, increases the risk of poor mental health, which further compounds the links between economic deprivation and psychological wellbeing. High frequencies of common mental disorders and suicide are associated with poverty, poor education, material disadvantage, social fragmentation and deprivation, and unemployment (De Vogli & Gimeno, 2009; Fryers, Melzer, Jenkins, & Brugha, 2005; Laaksonen et al., 2007). As people move down the socioeconomic ladder due to loss of jobs and income, without intervention their health can be at risk of being adversely affected (Pickett & Wilkinson, 2010; Wilkinson & Marmot, 2003). Men, in particular, are at increased risk of mental health problems (Artazcoz, Benach, Borrell, & Cortes, 2004) and death due to suicide (Berk, Dodd, & Henry, 2006) or alcohol use, as in Russia, (Men, Brennan, Boffetta, & Zaridze, 2003) during times of economic adversity.

Unmanageable debt is also increasingly recognized as a major concern. The number of highly indebted households, repossessions of houses, and evictions may well increase as a result of the economic crisis. There is much evidence that debts, financial difficulties, and housing payment problems lead to mental health problems (Brown, Taylor, & Price, 2005; Lee et al., 2010; Taylor, Pevalin, & Todd, 2007). The more debts people have, the higher the risk of many common mental disorders (Jenkins et al., 2008; Meltzer, Bebbington, Brugha, Farrell, & Jenkins, 2013). Debt can also potentially increase the risk of suicide; analysis of a sample of more than 4,600 adults in the Finnish population found that the risk of suicidal ideation was almost three times greater in people who had difficulty repaying their debts (Hintikka et al., 1998). In the United Kingdom individuals who initially had no mental health problems but found themselves having unmanageable debts within a 12-month period had a 33% higher risk of developing depression and anxiety-related problems compared to the general population who experienced no financial problems (Skapinakis, Weich, Lewis, Singleton, & Araya, 2006).

Increases in national and regional unemployment rates can be associated with increases in suicide rates (Barr, Taylor-Robinson, Scott-Samuel, McKee, & Stuckler, 2012; Economou, Nikolaou, & Theodossiou, 2008). Pooled evidence calls for protective interventions targeting both the newly and the long-term unemployed, especially men with low educational attainment—with U.S. evidence suggesting that they were more vulnerable to poor wellbeing and mortality during economic downturns in the 1980s and 1990s than better-educated people (Edwards, 2008). Economic downturns can also increase the social marginalization of vulnerable groups, including children, young people, single-parent families, the unemployed, ethnic minorities, migrants, and older people (World Health Organization, 2009).

The relationship between wellbeing and economic and societal conditions is, however, complex and far from clear-cut. For instance, while suicide rates remained very low by European standards during the initial onset of the economic crisis in Greece (Fountoulakis et al., 2012), the risk of suicidal ideation in the population has been on the rise in the more recent period following the threat to membership of the Euro (Economou et al., 2013; Economou, Madianos, Theleritis, Peppou, & Stefanis, 2011). In Spain, the rates of people seeking primary care in hospitals for mood, anxiety, somatoform, and alcohol-related disorders have increased following the onset of the economic crisis, with suggestions that about one third of this increased risk could be attributed to the threat of unemployment and/or housing foreclosure (Gili, Roca, Basu, McKee, & Stuckler, 2013). Yet, in Spain the overall suicide rate actually fell markedly between 2008 and 2011 (Instituto Nacional de Estadistica, 2013). In England, by contrast, even though the impacts of the economic crisis at national level have been much less severe, it has been argued that suicide rates are correlated with differences in the rate of unemployment between different regions (Barr et al., 2012). Work from South Korea reported increasing income-related inequalities in suicide and depression over a 10-year period following an economic crisis (Hong, Knapp, & McGuire, 2011).

In many countries, alcohol consumption is negatively associated with population mental health. For example, in Eastern Europe, alcohol consumption plays a considerable role in the suicide rate, especially in men (Norstrom & Ramstedt, 2005). In Russia, the societal changes seen after the collapse of the Soviet Union in 1991, as well as the breakdown of the ruble in 1998, were followed by increases in alcohol-related deaths (Zaridze et al., 2009). Likewise, high rises in unemployment were linked to a 28% increase in the risk of deaths from alcohol use in the European Union (Stuckler, Basu, Suhrcke, Coutts, & McKee, 2009). Binge drinking and alcohol-related deaths tend to increase in many countries during economic downturns (Dee, 2001; Johansson, Bockerman, Prattala, & Uutela, 2006), creating a need for governments to upgrade actions to control alcohol.

Families as a whole also feel the effects of an economic crisis. Poor families are especially hurt by cuts in health and education budgets. Family strain may lead to increases in family violence and child neglect. Children may also find themselves having to provide care and support for other family members. Economic stress, through its influence on parental mental health, marital interaction, and parenting, impacts on the mental health of children and adolescents (Conger, Ge, Elder, Lorenz, & Simons, 1994; Solantaus, Leinonen, & Punamaki, 2004). The impact of extreme poverty on children may include deficits in cognitive, emotional, and physical development, and the consequences for health and wellbeing may be lifelong (Marmot & Bell, 2009). Nationwide population follow-up data from Finland, which experienced a severe economic recession at the beginning of the 1990s, reveals gloomy figures: at age 21 one in four of those born in 1987 had committed a criminal offense and one in five had received psychiatric care (Paananen & Gissler, 2012).

What Can Be Done to Protect Mental Health and Wellbeing?

To protect the wellbeing of citizens against the impact of economic changes, governments will need to take a holistic Health in All Policies (HiAP) approach. HiAP is an approach to the development, implementation, and assessment of public policies across sectors that systematically takes into account the health implications of decisions, seeks synergies, and avoids harmful health impacts in order to improve population health and health equity (Puska, 2007).

We now go on to consider what can be done to protect mental health and wellbeing, given our knowledge of some of the heightened risk factors during times of economic shock. We build further on arguments we have made that many of the adverse associations between economic shocks, mental health, and wellbeing are avoidable through careful investment by governments and other actors in measures to promote resilience and coping skills as well as through the provision of a measure of financial security (Wahlbeck & McDaid, 2012). We will highlight effective measures that can be taken across the life course. These include family support and parenting programs, active labor market and social welfare programs, workplace mental health support, the provision of mental health services in primary care, alcohol control, promotion of social capital, and debt relief programs. We also discuss the emerging evidence base on the cost-effectiveness of these actions.

Family Support Interventions

As Chapter 8 has indicated, there are substantial opportunities for investing in cost-effective actions to promote the mental health and wellbeing of children. Children and adolescents are not immune from the effects of economic shocks, particularly where there are adverse impacts on their parents. The foundations of good mental health are laid during pregnancy, infancy, and childhood; there are long-term risks to psychological health in adulthood if psychological problems manifest themselves in childhood (Clark, Rodgers, Caldwell, Power, & Stansfeld, 2007; Werner, 2004). Yet, when finances are tight, governments (or parents) may be tempted to make cuts to pre-school support which may impact most on children in families who are already under great financial and psychological strain.

There are a number of different actions that might be of particular importance at a time of economic shocks. Family support programs, including support toward the costs associated with raising children as well as expenditure related to maternity and parental leave, have been associated with better levels of mental health. It has been estimated that in European Union countries, each US$100 per capita spent on family support programs reduced by 0.2% the effect of unemployment on suicides (Stuckler, Basu, et al., 2009).

There is a large body of literature indicating that investment in measures to support the wellbeing of parents and their children, both pre-school and in school, can be protective of mental health (Durlak & Wells, 1997). Many of these interventions have the potential for long-term economic gains outweighing short-term costs (McDaid & Park, 2011). A number of economic evaluations of parenting studies conducted alongside randomized controlled trials have been published, some set in schools, others focused on pre-school-age children. For example, an evaluation of the Webster-Stratton Incredible Years parenting program in Wales, found the intervention to be cost-effective for all 3–5-year-old children at risk of conduct disorder (Edwards, Ceilleachair, Bywater, Hughes, & Hutchings, 2007).

In England, modeling work for NICE (the National Institute for Health and Care Excellence) looked at the universal use of a teacher-delivered PATHS (Promoting Alternative Thinking Strategies) program for children (McCabe, 2008). It facilitates the development of self-control, emotional awareness, and interpersonal problem-solving skills, reduces aggression and behavior problems, enhances emotional development, and contributes to improved educational performance. Combining emotional and cognitive benefits in the model's base-case scenario, the cost per quality-adjusted life year (QALY) gained would be £5,500 (anything below £30,000 per QALY gained is generally considered to be cost-effective in an English context). There may also be additional benefits if the spillover effects of poor childhood mental health care can be averted: modeling work looking at the universal use of similar social and emotional learning interventions for 11–16-year-old children suggests that, if intervention reduces victimization by 15%, then it would have a 92% chance of having a cost per QALY <£30,000 (Hummel et al., 2009).

Social Welfare Measures

Another important area for action concerns social welfare protection systems. Reforms to social welfare to maintain or strengthen safety nets and taxation systems to reduce income inequalities can potentially help protect mental health and wellbeing. Evidence from different country contexts indicates that social protection responses may be crucial in mitigating poor mental health in any economic crisis (Uutela, 2010). In Finland and Sweden, during a period of deep economic recession and a large increase in unemployment, health inequalities remained broadly unchanged and suicide rates actually fell, possibly because social benefits and services broadly remained and buffered against the structural pressures toward widening health inequalities (Hintikka, Saarinen, & Viinamaki 1999; Lahelma et al., 2002; Ostamo & Lonnqvist, 2001). In the United States a reduction in spending by state welfare programs has been associated with an increase in suicide rates (Zimmerman, 2002).

Active Labor Market Support for Unemployed People

Active labor market programs can also mitigate the negative effects of economic shocks to wellbeing. These programs aim at improving people's prospects of finding gainful employment and include public employment services, labor market training, special programs for young people in transition from school to work, and programs to provide or promote employment for people with disabilities. In European Union countries, each additional $100 per head of population spent on active labor market programs per year reduced by 0.4% the effect of a 1% rise in unemployment on suicides (Stuckler, Basu, et al., 2009).

Psychological support for unemployed people to promote mental health can help increase reemployment rates (Proudfoot, Guest, Carson, Dunn, & Gray, 1997; Vuori & Silvonen, 2005). Cost-effectiveness evaluations of such interventions have reported savings for social welfare payers and employers alike, through increased rates of employment, higher earnings, and fewer job changes (Vinokur, Schul, Vuori, & Price, 2000).

Given the adverse economic impacts of unemployment on physical and mental health, there is a strong case for embedding these types of services routinely into redundancy packages provided by employers (Anaf, Baum, Newman, Ziersch, & Jolley, 2013). The onset of poor mental health can, in turn, reduce the chances of obtaining alternative employment. For instance, work in Sweden following more than 500 newly unemployed people found that those with greater levels of psychological distress and poor mental health were significantly less likely to be reemployed within a 1-year period (Skarlund, Ahs, & Westerling, 2012). In China, a study of 210 internal migrant workers who lost their jobs following the 2008 economic crisis found that more than 50% had some mental health problems and were at increased risk of poor mental wellbeing with increased duration of unemployment; those migrants with poorer coping strategies were most vulnerable (Chen et al., 2012). Special programs for young people in transition from school to work and re-employment training for young people left unemployed can be of benefit. Apprenticeship-type training in regular educational settings offer most mental health benefits (Morrell, Taylor, & Kerr, 1998).

Workplace Mental Health Promotion

It is not just those who lose their jobs that are at risk of poor mental wellbeing. Job insecurity and the fear of job loss are also associated with increased risks of poor psychological wellbeing (Burgard, Brand, & House, 2009; Laszlo et al., 2010). Occupational health services have an important role to play in providing psychological support to protect psychological wellbeing; there can also be economic benefits for business in the enhanced physical and psychological health of their employees. Employees who "survive" a downsizing process within a business can be as vulnerable to poor psychological wellbeing as those who lose their jobs (Campbell, Worral, & Cooper, 2000; Kivimäki et al., 2007). They can, therefore, also benefit from supportive interventions, including psychological support and better communication throughout the whole downsizing process (Vinten & Lane, 2002).

As noted in Chapter 9 of this volume, employers can also help by investing in measures to better recognize the risks of stress and to provide better line management and support for workers, including more flexible working arrangements where feasible; governments can help by providing advice and support, particularly to smaller business, which may not have any internal occupational health resources.

Refocusing Mental Health Systems

Many countries are facing pressure from the international financial community to cut borrowing and public expenditure, which inevitably puts strain on their health and welfare budgets. Government expenditures on health are being squeezed and are falling in real terms. For instance, data from the Organisation for Economic Cooperation and Development (OECD) indicates that overall health spending by European Union member states grew by 4.6% per year in real terms between 2000 and 2009, but expenditure decreased by 0.6% in 2010 (OECD, 2012). Mental health budgets can be hit very hard in times of austerity. In Ireland there has been a 10.5% real-terms decrease in publicly financed health expenditure since 2009 (Department of Health and Children, 2012) with much greater cuts made in spending on mental health (from €1.04 billion in 2008 to €0.71 billion in 2011).

Universal coverage by mental health services is a key element in reducing the impact of any economic crisis, and countering any growth in social inequalities in health (Lundberg et al., 2008). It is ironic that mental health budgets should come under threat, given the improved responsiveness of mental health services to changes in the social, employment, and income status of the population. Moreover, early recognition of mental health problems, suicidal ideas, and heavy drinking can help reduce the damage caused by economic shocks.

But it is not just about protecting budgets; there is scope for restructuring services to better meet the needs of the population. Well-developed community-based mental health services are linked to a reduction in suicides (Pirkola, Sund, Sailas, & Wahlbeck, 2009; While et al., 2012). An integrated care approach with a focus on service provision in primary care will increase access to mental health support, and shift the focus to prevention and early detection of mental health problems. Primary care doctors can play a key role in monitoring the health of people who have recently been made redundant or may have suffered other economic shocks, such as the loss of their home.

Primary care is another area where access to more mental health promotion programs can be made; more generally, there can be more opportunities to provide people with information on how to maintain good mental wellbeing. Community-oriented mental health services also need to liaise with resilience-strengthening elements in the community to create a comprehensive and accessible network. Perceived stigma is a barrier to help-seeking (Aromaa, Tolvanen, Tuulari, & Wahlbeck, 2011), and support services need to have high acceptability.

However, in many countries, mental health spending is still concentrated in hospitals. The current financial crisis may create the urgency and strengthen courage to eliminate the fundamental problems of hospital-dominated health care delivery and increase access to community-based services. Sound financial incentives are, however, needed to support the provision of high-quality community care and the optimal use of existing resources. One difficulty, when budgets are tight, is the need to continue to fund excess inpatient services at the same time as investing in other services during a transitional period (Thornicroft et al., 2010). Linking funding to accreditation systems and provider performance assessments can help support a shift in emphasis away from institutional care (Knapp, Beecham, McDaid, Matosevic, & Smith, 2011).

Control of Alcohol Price and Availability

We have noted increased risks of binge drinking in some population groups during times of economic change. Price increases represent the most cost-effective response to this problem throughout the world, reducing the harm done by alcohol, including heavy drinking, alcohol-related deaths, costs to the health and criminal justice systems, and lost productivity (Anderson, 2013; Österberg, 2012b). Increasing prices through alcohol-tax increases may be mitigated by illegal production, tax evasion, and illegal trading in some jurisdictions. Reducing this unrecorded consumption via concerted tax enforcement strategies by law enforcement and excise officers is estimated to cost more than a tax increase but produces similar levels of effect (Anderson, Chisholm, & Fuhr, 2009)

Restricting the availability of alcohol increases the time costs and inconvenience of obtaining it, which leads to reduced harm (Österberg, 2012a). Increasing alcohol sale times by as little as two hours, and increasing the number of places where alcohol can be bought in any given location, are linked to increases in alcohol consumption and harms, including injury, violence, crime, and medical harm. In contrast, reducing the number of hours of sale reduces violence and damage, assaults and murders. In many countries governments own retail outlets. These government monopolies, which limit outlet density and hours and days of sale as well as removing the private profit motive for increasing sales, result in reduced alcohol consumption and alcohol-related harm (Österberg, 2012b).

Control policies can be supplemented by the provision of services: heavy drinkers will benefit from the delivery of brief interventions in primary care. Opportunistic screening followed by brief interventions appears to be cost-effective in the context of high-income countries, with a cost per QALY gained of €5,400 in the Netherlands (Tariq, van den Berg, Hoogenveen, & van Baal, 2009). Measures to reduce the risk of driving while under the influence of alcohol, including better police enforcement measures, random breath tests, and alcohol-ignition locks also appear to be cost-effective and able to help counter the risks of road-traffic fatalities (Anderson, McDaid, & Park, 2013).

Tackling Unmanageable Debt

We have noted the increased risks to mental health arising from unmanageable debts. In the UK only about half of all people with debt problems seek advice, and, without intervention, almost two-thirds of people with unmanageable debt problems will still face such problems 12 months later (Pleasance et al., 2004). Actions to alleviate unmanageable debt can therefore be an important element of a policy to protect wellbeing during economic shocks; they can result in reduced distress and socioeconomic benefits. In Sweden, people in high debt who had been granted debt relief had better mental health than those who had not (Enforcement Authority, 2008). A controlled trial of access to debt management services in England and Wales was associated with positive improvements in respect of general health, anxiety, and optimism (Pleasance & Balmer, 2007). Use of debt advice services has also been associated with a reduction in the use of healthcare services (Williams & Sansom, 2007). Debt advice services can also be cost-effective, not only as a result of the reduction in use of health services, but also because of the reduced need for legal action and the avoidance of bankruptcy (Knapp, McDaid, Evans-Lacko, Fitch, & King, 2011).

Policymakers can strengthen cooperation and improve communication between health services and debt management agencies. Debt management advisers should be trained to refer clients to mental health care when needed (Wahlbeck & Awolin, 2009). On the other hand, health services need to acknowledge the burden of overindebtedness in clients and provide referral links to debt advice bureaus (Fitch, Hamilton, Basset, & Davey, 2009). Primary care practitioners can play a key role, if they receiving training to enable them to recognize unmanageable debt and to refer individuals to debt management services (Jenkins, Fitch, Hurlston, & Walker, 2009). Access to microcredit, through organizations such as credit unions, can also help (Fitch, Hamilton, Basset, & Davey, 2011). There may also be scope for looking at the provisions of bankruptcy laws in some countries and seeing whether they might also be reformed to try to protect mental health, as well as investing in more financial literacy initiatives as part of the school curriculum.

Strengthening Social Capital

Social capital can be defined in different ways, but, in general terms, it covers the resources available to individuals and society provided by social relationships or social networks. In times of economic crisis, social capital can be an important protective factor. In economic crises, social capital may paradoxically grow stronger, due to more opportunities for voluntary work and by mobilizing neighborhoods to mutual support actions and charity work. Social networks, as represented by trade unions, religious congregations, and sport clubs, seem to constitute a safety net against the adverse effect of rapid macroeconomic changes (Stuckler, King, & McKee, 2009). Participation in group activities and greater levels of perceived helpfulness within communities have been associated with better levels of mental health (Han & Lee, 2012). In contrast, a poor level of interpersonal trust between individuals is associated with increased risk of depression (Forsman, Nyqvist, & Wahlbeck 2011).

Responsible Media Coverage of Suicides

Another, often overlooked, area for action, concerns the reporting of suicide in the media. The current economic crisis has been accompanied by the publication of dramatic stories of suicide as a protest against economic circumstances. Evidence indicates that highly sensationalized reporting of suicides, providing detailed descriptions of methods, can and does lead to "copycat" suicides. On the other hand, responsible reporting reduces copycat suicide (Niederkrotenthaler & Sonneck, 2007; Sonneck, Etzersdorfer, & Nagel-Kuess, 1994), especially among adolescents (Hawton & Williams, 2001). Media guidelines for reporting suicides and the monitoring of stigmatizing media reports have been linked with reduced stigmatization in the press and reduction of suicides (Hawton & Williams, 2001; Sonneck et al., 1994). In economic crises, increased media coverage of possible increases in suicides may thus have detrimental consequences and contribute to a "snowball" effect. A close collaboration between media representatives and mental health experts as well as commonly agreed suicide reporting guidelines are needed at all times, but never more so than during times of economic hardship.

The Challenge of Implementation

It is insufficient, of course, to highlight the evidence base supporting actions to protect mental health and promote mental wellbeing. There remains the challenge of implementation. Psychological health and wellbeing are not perceived as a priority for investment when budgets are under pressure (Matschinger & Angermeyer, 2004; Saxena, Thornicroft, Knapp, & Whiteford, 2007; Schomerus, Matschinger, & Angermeyer, 2006) and we can point to the sharp decrease in funding for mental health in Ireland relative to other parts of the health budget. One reason for the apparent low funding priority and neglect may be the high level of stigma associated with mental health problems. Countering this stigma and discrimination remains one of the most critical challenges for improving mental health at a time of economic crisis, because they may impact on the willingness of public policy makers to invest in mental health (Sharac, McCrone, Clement, & Thornicroft, 2010).

Demonstrating the economic benefits of protecting wellbeing can help governments justify new investments in mental health, as in the case of the mental health strategy in England (Department of Health, 2011). Investing in mental health actions, both within and outside the health sector, can have economic payoffs. This is not just an issue affecting high-income countries, there are significant economic impacts that can be achieved right across the globe (McDaid, Knapp, & Raja, 2008). Population wellbeing (i.e., mental capital) is a crucial prerequisite for a flourishing economy with high productivity (Beddington et al., 2008; Weehuizen, 2008). As many of the above-mentioned economic benefits fall to sectors outside the health system, it is crucial to communicate the idea that investment in wellbeing and mental health can have broad benefits for the public purse as a whole to ministries of finance (McDaid & Knapp, 2010).

Conclusion: Every Cloud Has a Silver Lining

The current economic crisis presents an opportunity to strengthen policies that would not only mitigate the impact of the recession on wellbeing, but also help promote wellbeing at any point in the economic cycle. We have argued that investment in supports for wellbeing and mental health are just as relevant in times of economic boom as in times of economic bust.

Economic change will, without any corrective actions, inevitably be followed by an uneven distribution of wealth gains and not all of the population will benefit to the same extent—if at all, as was seen during the Celtic Tiger boom years in Ireland (Corcoran & Arensman, 2011).

There are powerful public health and economic arguments for investment in family and parenting support, adequate social protection systems, active labor market programs, psychological support for those at risk of losing their jobs, or who have "survived" downsizing, as well as for the newly unemployed, more primary and community-oriented mental health services, general mental-health-promoting activities, debt relief, an alcohol-control policy, and more responsible reporting of suicides.

Governments could consider reorienting budgets to protect populations now and in the future by budgeting for measures that keep people employed, which would help those who lose their jobs and their families with the negative effects of unemployment and enable unemployed people to regain work quickly. Business under strain may also be able to help by offering reduced working hours or temporary sabbaticals from employment rather than making workers redundant.

Economic change can also present opportunities to revaluate our lives and contribute to positive lifestyle changes. Fewer hours spent at work could mean more leisure hours spent with children, family, and friends. Less economic activity may contribute to a slower pace of life and strengthen social capital by providing more opportunities for civic participation and social networking. Positives can be taken from the Icelandic experience of economic shock post 2008. Some Icelanders saw the crisis as a "blessing in disguise for a nation that had lost its basic values to greed and narcissism," offering a chance to "recover to become a more democratic, human and fair society" (Olafsdottir, 2009, p. 189). Indeed, due to the preservation of well-developed basic social welfare and good social networks in Iceland even at the height of the crisis, as Ásgeirsdóttir and colleagues describe in Chapter 6 in this volume, some positive impacts on health and wellbeing were achieved. One challenge will be to try and maintain any positive changes as economic conditions change.

It is still not too late to influence outcomes from the current economic shock, but we need to look to the future and would do well to learn the lessons of this and previous economic crises. Not enough of this learning from the past has influenced policy responses in the post-2008 world. A real silver lining from the economic cloud over the globe would be better institutional learning, giving mental health a place in all policies—not only to protect wellbeing in general, but so as to have plans for a rapid response to subsequent economic shocks.

References

Anaf, J., Baum, F., Newman, L., Ziersch, A., & Jolley, G. (2013). The interplay between structure and agency in shaping the mental health consequences of job loss. *BMC Public Health, 13*, 110.

Anderson, P. (2013). Making the economic case for reducing the harm done by alcohol. In D. McDaid, F. Sassi & S. Merkur (Eds.), *Promoting health, preventing disease: The economic case*. Maidenhead: Open University Press.

Anderson, P., Chisholm, D., & Fuhr, D. C. (2009). Effectiveness and cost-effectiveness of policies and programmes to reduce the harm caused by alcohol. *The Lancet, 373*(9682), 2234–2246.

Anderson, R., McDaid, D., & Park, A. -L. (2013). Road related injuries. In D. McDaid, F. Sassi, & S. Merkur (Eds.), *Promoting health, preventing disease: The economic case*. Maidenhead: Open University Press.

Aromaa, E., Tolvanen, A., Tuulari, J., & Wahlbeck, K. (2011). Personal stigma and use of mental health services among people with depression in a general population in Finland. *BMC Psychiatry, 11*, 52.

Artazcoz, L., Benach, J., Borrell, C., & Cortes, I. (2004). Unemployment and mental health: Understanding the interactions among gender, family roles, and social class. *American Journal of Public Health, 94*(1), 82–88.

Barr, B., Taylor-Robinson, D., Scott-Samuel, A., McKee, M. & Stuckler, D. (2012). Suicides associated with the 2008–10 economic recession in England: Time trend analysis. *British Medical Journal, 345*, e5142.

Beddington, J., Cooper, C. L., Field, J., Goswami, U., Huppert, F. A., Jenkins, R., . . . Thomas, S. M. (2008). The mental wealth of nations. *Nature, 455*(7216), 1057–1060.

Berk, M., Dodd, S., & Henry, M. (2006). The effect of macroeconomic variables on suicide. *Psychological Medicine, 36*(2), 181–189.

Brenner, M. H. (1987). Economic instability, unemployment rates, behavioral risks, and mortality rates in Scotland, 1952–1983. *International Journal of Health Services, 17*(3), 475–487.

Brenner, M. H. (2005). Commentary: Economic growth is the basis of mortality rate decline in the 20th century—Experience of the United States 1901–2000. *International Journal of Epidemiology, 34*(6), 1214–1221.

Brown, S., Taylor, K., & Price, S. W. (2005). Debt and distress: Evaluating the psychological cost of credit. *Journal of Economic Psychology, 26*, 642–663.

Burgard, S. A., Brand, J. E., & House, J. S. (2009). Perceived job insecurity and worker health in the United States. *Social Science and Medicine, 69*(5), 777–785.

Campbell, F., Worral, L., & Cooper, C. (2000). *The psychological effects of downsizing and privatisation (Wolverhampton Business School working paper series WP001/00)*. http://www.wlv.ac.uk/PDF/uwbs_WP001-00%20Campbell%20Worrall%20Cooper.pdf.

Chen, L., Li, W., He, J., Wu, L., Yan, Z., & Tang, W. (2012). Mental health, duration of unemployment, and coping strategy: A cross-sectional study of unemployed migrant workers in eastern China during the economic crisis. *BMC Public Health*, *12*, 597.

Clark, C., Rodgers, B., Caldwell, T., Power, C., & Stansfeld, S. (2007). Childhood and adulthood psychological ill health as predictors of midlife affective and anxiety disorders: The 1958 British Birth Cohort. *Archives of General Psychiatry*, *64*(6), 668–678.

Conger, R. D., Ge, X., Elder, G. H., Jr., Lorenz, F. O., & Simons, R. L. (1994). Economic stress, coercive family process, and developmental problems of adolescents. *Child Development*, *65*(2), 541–561.

Corcoran, P., & Arensman, E. (2011). Suicide and employment status during Ireland's Celtic Tiger economy. *European Journal of Public Health*, *21*(2), 209–214.

De Vogli, R., & Gimeno, D. (2009). Changes in income inequality and suicide rates after "shock therapy": Evidence from Eastern Europe. *Journal of Epidemiology and Community Health*, *63*(11), 956.

Dee, T. S. (2001). Alcohol abuse and economic conditions: Evidence from repeated cross-sections of individual-level data. *Health Economy*, *10*(3), 257–270.

Department of Health (2011). *No health without mental health: A cross-government mental health outcomes strategy for people of all ages. Supporting document—The economic case for improving efficiency and quality in mental health*. London: Department of Health.

Department of Health and Children (2012). *Health in Ireland. Key trends 2012*. Dublin: Department of Health and Children.

Durlak, J. A., & Wells, A. M. (1997). Primary prevention mental health programs for children and adolescents: A meta-analytic review. *American Journal of Community Psychology*, *25*(2), 115–152.

Dyer, C. (1989). *Standards of living in the later Middle Ages*. Cambridge: Cambridge University Press.

Economou, A., Nikolaou, A., & Theodossiou, I. (2008). Are recessions harmful to health after all? Evidence from the European Union. *Journal of Economic Studies*, *35*, 368–384.

Economou, M., Madianos, M., Peppou, L. E., Theleritis, C., Patelakis, A., & Stefanis, C. (2013). Suicidal ideation and reported suicide attempts in Greece during the economic crisis. *World Psychiatry*, *12*(1), 53–59.

Economou, M., Madianos, M., Theleritis, C., Peppou, L. E., & Stefanis, C. (2011). Increased suicidality amid economic crisis in Greece. *The Lancet*, *378*(9801), 1459.

Edwards, R. (2008). Who is hurt by procyclical mortality? *Social Science and Medicine, 67*(12), 2051–2058.

Edwards, R. T., Ceilleachair, A., Bywater, T., Hughes, D. A., & Hutchings, J. (2007). Parenting programme for parents of children at risk of developing conduct disorder: Cost effectiveness analysis. *British Medical Journal, 334*(7595), 682.

Enforcement Authority (2008). *Everyone wants to pay their fair share: Causes and consequences of overindebtedness.* Stockholm: Enforcement Authority.

Fitch, C., Hamilton, S., Basset, P., & Davey, R. (2009). *Debt and mental health: What do we know? What should we do?* London: Royal College of Psychiatrists and Rethink.

Fitch, C., Hamilton, S., Basset, P., & Davey, R. (2011). The relationship between personal debt and mental health: A systematic review. *Mental Health Review Journal, 16,* 153–166.

Forsman, A. K., Nyqvist, F., & Wahlbeck, K. (2011). Cognitive components of social capital and mental health status among older adults: A population-based cross-sectional study. *Scandinavian Journal of Public Health, 39*(7), 757–765.

Fountoulakis, K. N., Savopoulos, C., Siamouli, M., Zaggelidou, E., Mageiria, S., Iacovides, S., & Hatzitolios, A. I. (2012). Trends in suicidality amid the economic crisis in Greece. *European Archives of Psychiatry and Clinical Neuroscience.* doi: 10.1007/s00406-012-0385-9.

Fryers, T., Melzer, D., Jenkins, R., & Brugha, T. (2005). The distribution of the common mental disorders: Social inequalities in Europe. *Clinical Practice and Epidemiology in Mental Health, 1,* 14.

Garcy, A. M., & Vagero, D. (2012). The length of unemployment predicts mortality, differently in men and women, and by cause of death: A six year mortality follow-up of the Swedish 1992–1996 recession. *Social Science and Medicine, 74*(12), 1911–1920.

Garcy, A. M., & Vagero, D. (2013). Unemployment and suicide during and after a deep recession: A longitudinal study of 3.4 million Swedish men and women. *American Journal of Public Health, 103*(6), 1031–1038.

Gili, M., Roca, M., Basu, S., McKee, M., & Stuckler, D. (2013). The mental health risks of economic crisis in Spain: Evidence from primary care centres, 2006 and 2010. *European Journal of Public Health, 23*(1), 103–108.

Han, S., & Lee, H. S. (2012). Individual, household and administrative area levels of social capital and their associations with mental health: A multilevel analysis of cross-sectional evidence. *International Journal of Social Psychiatry.* doi: 10.1177/0020764012453230.

Hawton, K., & Williams, K. (2001). The connection between media and suicidal behavior warrants serious attention. *Crisis, 22*(4), 137–140.

Herrman, H., Saxena, S., & Moodie, R. (2005). *Promoting mental health: Concepts, emerging evidence, practice.* Geneva: World Health Organization.

Hintikka, J., Kontula, O., Saarinen, P., Tanskanen, A., Koskela, K., & Viinamaki, H. (1998). Debt and suicidal behaviour in the Finnish general population. *Acta Psychiatrica Scandinavica, 98*(6), 493–496.

278

Hintikka, J., Saarinen, P. I., & Viinamaki, H. (1999). Suicide mortality in Finland during an economic cycle, 1985–1995. *Scandinavian Journal of Public Health*, *27*(2), 85–88.

Hong, J., Knapp, M., & McGuire, A. (2011) Income-related inequalities in the prevalence of depression and suicidal behaviour: A 10-year trend following economic crisis. *World Psychiatry*, *10*(1), 40–44.

Hummel, S., Naylor, P., Chilcott, J., Guillaume, L., Wilkinson, A., Blank, L., . . . Goyder, E. (2009) *Cost-effectiveness of universal interventions which aim to promote emotional and social wellbeing in secondary school*. Sheffield: ScHARR Public Evidence Report, 1.2.

Instituto Nacional de Estadistica (2013). *Salud: Defunciones según la causa de muerte* [Health: Mortality statistics by cause of death]. Madrid: INES.

Jenkins, R., Bhugra, D., Bebbington, P., Brugha, T., Farrell, M., Coid, J., . . . Meltzer, H. (2008). Debt, income and mental disorder in the general population. *Psychological Medicine*, *38*(10), 1485–1493.

Jenkins, R., Fitch, C., Hurlston, M., & Walker, F. (2009). Recession, debt and mental health: Challenges and solutions. *Mental Health in Family Medicine*, *6*(2), 85–90.

Johansson, E., Bockerman, P., Prattala, R., & Uutela, A. (2006). Alcohol-related mortality, drinking behavior, and business cycles: Are slumps really dry seasons? *European Journal of Health Economics*, *7*(3), 215–220.

Kentikelenis, A., Karanikolos, M., Papanicolas, I., Basu, S., McKee, M., & Stuckler, D. (2011). Health effects of financial crisis: Omens of a Greek tragedy. *The Lancet*, *378*(9801), 1457–1458.

Kivimäki, M., Honkonen, T., Wahlbeck, K., Elovainio, M., Pentti, J., Klaukka, T., . . . Vahtera, J. (2007). Organisational downsizing and increased use of psychotropic drugs among employees who remain in employment. *Journal of Epidemiology and Community Health*, *61*(2), 154–158.

Knapp, M., Beecham, J., McDaid, D., Matosevic, T., & Smith, M. (2011). The economic consequences of deinstitutionalisation of mental health services: Lessons from a systematic review of European experience. *Health and Social Care in the Community*, *19*(2), 113–125.

Knapp, M., McDaid, D., Evans-Lacko, S., Fitch, C., & King, D. (2011). Debt and mental health. In M. Knapp, D. McDaid & M. Parsonage (Eds.), *Mental health promotion and mental illness prevention: The economic case* (pp. 24–25). London: Department of Health.

Kondo, N., Subramanian, S. V., Kawachi, I., Takeda, Y., & Yamagata, Z. (2008). Economic recession and health inequalities in Japan: Analysis with a national sample, 1986–2001. *Journal of Epidemiology and Community Health*, *62*(10), 869–875.

Laaksonen, E., Martikainen, P., Lahelma, P., Lallukka, T., Rahkonen, O., Head, J., & Marmot, M. (2007). Socioeconomic circumstances and common mental disorders among Finnish and British public sector employees: Evidence from the Helsinki Health Study and the Whitehall II Study. *International Journal of Epidemiology*, *36*(4), 776–786.

Lahelma, E., Kivela, K., Roos, E., Tuominen, T., Dahl, E., Diderichsen, F., . . . Yngwe, M. A. (2002). Analysing changes of health inequalities in the Nordic welfare states. *Social Science and Medicine*, *55*(4), 609–625.

Laszlo, K. D., Pikhart, H., Kopp, M. S., Bobak, M., Pajak, A., Malyutina, S., . . . Marmot, M. (2010). Job insecurity and health: A study of 16 European countries. *Social Science and Medicine*, *70*(6), 867–874.

Lee, S., Guo, W. J., Tsang, A., Mak, A. D., Wu, J., Ng, K. L., & Kwok, K. (2010). Evidence for the 2008 economic crisis exacerbating depression in Hong Kong. *Journal of Affective Disorders*, *126*(1–2), 125–133.

Lundberg, O., Yngwe, M. A., Stjarne, M. K., Elstad, J. I., Ferrarini, T., Kangas, O., . . . Fritzell, J. (2008). The role of welfare state principles and generosity in social policy programmes for public health: An international comparative study. *The Lancet*, *372*(9650), 1633–1640.

Marmot, M. G., & Bell, R. (2009). How will the financial crisis affect health? *British Medical Journal*, *338*, b1314.

Matschinger, H., & Angermeyer, M. C. (2004). The public's preferences concerning the allocation of financial resources to health care: Results from a representative population survey in Germany. *European Psychiatry*, *19*(8), 478–482.

McCabe, C. (2008). *Estimating the short-term cost effectiveness of a mental health promotion intervention in primary schools*. London: NICE.

McDaid, D., & Knapp, M. (2010). Black-skies planning? Prioritising mental health services in times of austerity. *British Journal of Psychiatry*, *196*(6), 423–424.

McDaid, D., Knapp, M., & Raja, S. (2008). Barriers in the mind: Promoting an economic case for mental health in low- and middle-income countries. *World Psychiatry*, *7*(2), 79–86.

McDaid, D., & Park, A.-L. (2011). Investing in mental health and well-being: Findings from the DataPrev project. *Health Promotion International*, *26*(suppl. 1), i108–i139.

Meltzer, H., Bebbington, P., Brugha, T., Farrell, M., & Jenkins, R. (2013). The relationship between personal debt and specific common mental disorders. *European Journal of Public Health*, *23*(1), 108–113.

Men, T., Brennan, P., Boffetta, P., & Zaridze, D. (2003). Russian mortality trends for 1991–2001: Analysis by cause and region. *British Medical Journal*, *327*(7421), 964.

Morrell, S. L., Taylor, R. J., & Kerr, C. B. (1998). Jobless. Unemployment and young people's health. *Medical Journal of Australia*, *168*(5), 236–240.

Niederkrotenthaler, T., & Sonneck, G. (2007). Assessing the impact of media guidelines for reporting on suicides in Austria: Interrupted time series analysis. *Australia and New Zealand Journal of Psychiatry*, *41*(5), 419–428.

Norstrom, T., & Ramstedt, M. (2005). Mortality and population drinking: A review of the literature. *Drug Alcohol Review*, *24*(6), 537–547.

Olafsdottir, H. (2009). Current concerns in Icelandic psychiatry; Nation in crisis. *Nordic Journal of Psychiatry*, *63*(2), 188–189.

OECD (Organization for Economic Cooperation and Development) (2012). *OECD health data 2012*. Paris: OECD.

Ostamo, A., & Lonnqvist, J. (2001). Attempted suicide rates and trends during a period of severe economic recession in Helsinki, 1989–1997. *Social Psychiatry and Psychiatric Epidemiology, 36*(7), 354–360.

Österberg, E. (2012a). Availability of alcohol. In P. Anderson, L. Møller, & G. Galea (Eds.), *Alcohol in the European Union*. Copenhagen: World Health Organization Regional Office for Europe.

Österberg, E. (2012b). Pricing of alcohol. In P. Anderson, L. Møller & G. Galea (Eds.), *Alcohol in the European Union*. Copenhagen: World Health Organization Regional Office for Europe.

Paananen, R., & Gissler, M. (2012). Cohort profile: The 1987 Finnish birth cohort. *International Journal of Epidemiology, 41*(4), 941–945.

Pickett, K. E., & Wilkinson, R. G. (2010). Inequality: An underacknowledged source of mental illness and distress. *British Journal of Psychiatry, 197*(6), 426–428.

Pirkola, S., Sund, R., Sailas, E., & Wahlbeck, K. (2009). Community mental-health services and suicide rate in Finland: A nationwide small-area analysis. *The Lancet, 373*(9658), 147–153.

Pleasance, P., & Balmer, N. (2007). Changing fortunes: Results from a randomized trial of the offer of debt advice in England and Wales. *Journal of Empirical Legal Studies, 4*, 651–673.

Pleasance, P., Buck, A., Balmer, N., O'Grady, A., Genn, H., & Smith, M. (2004). *Causes of action: Civil law and social justice*. London: Legal Services Commission.

Proudfoot, J., Guest, D., Carson, J., Dunn, G., & Gray, J. (1997). Effect of cognitive-behavioural training on job-finding among long-term unemployed people. *The Lancet, 350*(9071), 96–100.

Puska, P. (2007). Health in all policies. *European Journal of Public Health, 17*(4), 328.

Roelfs, D. J., Shor, E., Davidson, K. W., & Schwartz, J. E. (2011). Losing life and livelihood: A systematic review and meta-analysis of unemployment and all-cause mortality. *Social Science and Medicine, 72*(6), 840–854.

Saxena, S., Thornicroft, G., Knapp, M., & Whiteford, H. (2007). Resources for mental health: Scarcity, inequity, and inefficiency. *The Lancet, 370*(9590), 878–889.

Schomerus, G., Matschinger, H., & Angermeyer, M. C. (2006). Preferences of the public regarding cutbacks in expenditure for patient care: Are there indications of discrimination against those with mental disorders? *Social Psychiatry and Psychiatric Epidemiology, 41*(5), 369–377.

Sharac, J., McCrone, P., Clement, S., & Thornicroft, G. (2010). The economic impact of mental health stigma and discrimination: A systematic review. *Epidemiologia e Psichiatrica Sociale, 19*(3), 223–232.

Skapinakis, P., Weich, S., Lewis, G., Singleton, N., & Araya, R. (2006). Socio-economic position and common mental disorders. Longitudinal study in the general population in the UK. *British Journal of Psychiatry, 189*, 109–117.

Skarlund, M., Ahs, A., & Westerling, R. (2012). Health-related and social factors predicting non-reemployment amongst newly unemployed. *BMC Public Health, 12*, 893.

Solantaus, T., Leinonen, J., & Punamaki, R. L. (2004). Children's mental health in times of economic recession: Replication and extension of the family economic stress model in Finland. *Developmental Psychology, 40*(3), 412–429.

Sonneck, G., Etzersdorfer, E., & Nagel-Kuess, S. (1994). Imitative suicide on the Viennese subway. *Social Science and Medicine, 38*(3), 453–457.

Stuckler, D., Basu, S., Suhrcke, M., Coutts, A., & McKee, M. (2009). The public health effect of economic crises and alternative policy responses in Europe: An empirical analysis. *The Lancet, 374*(9686), 315–323.

Stuckler, D., King, L., & McKee, M. (2009). Mass privatisation and the post-communist mortality crisis: A cross-national analysis. *The Lancet, 373*(9661), 399–407.

Stuckler, D., Meissner, C., Fishback, P., Basu, S., & McKee, M. (2012). Banking crises and mortality during the Great Depression: Evidence from US urban populations, 1929–1937. *Journal of Epidemiology and Community Health, 66*(5), 410–419.

Tariq, L., van den Berg, M., Hoogenveen, R. T., & van Baal, P. H. (2009). Cost-effectiveness of an opportunistic screening programme and brief intervention for excessive alcohol use in primary care. *PLoS One, 4*(5), e5696.

Taylor, M. P., Pevalin, D. J., & Todd, J. (2007). The psychological costs of unsustainable housing commitments. *Psychological Medicine, 37*(7), 1027–1036.

Thornicroft, G., Alem, A., Antunes Dos Santos, R., Barley, E., Drake, R. E., Gregorio, G., . . . Wondimagegn, D. (2010). WPA guidance on steps, obstacles and mistakes to avoid in the implementation of community mental health care. *World Psychiatry, 9*(2), 67–77.

Uutela, A. (2010). Economic crisis and mental health. *Current Opinion in Psychiatry, 23*(2), 127–130.

Vinokur, A. D., Schul, Y., Vuori, J., & Price, R. H. (2000). Two years after a job loss: Long-term impact of the JOBS program on reemployment and mental health. *Journal of Occupational Health Psychology, 5*, 32–47.

Vinten, G., & Lane, D. A. (2002). Counselling remaining employees in redundancy situations. *Career Development, 7*(7), 430–437.

Vuori, J., & Silvonen, J. (2005). The benefits of a preventive job search program on re-employment and mental health at 2-year follow-up. *Journal of Occupational Health Psychology, 78*, 43–52.

Wahlbeck, K., & Awolin, M. (2009). *The impact of economic crises on the risk of depression and suicide: A literature review.* Supporting Document for the EU Thematic Conference on Preventing Depression and Suicide, Budapest. http://www.thl.fi/thl-client/pdfs/c39bd6b8-56ad-4ca2-8d87-0e7cdeb50b9f.

Wahlbeck, K., & McDaid, D. (2012). Actions to alleviate the mental health impact of the economic crisis. *World Psychiatry, 11*(3), 139–145.

Weehuizen, R. (2008). *Mental capital. The economic significance of mental health.* Maastricht: University of Maastricht.

Werner, E. E. (2004). Journeys from childhood to midlife: Risk, resilience, and recovery. *Pediatrics, 114*(2), 492.

While, D., Bickley, H., Roscoe, A., Windfuhr, K., Rahman, S., Shaw, J., . . . Kapur, N. (2012). Implementation of mental health service recommendations in England and Wales and suicide rates, 1997–2006: A cross-sectional and before-and-after observational study. *The Lancet, 379*(9820), 1005–1012.

Wilkinson, R., & Marmot, M. (2003). *Social determinants of health: The solid facts.* Copenhagen: World Health Organization, Regional Office for Europe.

Williams, K., & Sansom, A. (2007). *Twelve months later: Does advice help? The impact of debt advice—Advice agency client study.* London: Ministry of Justice.

World Health Organization (2009). *Financial crisis and global health: Report of a high-level consultation.* Geneva: World Health Organization.

Zaridze, D., Brennan, P., Boreham, J., Boroda, A., Karpov, R., Lazarev, A., . . . Peto, R. (2009). Alcohol and cause-specific mortality in Russia: A retrospective case–control study of 48,557 adult deaths. *The Lancet, 373*(9682), 2201–2214.

Zimmerman, S. L. (2002). States' spending for public welfare and their suicide rates, 1960 to 1995: What is the problem? *Journal of Nervous Mental Disease, 190*(6), 349–360.

Further Readings

Foresight Mental Capital and Wellbeing Project (2008). *Final project report.* London: Government Office for Science.

Knapp, M., McDaid, D., & Parsonage, M. (Eds.) (2011). *Mental health promotion and mental illness prevention: The economic case.* London: Department of Health.

Ståhl, T., Wismar, M., Ollila, E., Lahtinen, E., & Leppo, K. (Eds.). (2006). *Health in all policies. Prospects and potentials.* Helsinki: European Observatory on Health Systems and Policies & Ministry of Social Afffairs and Health, Finland.

Stuckler, D., & Basu, S. (2013). *The body economic. Why austerity kills.* London: Allen Lane.

Winters, L., McAteer, S., & Scott-Samuel, A. (2012). *Assessing the impact of the economic downturn on mental health and wellbeing* (Observatory report series 88). Liverpool: Liverpool Public Health Observatory.

12

Making Use of Evidence from Wellbeing Research in Policy and Practice

David McDaid

London School of Economics and Political Science, U.K.

I do think we have got to recognise, officially, that economic growth is a means to an end. If your goal in politics is to help make a better life for people—which mine is—and if you know, both in your gut and from a huge body of evidence that prosperity alone can't deliver a better life, then you've got to take practical steps to make sure government is properly focused on our quality of life as well as economic growth, and that is what we are trying to do.

British Prime Minister David Cameron, November 25, 2010

Introduction

The launch in 2010 of an initiative by British Prime Minister David Cameron to develop a measure of national wellbeing can be highlighted as one example of how wellbeing has risen to the top of the political agenda. As the quotation above highlights, the Prime Minister acknowledged that "prosperity alone can't deliver a better life" (Cameron, 2010). This launch came hot on the heels of the publication of the report of the Commission on the Measurement of Economic Performance and Social Progress, an international academic body led by two Nobel-Prize-winning economists that had been set up by the French President, Nicolas Sarkozy, in 2008. It also concluded that wellbeing was about an awful lot more than just

The Economics of Wellbeing: Wellbeing: A Complete Reference Guide, Volume V.
Edited by David McDaid and Cary L. Cooper.
© 2014 John Wiley & Sons, Ltd. Published 2014 by John Wiley & Sons, Inc.
DOI: 10.1002/9781118539415.wbwell12

economic growth (Stiglitz, Sen, & Fitoussi, 2010). Initiatives in a number of other countries including the United States, Canada, Australia, and Italy can also be identified (Kroll, 2011).

Welcome though this increased recognition of the importance of wellbeing is, it is of little use unless research on wellbeing actually makes a difference to policy and practice. In this concluding chapter to the volume, three issues to help foster its use in policy making are considered. First, issues in the measurement of wellbeing. Measures will need to have broad acceptance by policy makers and the public if they are to be sustained. The chapter then looks at how information about wellbeing, including its economic impact, can be used to aid in making policy. It then focuses in more detail on the fundamental issue of knowledge exchange. This is a means of facilitating the use of wellbeing research and other information as part of a process of evidence-informed policy making.

Getting the Measurement Right

Many of the chapters in this volume have focused on different issues in the measurement of wellbeing. They all firmly recognize that conventional measures of economic growth do have an important impact on personal and societal wellbeing. A survey of more than 1,000 members of the general population of the United Kingdom asked respondents to rank in importance seven different potential indicators of wellbeing; the state of the economy was still seen as most important, followed by health, with measurement of happiness coming in third, although there was a considerable amount of variation in responses (see Table 12.1) (Dolan & Metcalfe, 2011). Depression, an issue that has been highlighted throughout this volume as an important aspect of wellbeing, was lowest ranked, which might also reflect public attitudes towards mental health. (In fact there is perhaps an element of stigmatization in the survey itself in that it separates depression from other aspects of peoples' health.)

Some of these components of wellbeing can be measured using objective measures (e.g., educational qualifications achieved, the rate of unemployment, or life expectancy across countries). More care needs to be taken with other domains of wellbeing, where question-framing effects could influence the responses made, for example, in respect of opinions on levels of satisfaction with life or the quality of personal relationships. Work continues in order to overcome these challenges: the Organisation for Economic

Table 12.1. What Matters in Ranking Progress in Wellbeing in the United Kingdom?

Aspect of subjective wellbeing	Mean ranking	Standard deviation
State of the economy	2.38	1.74
Peoples' health	2.90	1.48
Peoples' happiness	3.75	2.03
Crime rates	3.93	1.65
Education levels	4.2	1.59
The environment	5.22	1.7
Depression rates	5.61	1.59

Adapted from Dolan and Metcalfe (2011).

Cooperation and Development (OECD), for instance, has produced guidelines on how best to measure subjective wellbeing, cautioning that these aspects of wellbeing are only part of the picture and they must be complemented by objective measures (OECD, 2013). GDP measurement still has an important contribution to make (Delhey & Kroll, 2012). The complexity inherent in the measurement of wellbeing may militate against the development of an all-encompassing index, but rather favor the presentation of a range of values for different components of wellbeing, as used, for instance, by the U.K. Office for National Statistics' National Wellbeing Wheel of Measures.[1]

How Can Wellbeing Inform Policy and Practice?

Wellbeing information can be used in several ways to inform policy and practice. Key audiences include policy makers at all levels of government, public and private sector employers, key service providers in, for example, health and education, civil society organizations, the media, and the general public.

If governments and other stakeholders make a commitment to the routine collection of data from large representative samples of national populations using agreed key indicators of wellbeing over time, then trends in wellbeing can be monitored and potentially benchmarked internationally. This information could also be unpacked to look at wellbeing changes in population subgroups, such as in older people, minority groups, or rural dwellers, or to look at the extent of inequalities in wellbeing and how these are changing over time. Differences in the relative importance of different components of wellbeing might also be identified across the lifespan.

By looking at these trends it may become possible to identify how various policy and societal changes may impact on different aspects of wellbeing, and thus consider different policy interventions to mitigate any adverse impacts on wellbeing for the population as a whole or for specific at-risk groups.

Stoll and colleagues highlight numerous studies that have looked at the relationship between wellbeing and economic variables such as income, income inequality, access to social welfare benefit, unemployment, and the number of hours worked (Stoll, Michaelson, & Seaford, 2012). They also provide a review of research on the associations between wellbeing and other domains of interest such as health, social networks, the environment, and education. This includes work on the relative impacts of different variables to wellbeing such as unemployment, civil status, and health. This information, while predominantly of use at policy-making level, for example, to national or local governments, might also be used by other key stakeholders such as employers looking to protect the wellbeing of their employees or not-for-profit organizations looking to see how best they can make a difference to society.

Standardized measures of wellbeing can also be used in research to look at the cost-effectiveness of different interventions in achieving improvements in levels of wellbeing. To date, comparatively little research of this type has been done. Even though earlier chapters in this volume have looked at the economic case for investing in measures to promote wellbeing for young people, in workplaces, and for older people, most of the research they cite has had to look at the impacts of interventions on risk factors for poor wellbeing, such as poor performance in school, lack of rewards for effort in workplaces, or social isolation in older people. What is also needed is economic analysis showing the true return on investment for each additional unit of wellbeing gained.

This type of analysis is certainly possible to conduct. In formal cost–benefit analyses, where monetary values are placed on outcomes as well as costs, specific economic techniques could be used to value aspects of wellbeing that typically have often not been included in analyses of the type mentioned in the previous paragraph (Fujiwara & Campbell, 2011). This could help to ensure a more level playing field in assessing the economic benefits of actions whose principal outcomes are not, for instance, focused on improvements in economic productivity, but rather on other benefits that are valued by society, such as a greater level of community coherence, trust in one's neighbors or greater levels of life satisfaction.

This, incidentally, poses interesting challenges for those assessing wellbeing interventions within the context of health technology assessment where a common outcome metric, based on quality of life, is used to compare two or more health interventions. However, quality of life measures in common use, such as the EuroQol EQ-5D or the SF-36, do not cover all of the dimensions of wellbeing, for instance, the environment, that have been suggested in recent international work. A way round this might be to move to formal cost–benefit analysis, but this method of economic analysis has not been favored by health policy makers, in contrast to economists working in other sectors such as the environment or education.

What Needs to Be Done to Facilitate the Use of Wellbeing Information in Policy and Practice?

The nineteenth-century American education reformer, Horace Mann, stated that "every addition to true knowledge is an addition to human power" (Mann, 1845). While the sentiments behind this statement may resonate with many, reality is rather more complex. Notwithstanding the challenges both in the measurement of wellbeing and in generating information of policy relevance, this knowledge is of little use unless it has an opportunity to inform the development of policy and practice. Sadly, the process of exchanging knowledge between knowledge producers, policy makers, and practitioners is far from straightforward.

Recognition of this challenge is far from new; Carol Weiss suggested seven different routes for the transfer of knowledge to policy and practice more 30 years ago (Weiss, 1979), while at around the same time work on different stages in the research utilization process (Knott & Wildavsky, 1980), highlighted the importance of tackling inattention and resistance to new knowledge by different target groups.

There appears to have been little discussion of these issues thus far in respect of wellbeing research. This needs to change if a good level of research uptake is to be achieved. Too often this issue of knowledge exchange is overlooked or dismissed as being of little importance, yet when it comes to wellbeing research it remains the case that some policymakers, as well as parts of the media and members of the public might, to quote David Cameron, have a "suspicion that, frankly, the whole thing is a bit woolly, a bit impractical. You can't measure wellbeing properly, so why bother doing it at all?" (Cameron, 2010). Such skepticism makes it more difficult to allocate resources to wellbeing initiatives. This section briefly looks, therefore, at some of the barriers and facilitators to the exchange and use of wellbeing research findings and considers how to better facilitate their use in policy and practice.

Barriers to Knowledge Exchange

Work looking at the dissemination, diffusion, and uptake of research knowledge suggests that there remains too little dialogue or use of a common language between the different research and policy making communities (Abelson, Lavis, McLeod, Robertson, & Woodside, 2003; Innvaer, Vist, Trommald, & Oxman, 2002; Lavis, 2006; Lomas, 1997). Research results may be poorly presented to the policy-making community, while policy makers may pose questions to researchers that cannot be evaluated. Research evidence also has to compete with many different sources of information, including media myths and lobbying from various organizations.

It usually takes considerable time for research-based information to have an impact. It is very rare for policy makers to have a Eureka moment and immediately implement something on the basis of research received. It is much more likely to be a gradual process, with impact achieved over time as a result of regular interaction, feedback, and dialogue between research producers, policy makers, and other stakeholders.

Another challenge is that, since wellbeing is a multidimensional concept, actions to improve or protect wellbeing are likely to require interventions in many different sectors. This means having to liaise with many different policy makers, who will be much more interested in achieving the primary goals of their own sector rather than being unduly concerned about levels of wellbeing. The different government departments and other institutions in these multiple sectors often may not talk with each other very much.

These sectors will usually have their own separate budgets, perhaps with tight restrictions on how funding can be used and subject to different financial incentives and cost-containment concerns. This structural issue can also act as a major impediment to the use of wellbeing research in policy and practice. Budget holders will have incentives to concentrate on achieving internal departmental goals and policy targets rather than achieving broader cross-sectorial aims. For example, education budget holders are more likely to be concerned with changes in average examination grade scores on national tests or with the level of truancy in schools, while labor ministries may focus on the rate of employment. The predominance of vertical policy structures (e.g., a ministry of education, ministry of employment, ministry for health) with their own funding silos means that, unchallenged, many wellbeing concerns may be neglected. This may particularly be the case for actions that should be addressed outside the health sector.

Facilitators to Knowledge Exchange

Packaging of information.
How can these challenges be overcome? One key issue concerns how research information is packaged. Written documentation should be tailored to each target audience to be reached so that the content of the message is relevant and directly applicable to the decision or practice issue faced by the target audience (Dobbins, Hanna, et al., 2009). Care must be taken, as far as language is concerned, to avoid using unnecessary jargon and to make sure that any particular form of words will not be viewed with suspicion by the target audience. This is especially important when preparing information for the media; this should be put together in such a way that it can be reported accurately without the need to use jargon or complex statistics.

An approach that has been shown to be effective in conveying ideas to policy makers is to prepare short briefing papers (Dobbins, Hanna, et al., 2009). These papers are prepared using a graded entry format that consists of a one-page take-home message targeted directly at the time-precious policy maker, a three-page executive summary, and a report of up to 25 pages which is more likely to be read by senior policy advisors than policy makers. Typically, these briefing papers would address a specific policy question, provide some background, then provide policy makers with a least three options on how to address the issue, including information on the strengths and weakness of each approach and consideration of implementation issues. The aim should be that the policy options presented are based on previous robust reviews of evidence.

Issues of the transferability of research findings between different contexts should form part of these policy briefs where relevant. Much of the research on the effectiveness of interventions has taken place in the United States. Just because an intervention has been effective in one country or culture, this does not mean that it will necessarily be effective elsewhere. It is essential to explore the transferability of preventive practices to different cultural situations. From a research design perspective, this also highlights the important role that qualitative research methods can play in providing essential insights into any adaptations that are needed for implementation.

Interactive dialogue and collaboration.
A second area to address is collaboration and interactive communication between researchers and policy makers. This can help enhance linkage and exchange and build trust (Baumbusch et al., 2008; Jbilou, Amara, & Landry, 2007), which, in turn, can help stimulate ongoing dialogue on wellbeing research. Timing is important. Mutual engagement of all stakeholders early on in the research cycle can help to ensure that research is relevant to policy and/or practice and can also engender a sense of ownership of different stakeholders in the research process, which subsequently can aid in uptake and implementation (McDonald & Viehbeck, 2007). It can also help researchers gain a better appreciation of the context in which policymakers function. Interaction with different stakeholders must then be an ongoing process. It requires an investment of time and resources by all parties. The aim is to create repeated opportunities to work together and to establish an environment of open communication, mutual respect, and trust.

It should be recognized that it may not be easy for all researchers to directly engage with policy makers. There are countries where such dialogues are rare for cultural reasons; but, even in countries like the UK where there are many examples of interactions between researchers and policymakers, not all researchers will be able to establish these connections. It is important to think carefully about how researchers can be incentivized to link up with policy makers and vice versa (Brown, 2012).

One way of overcoming this issue may be to rely on intermediary organizations to move between research and policy. These organizations would be "knowledge brokers"; their staff would have skills in interpreting and conducting research, while also being familiar with policy-making environments. They would be able to move comfortably and engage iteratively in discussions between the research and policy/practice-making communities (Dobbins, Robeson, et al., 2009; Lomas, 2007). They could set out the strengths and weaknesses of different types of research knowledge, as well as other sources of information, and dispel myths in the media. Such organizations might be in a good position to set up informal policy dialogues and workshops that bring researchers, policy makers, and practitioners together to discuss issues (Boyko, Lavis, Abelson, Dobbins, & Carter, 2012). Policy briefs, for example, could be used as a catalyst for discussion at these events.

Highlighting sector-specific benefits of investment in wellbeing.
When trying to persuade a sector to invest its limited budgetary resources in wellbeing, it is helpful to be able to demonstrate that this will have

sector-specific benefits. Take, for instance, the case for action to improve the wellbeing of children at school. In this volume we have indicated that interventions in school to promote emotional wellbeing can be highly cost-effective. They have the potential, not only for better health, but also to generate economic gains to the economy arising from a reduction in the use of specialist health-care services, and in the need for specialist social and foster care services or contacts with the juvenile criminal justice system. However, if none of these benefits accrue to the education sector then it may be reluctant to make an investment, preferring to spend its resources on explicitly education-related activities.

This is something that researchers (and commissioners of research) need to bear in mind when designing evaluative studies. When evaluating the impacts of interventions delivered in schools, it can be helpful to ensure that outcomes of direct interest to the sector are among data that will be collected. So, when looking at the merits of an emotional resilience program, this might mean collecting data on outcomes such as classroom disruption, teacher sickness leave, use of special educational need services, and performance in academic tests, in addition to measures of subjective wellbeing. If the intervention has a positive effect on wellbeing, this message might be persuasively reinforced by any positive improvements of direct interest to the education sector. An alternative approach, when there are few positive benefits to the sector where the intervention is delivered, may be to create dedicated budgets for some wellbeing activities, bringing together resources from different sectors, or to set up mechanisms so that the sectors that benefit from a school-based intervention compensate the education sector.

This can be illustrated by looking at the evaluation of the long-term effects of a universal, comprehensive, community-based prevention project for primary school children and families living in three disadvantaged communities in Ontario, Canada—the Better Beginnings, Better Futures (BBBF) project (Peters et al., 2010). This has so far monitored changes in a broad range of outcomes at 1, 4, and 7 years after program participation in comparison with control school populations. In addition to looking at social, emotional and behavioral outcomes for children and their parents, the evaluation also considered a number of outcomes related to school performance. Levels of current academic achievement were measured in terms of each child's relative position in their class and in their performance on a standardized maths test. The long-term economic costs and benefits of the program were also considered, including the costs of special educational services and any need to repeat a year of school.

The evaluation reported significant improvements in these educational outcomes (Peters et al., 2010); moreover the children were less likely to need to repeat school years or to use special educational needs services compared with their control school counterparts. The overall economic analysis demonstrated that the program had net benefits of US$3,777 (2010 prices) per child, nearly all of which was due to better school performance. These benefits are conservative, as any eventual benefits of achieving higher levels of qualification at school leaving age cannot yet be calculated. However, this data will subsequently be available to policy makers as the study will follow participants for up to 25 years. Nonetheless, this analysis already can be very persuasive to budget holders in the education sector as they can see that a program to improve emotional wellbeing in school has substantial benefits to the education sector.

Modeling the long-term impacts of interventions to promote wellbeing.
The costs and benefits of some wellbeing interventions may take many years to be realized. While it is important to invest in longer term studies to look at these impacts, decision-modeling techniques can be a very useful aid to the policy-making process. Available data on short-term impacts and costs can be used to make projections of the long-term costs and consequences of different programs. Assumptions made in the model about long-term effects can be varied—if an intervention appears to be cost-effective using very conservative assumptions, this may provide powerful support for investment. Models can also be used to add data on cost consequences to already available data on long-term effectiveness outcomes. This, for instance, could be used to look at some of the potential financial benefits of research from the United States, which indicates that good wellbeing reduces the risk of mortality and health problems 10 years down the line (Keyes & Simoes, 2012).

Conclusion

Wellbeing is now firmly on the agendas of many governments around the world, but this is of little use unless research on wellbeing is actually used to inform policy and practice. Measures will need to have broad acceptance by policy makers and the public if they are to be sustained. Where wellbeing research has been used in the policy-making process, this has focused largely on looking at the associations between wellbeing and issues such as income, income inequality, access to social welfare benefits, unemployment, and the number of hours worked. More attention needs to be paid to assessing the economic case for investing in actions to promote or protect wellbeing.

It is critical not to overlook the process of actually ensuring that wellbeing research has the best possible opportunity to be considered as part of the policy-making process. Key barriers to address include the way in which information is packaged and presented, as well as a divided policy-making landscape, where many different actors in different sectors with different motivations and incentive structures need to be persuaded of the merits of investing in the promotion of wellbeing. To overcome these barriers, information must be tailored to the target audience. It should be succinct, written in clear language that minimizes jargon.

Opportunities for dialogue between researchers and policy makers should be maximized to increase the likelihood of research uptake; this may not be easy to achieve if either party does not have an incentive to engage. One option might be for specialist "knowledge broking" organizations to act as conduits bringing together researchers and policy makers. It can help foster the scale-up of any effective wellbeing intervention if it generates benefits to the funding sector. Modeling techniques can also be used to look at longer-term costs and benefits in the absence of longitudinal data. Ensuring that sufficient attention is devoted to issues of research uptake should help to keep wellbeing research firmly on the agenda for many years. This can hone and help maximize research benefits through the implementation of cost-effective actions to promote and protect wellbeing.

Note

1. At time of writing an interactive version of this wheel was available at http://www.ons.gov.uk/ons/interactive/well-being-wheel-of-measures/index.html.

References

Abelson, J., Lavis, J. N., McLeod, C. B., Robertson, D., & Woodside, J. M. (2003). How can research organizations more effectively transfer research knowledge to decision makers? *Milbank Quarterly, 81*(2), 221–248.

Baumbusch, J. L., Kirkham, S. R., Khan, K. B., McDonald, H., Semeniuk, P., Tan, E., & Anderson, J. M. (2008). Pursuing common agendas: A collaborative model for knowledge translation between research and practice in clinical settings. *Research in Nursing and Health, 31*(2), 130–140.

Boyko, J. A., Lavis, J. N., Abelson, J., Dobbins, M., & Carter, N. (2012). Deliberative dialogues as a mechanism for knowledge translation and exchange in health systems decision-making. *Social Science and Medicine, 75*(11), 1938–1945.

Brown, C. (2012). The "policy-preferences model": A new perspective on how researchers can facilitate the take-up of evidence by educational policy makers. *Evidence & Policy, 8*(4), 455–472.

Cameron, D. (2010). Speech on wellbeing. London: Cabinet Office. https://www.gov.uk/government/speeches/pm-speech-on-wellbeing.

Delhey, J., & Kroll, C. (2012). *A "happiness test" for the new measures of national wellbeing: How much better than GDP are they?* Berlin: Social Science Research Centre.

Dobbins, M., Hanna, S. E., Ciliska, D., Manske, S., Cameron, R., Mercer, S. L., . . . Robeson, P. (2009). A randomized controlled trial evaluating the impact of knowledge translation and exchange strategies. *Implementation Science, 4*(1), 61.

Dobbins, M., Robeson, P., Ciliska, D., Hanna, S., Cameron, R., O'Mara, L., . . . Mercer, S. (2009). A description of a knowledge broker role implemented as part of a randomized controlled trial evaluating three knowledge translation strategies. *Implementation Science, 4,* 23.

Dolan, P., & Metcalfe, R. (2011). *Comparing measures of subjective wellbeing and views about the role they should play in policy.* London: Office for National Statistics.

Fujiwara, D., & Campbell, R. (2011). *Valuation techniques for social cost benefit analysis: Stated preference, revealed preference and subjective wellbeing approaches.* London: HM Treasury.

Innvaer, S., Vist, G., Trommald, M., & Oxman, A. (2002). Health policy-makers' perceptions of their use of evidence: A systematic review. *Journal of Health Services Research and Policy, 7*(4), 239–244.

Jbilou, J., Amara, N., & Landry, R. (2007). Research-based decision-making in Canadian health organizations: A behavioural approach. *Journal of Medical Systems, 31*(3), 185–196.

Keyes, C. L., & Simoes, E. J. (2012). To flourish or not: Positive mental health and all-cause mortality. *American Journal of Public Health, 102*(11), 2164–2172.

Knott, J., & Wildavsky, A. (1980). If dissemination is the solution, what is the problem? *Knowledge: Creation, Diffusion, Utilization, 1*(4), 537–578.

Kroll, C. (2011). *Measuring progress and wellbeing. Achievements and challenges of a new global movement.* Berlin: Friedrich-Ebert-Stiftung.

Lavis, J. (2006). Research, public policymaking, and knowledge-translation processes: Canadian efforts to build bridges. *Journal of Continuing Education in the Health Professions, 26*(1), 37–45.

Lomas, J. (1997). *Improving research dissemination and uptake in the health sector: Beyond the sound of one hand clapping.* Hamilton: McMaster University Press.

Lomas, J. (2007). The in-between world of knowledge brokering. *British Medical Journal, 334*(7585), 129–132.

Mann, H. (1845). *Lectures on education.* Boston: Fowle & Capen.

McDonald, P. W., & Viehbeck, S. (2007). From evidence-based practice making to practice-based evidence making: Creating communities of (research) and practice. *Health Promotion Practice, 8*(2), 140–144.

OECD (Organisation for Economic Co-operation and Development) (2013). *Guidelines on measuring subjective wellbeing.* Paris: OECD Publishing.

Peters, R. D., Bradshaw, A. J., Petrunka, K., Nelson, G., Herry, Y., Craig, W. M., . . . Rossiter, M. D. (2010). *The Better Beginnings, Better Futures project: Findings from Grade 3 to Grade 9.* Monographs of the Society for Research in Child Development no. 75(3). New York: Wiley.

Stiglitz, J., Sen, A., & Fitoussi, J.-P. (2010). *Mismeasuring our lives: Why GDP doesn't add up. The report by the Commission on the Measurement of Economic Performance and Social Progress.* New York: The New Press.

Stoll, L., Michaelson, J., & Seaford, C. (2012). *Wellbeing evidence for policy: A review.* London: New Economics Foundation.

Weiss, C. (1979). The many meanings of research utilisation. *Public Administration Review, 39*(5), 426–431.

Index

Notes: Page numbers in *italics* denote Figures. Page numbers in **bold** denote Tables.